Object-Oriented
Programming in
Turbo Pascal® 5.5

Object-Oriented Programming in Turbo Pascal® 5.5

BEN EZZELL

Addison-Wesley Publishing Company, Inc.
Reading, Massachusetts   Menlo Park, California   New York
Don Mills, Ontario   Wokingham, England   Amsterdam   Bonn
Sydney   Singapore   Tokyo   Madrid   San Juan

Many of the designations used by manufacturers and sellers to distinguish their products are claimed as trademarks. Where those designations appear in this book and Addison-Wesley was aware of a trademark claim, the designations have been printed in initial capital letters.

Library of Congress Cataloging-in-Publication Data

Ezzell, Ben.
    Object-oriented programming in Turbo Pascal 5.5 / by Ben Ezzell
        p.   cm.
    ISBN 0-201-52375-2
    1. Object-oriented programming.   2. Pascal (Computer program
language) 3. Turbo Pascal (computer program)   I. Title.
QA76.64.E99   1989
005.1--dc20   89-27578
                                                                    CIP

Production Editor: Amorette Pedersen
Cover Design by: Doliber Skeffington Design
Set in 11.5 Times by Benchmark Productions

ABCDEFGHIJ-AL-89
First Printing, November, 1989

This volume is dedicated to the memory of an early pioneer of mathematics who, motivated by a fervent hatred of organ grinders, once proposed the ultimate computing object which was capable of "eating its own tail."

In more serious endeavors, this same inventor/mathematician was unfortunately unsuccessful in his attempts to construct the first digital computer (which, once completed, might well have become a steam powered computer). While incomplete, his device may still be viewed at the Kensington Museum.

Charles Babbage
Lucasian Professor of Mathematics at Cambridge
Inventor of the Analytic Engine

Had the execution of the times been equal to Babbage's concept, the Age of Computers might well have preceded the Age of the Automobile.

For a moment, consider the most novel image of an Analytic Engine composed of gleaming brass gears and cogs, driven by a steam engine and complete with Elizabethan ornamentation in the full baroque glory of the period. That's style!

TABLE OF CONTENTS

INTRODUCTION
INTRODUCTION TO OBJECT PASCAL   XIII

Object-Oriented Pascal   XV
The Object in Object Programming   XV
Topics and Treatment   XVI

CHAPTER 1
OBJECT-ORIENTED PRACTICES   1

Inheritance   2
OOPTest1 — Using Records   5
OOPTest2 — Using Objects   7
Methods   10
OOPTest3 — Using Methods   12
Encapsulation   16
Program Organization   17
OOPTest4 — Using Polymorphism   19
Summary   26

CHAPTER 2
AN OBJECT-ORIENTED MOUSE   35

Creating an Object-Mouse Unit   36
The Object Definitions   39

The Implementation Section   41
The GenMouse Implementation   42
The GraphicsMouse Implementation   49
The TextMouse Implementation   51
The LightPen Implementation   54
The Mouse Pointer Utility   55
Conventional Style Button Operations   58
Summary   60

CHAPTER 3
OBJECT BUTTON CONTROLS   **97**

Graphics and Text Button Operations   97
The TBoxes Unit   100
The Buttons Unit   106
The Button Test Program   115
Summary   116

CHAPTER 4
INTRODUCTION TO OBJECT-ORIENTED PASCAL   **139**

Object Data Abstraction   139
Extending Objects   145
Global Variables   151
Compiler Operations for Static Methods   152
Static vs. Virtual Methods   154
Summary   155

CHAPTER 5
VIRTUAL OBJECT METHODS   **157**

Creating Virtual Methods   169
Summary   173

CHAPTER 6
SCROLLBARS AND OBJECT EXTENSIBILITY   **181**

Object Extensibility   181
Programming for Extensibility   182
The ScrollBar Object   185
The ScrlTest Demo   200
Omissions   201
Summary   202

CHAPTER 7
DYNAMIC OBJECT INSTANCES   **217**

Advantages of Dynamic Objects   218
Pointers to Objects   218
Allocation and Initialization   219
Disposing of Dynamic Objects   221
The Destructor Method   221
Using the Destructor Method   223
The Destructor Mechanism   224
Extended Type Compatibility   226
Summary   226

CHAPTER 8
DYNAMIC OBJECTS AND LINKED LISTS   **229**

A Brief Explanation of Pointers   230
Sorting Lists   232
The Precede Utility   236
The Phone1 Demo Program   237
The Phone2 Demo Program   241
The LinkObj Methods   244
Memory Usage   249
Summary   249

CHAPTER 9
LINKED LISTS AND MIXED OBJECTS   **265**

   Mixing Objects Within a List   266
   Three Data Object Types   277
   Summary   281

CHAPTER 10
BINARY TREE OBJECTS   **299**

   Binary Tree Structures   300
   A Binary Tree Application   302
   Implementing a Binary-Tree Object   306
   Building the Tree   307
   Disposing of the Tree   309
   Printing the Tree   311
   Binary Searches, Insertions and Deletions   312
   Removing an Item from the Tree   316
   The DeleteItem Method   319
   Other Methods   322
   Summary   325

CHAPTER 11
DEBUGGING OBJECT-ORIENTED PASCAL   **341**

   Debugging in the IDE   341
   The Turbo (Stand-Alone) Debugger   344
   The Object Hierarchy Window   346
   The Object Type Inspector Window   348
   The Module Window   349
   The Object Instance Inspector Window   350
   New Error Messages   352

APPENDIX A
OOP TERMINOLOGY   **353**

APPENDIX B
THE OBJECT MOUSE UTILITY   **361**

General Mouse Procedures and Functions   363
The Text Mouse Object   368
The Graphic Mouse Object   369
The LightPen Mouse Object   370

INDEX   **371**

INTRODUCTION

INTRODUCTION TO OBJECT PASCAL

The history of computers over the past two decades has been a race between technology and imagination, with imagination running second. One authority, speaking of automata and computer capabilities in general, pronounced an upper limit, saying "it is not likely that 10,000 (or perhaps a few times 10,000) switching organs will be exceeded ... about 10^4 switching organs seem to be the proper order of magnitude for a computing machine."

A very few years later, an IBM marketing survey indicated that a mere nine SSECs — the Selective Sequence Electronic Calculator using 12,500 vacuum tubes, 21,400 relays and (shudder) punched paper tape memory — would serve the entire world's computational needs for several decades to come.

A similar pronouncement was made by the mayor of a major U.S. city who regarded the telephone as a marvelous invention and said, "I can foresee the day when every city will have one." About the same time, the postmaster general of Great Britain offered his own opinion, stating, "Telephones are all very well for the colonies, but we (the English) have plenty of messenger boys.'

If the technology has outrun the imagination, the development of computer languages has kept better pace with realities.

In the beginning, there was assembly language programming which concentrated on processor opcodes, manipulating register values and memory addresses. At the same time, the primary emphasis was on compact code, minimum memory requirements and, lastly, speed of execution. Considerations such as order and organization were, though not totally ignored, secondary in importance.

Later, with the appearance of higher level languages such as C and Pascal, the programmer's focus shifted to procedures and functions together with variables and data types. At the same time, the emphasis on structured programming appeared and imposed order on what had often been near chaos.

Concomitant to this was the fact that programs became modular in construction (sometimes assembly language was also modular) while data was subjected to abstraction and many details of the program/data structures became obscured and even hidden entirely from cursory examination. Speed of execution and memory usage remained important considerations, but were now secondary in many respects to the programmer's speed and convenience in development and debugging.

Of the two examples shown in Chapter 1, after compiling, OppTest2.EXE — using simple OOP structures — is 41 bytes larger than OppTest1.EXE, which uses conventional record structures.

Now, with the appearance of Object-Oriented-Programming (commonly called OOP for short), abstraction is taken a step further while many details of a program's operation are hidden almost entirely from view (or may — for proprietary reasons — be deliberately concealed without being inaccessible). Also, with OOP programming, modularity becomes the rule rather than the exception, however, as you will see, it is also modularity on a new level.

Previously, object-oriented programming was largely restricted to specialized and/or experimental applications such as Artificial Intelligence and Expert Systems, appearing in the form of an interpreted language called SmallTalk and in the C++ compiler superset extension created by Bjarne Stroustrup at Bell Labs.

For various reasons, none of the previous object-oriented systems have come into general use, partially because of a lack of general information about what OOP is, why object programming offers advantages and, probably not least, because programmers have simply been too busy to find time to experiment with an entirely new programming language ... or what can appear to be a new language.

In some ways, OOP is very new, but now it is also familiar.

Object-Oriented Pascal

Turbo Pascal 5.5 (aka Object Pascal) brings the advantages of OOP programming to a familiar language and programming vehicle while retaining the conveniences of the Borland Graphic Interface (BGI), Turbo's Integrated Development Environment and the Integrated Debugger (the Turbo Debugger Version 1.5 also supports the OOP extensions).

But not everything is new. Turbo Pascal 5.5 provides complete backwards compatibility for versions 4.0 and 5.0 (and for version 3.x programs via either the UPGRADE utility or the 3.0 compatibility units).

However, if not everything is new, the OOP extensions certainly are and, as a result, you may have to "unlearn" some of what you know about Pascal in order to learn Object-Oriented Pascal.

If you know a little bit about object-oriented programming, your best bet may be simply to forget what you've been told, read or imagined about the theory of object-oriented programming.

Instead, in *Object-Oriented Programming in Turbo Pascal 5.5*, OOP will be explained by illustration and example — a hands-on approach demonstrating not just the theory, but also the mechanisms and advantages of object programming and its place in production programming — not just in experimental applications.

The Object in Object Programming

The *object* in object-oriented programming is simply a generic label for a programming element, but the *object* in question is defined, in part, by what it is *not*. This is because the object is not individually either a procedure or a function nor is the object a variable or a data type.

Instead, the *object* in question *is* composed of all of these elements and the relationship between these elements. This encompasses a new degree of modularity in which data, variables, procedures and their relationships comprise a new modular element called an object.

Centuries ago, chemistry (then called alchemy) dealt with a series of relationships and qualities that were sometimes called influences, sometimes primal substances (air, earth, water and fire were four of these). Later, chemists began to identify, first, chemical compounds, then chemical elements and, a few decades ago, sub-atomic elements and elementary particles.

With computers, however, we have been working in the opposite direction. We began with our 'primal' particles, simple binary switches, proceeded by building 'atoms' in the form of computer instructions, began combining these 'atoms' into chemical-equivalents called programs (we are presently at the level of creating aspirin ... and needing it!), and are moving toward the discovery of tailored constructs of the complexity level of plastics. If you remember punch cards — as I do — don't let the white beard get in your way, experience still counts for something.

Object-oriented programming is the next big advance, allowing us to tailor our 'atoms' in order to create custom materials of greater complexity than previously possible and to do so with greater ease and convenience than previous languages.

Incidentally, if you have been a programmer or even a computer hobbyist for five years or more, take a moment to remember what programming was like when you first entered the field, remember those early days?

Welcome to the next step forward!

Topics and Treatment

Object-oriented programming is a tool that can be applied to virtually any task and the first object-oriented language, Simula-67, was a tool designed to model the operation of mechanisms — or objects. Object-oriented programming is not so restricted in its uses and the applications shown here will be far more general and diverse.

The first examples used to demonstrate principles of object-oriented programming will be simple graphics applications because graphics provide a natural environment for teaching object-oriented program-ming, allowing you to, quite literally, see what the objects are doing.

And, because many programs — with the recent advances in both computers and languages — are becoming graphic-oriented, object-ori-ented graphics will be one of the topics covered at further length.

The new OS/2–Presentation Manager system is almost totally graph-ics-oriented even for routine text displays and, incidentally, is also object-oriented though more restrictively so than Object Pascal (Turbo Pascal 5.5).

Graphics imply the use of a mouse as an input device, therefore, one of the first object applications will be an object-oriented mouse that will later be used with control objects in the form of graphics buttons.

Object-oriented programming is far from limited to graphics and more conventional programming operations will also be covered, including using the mouse and button controls in text as well as graphics applica-tions.

But this is enough preface — let's move on to theory and practice and see how object-oriented programming works and how it can be used to improve and enhance your programming practices.

CHAPTER 1

OBJECT-ORIENTED PRACTICES

In this chapter, several example programs will be used to demonstrate the basic elements of object-oriented programming without attempting to accomplish any overly complex tasks. At the same time, the precepts governing object-oriented programming will be explained and illustrated; together with their possible problems and pitfalls.

First, here is an overview of the three principal properties that dominate object-oriented programming: inheritance, encapsulation and polymorphism.

- **Inheritance** is a property of objects. It allows for the creation of a hierarchy of objects with descendants of objects inheriting access to their ancestors' code and data structures.

- **Encapsulation** is modularity applied to data. It combines records with procedures and functions — called **methods** — that manipulate data, forming a new data type called an **object**.

- **Polymorphism** is the property of sharing a single action (and action name) throughout an object hierarchy. Each object in the hierarchy implements the action in a manner appropriate to its specific requirements.

Inheritance

Much of science is concerned with hierarchies and relationships (or artificial relationships), between objects. Fossil archaeology looks for relationships between extinct species and historians record sequences of events and dynasties and seek to understand relationships between causes and events. Biologists classify insects, plants and animals by taxonomy; genealogists draw and study family trees and stock market analysts study price fluctuations. All of these are studies of relationships between individual events, studies that may, in some way, provide predictive information.

All of these "charts," however, are based on the concept that objects lower in the hierarchy are influenced by, inherit characteristics from, or are descended from those above them in the chart.

Figure 1-1 shows a classification hierarchy for objects of type *vehicle*. On the top level, we find the object "vehicles" and, in the first generation of descendants, the vehicles object is broken down into four very different operating mediums: water, land, air and space, which seem to have little in common.

Objects in each of these second generation categories have inherited one principal characteristic from their parent object; each has the characteristic defined as "vehicle" and; therefore, has inherited some property that separates a vehicle from, for example, a plant, mineral or animal.

In the third generation, objects of the class "surface" and "submarine" appear below "aquatic," but both have inherited the characteristics "vehicle" and "aquatic" from their parent generation. This classification tree can be carried further, but in each case, any specific object inherits all of the characteristics that defined its parent object, and its parent's parent.

Figure 1-1: Vehicular Family Tree

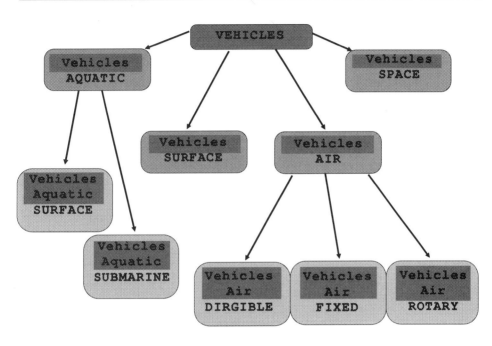

Object Inheritance by Declaration

As an example of how object inheritance operates, four variable types have been declared (in Table 1-1), on the left as **record** types and, on the right, as **object** types. A taxonomy chart appears in Figure 1-1.

Table 1-1: Record Declarations vs. Object Declarations

RECORD DECLARATION	OBJECT DECLARATION
| ```
Loc = record
      x, y : integer;
   end;
``` | ```
Loc = object
      x, y : integer;
   end;
``` |

Table 1-1: Record Declarations vs. Object Declarations

RECORD DECLARATION	OBJECT DECLARATION
`Point = record`	`Point = object( Loc )`
`        Where : Loc;`	`        Color : integer;`
`        Color : integer;`	`    end;`
`    end;`	
`Rect = record`	`Rect = object( Point )`
`        Pixel : Point;`	`        sx, sy : integer;`
`        sx, sy : integer;`	`    end;`
`    end;`	
`Circl = record`	`Circl = object (Point)`
`        Pixel : Point;`	`        rx : integer;`
`        rx : integer;`	`    end;`
`    end;`	
`Ellip = record`	`Ellip = object (Circl)`
`        Pixel ; Point;`	`        ry : integer;`
`        rx, ry : integer;`	`    end;`
`    end;`	

In Figure 1-2, the four object variables appear in a tree relationship. As you can see, these four variable types can be declared either as records or as objects. The advantage of declaring them as objects is not because the source code is slightly shorter (the .EXE code will be slightly longer); instead, look at the two source code listings for OOPTest1 and OOPTest2:

Figure 1-2: An Object Hierarchy with Inheritance

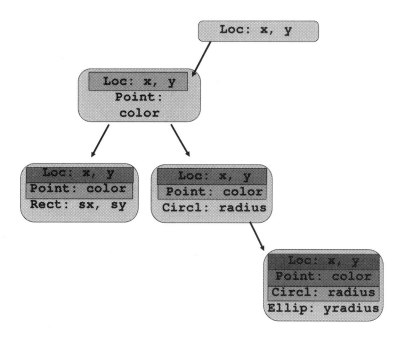

OOPTest1 — Using Records

In the first example, the variables are declared as record types similar to the examples in the left column in Table 1-1, and in the second case, as object types similar to the examples in the right column of Table 1-1.

```
program OOPTest1;

   uses Crt;

   type
       Location = record  x, y   : integer;  end;
       Point    = record  Pixel  : Location;
```

```
                        Color  : integer;  end;
    Circle   = record  Place  : Point;
                        radius : integer;  end;
  var
     TestPt  : Location;
     ACircle : Circle;
begin
  TestPt.x := 10;
  TestPt.y := 20;
```

Assigning values to the *TestPt* variable is simple (and it should also be a familiar practice). The values for the variable *ACircle* are not so easily referenced.

```
{  ACircle.x := 30; {} Field identifier expected }
{  ACircle.Pixel.x := 30; } { "  "      "  "        " "    }
```

Either of the two preceding attempts to reference the field element *x* would produce the error message shown.

For the record type variable, the entire genealogy of the record structure has to be explicitly referenced to both assigned values:

```
ACircle.Place.Pixel.x  := 30;
ACircle.Place.Pixel.y  := 40;
ACircle.Place.Color    := 50;
ACircle.radius         := 60;
```

and to subsequently access the assigned values:

```
   ClrScr;
   writeln( ACircle.Place.Pixel.x );
   writeln( ACircle.Place.Pixel.y );
```

```
    writeln( ACircle.Place.Color );

    writeln( ACircle.radius );

    writeln( TestPt.x );

    writeln( TestPt.y );

    writeln; write('Press ENTER to proceed'); readln;
end.
```

OOPTest2 — Using Objects

In the second example, the same record structures and variables are created, but this time, the variables are of type object.

```
program OOPTest2;

    uses Crt;

    type
        Location = object  x, y : integer;    end;
        Point     = object( Location )
                              Color: integer;    end;
        Circle    = object( Point )
                              radius : integer; end;
```

The parenthetical expressions following object — (Location) in one case and (Point) in the other — name the immediate ancestors of the objects being declared. Notice also that the object Location has no ancestor while, unlike humans, objects have one immediate ancestor at most.

At this point, the data type Circle has inherited the same equivalent data fields as if it had been declared as:

```
Circle   = record

                  x,  y,  Color,  radius : integer;

              end;
```

Note the qualifier, equivalent; in this simple example. Equivalence is easy, but as the object types become less simple, the equivalence will be less apparent and less real. For the moment, however, let's continue with the example:

```
var

    TestPt   : Location;

    ACircle  : Circle;
begin
    TestPt.x        := 10;
    TestPt.y        := 20;
    ACircle.x       := 30;
    ACircle.y       := 40;
    ACircle.Color   := 50;
    ACircle.radius  := 60;
```

Even though the structure elements in *ACircle* were not explicitly declared in the type declarations and their even though genealogy is not referenced in the value assignments, the elements *x*, *y* and *Color* accept values without difficulty. In actual fact, I do not have to know the genealogy of the data type Circle at all — just as long as I know what elements exist in the object Circle. These same record elements are read back with no more difficulty than they were originally assigned.

```
ClrScr;
writeln(ACircle.x);
writeln(ACircle.y);
writeln(ACircle.Color);
writeln(ACircle.radius);
writeln(TestPt.x);
writeln(TestPt.y);
```

```
    writeln; write('Press ENTER to proceed'); readln;
end.
```

Please note, while it is possible to assign values to an object's fields — as shown in the preceding example — this is very bad practice and *should not be followed*. The reasons for this caution and the practices that should be used will be demonstrated momentarily (see the Methods section). This shortcut was employed here to provide an uncomplicated example of the nature of inheritance fields.

As with conventional Pascal records, the data fields could also have been assigned using the *with...do* statements:

```
with ACircle do

begin

    x       := 30;

    y       := 40;

    Color   := 50;

    radius  := 60;

end;
```

Again, the same caution applies: while this form will work, it is not good practice and should not be employed as normal procedure.

Object Inheritance Terminology

In the example OOPTest2, the record type Loc was declared as an object type and the variables *TestPt* and *ACircle* became object variables.

The data type, Location is the **ancestor** of the data type Point, while the data type Circle is the **descendant** of Point, which is the **descendant** of Location.

In similar fashion, in Figure 1-2, both Circl and Rect were descendants of Point. Note that sibling relationships are not relevant, only descendance and ancestry and the inheritance from ancestor to descendant.

Methods

To object-oriented programming, **methods** or **object methods** are the equivalent of procedures and functions in conventional programming and, in actual fact, they are composed of procedures and functions that are similar, but work in a new way. As with all programming, they require recognition of their capacities and of their limitations.

Previously, the data fields of the objects TestPt and ACircle were initialized with direct assignment references:

```
TestPt.x = 10;
```

and:

```
ACircle.x = 30;
```

A second instance was shown using a *with...do* assignment. A caution was appended, however, stating that neither was the best form for assigning values to objects.

Granted, both assignments worked, but each descendant of the object type Location required separate and specific instructions to assign values to each data field — a process that is tedious and repetitive at best and, in real programming practices, can quickly become an annoyance.

The obvious alternative would be to create a procedure containing generalized assignment statements and to pass objects of type Location (or objects that have inherited Location's data structure) as variable parameters:

```
procedure SetLoc( var Coordinate : Location;
                      PtX, PtY : integer );
begin
   Coordinate.x = PtX;
   Coordinate.y = PtY;
end;
```

Now, assignments can be carried out in the form:

```
SetLoc( TestPt, 10, 20 );
```

and:

```
SetLoc( ACircle, 30, 40 );
```

This will work for all objects of type Location and for all descendants of objects of type Location, but it is still not the best way to assign values. As the objects become more complex, in many cases, this approach will not work at all or will work very awkwardly. This is neither the intent nor the objective of object-oriented programming.

Instead, to manipulate data belonging to objects, methods are created. A method is a procedure or a function that becomes integral to a specific object type (and, of course, it is subject to the same rule of inheritance for descendants). In this fashion, the data structure — the object — and the procedures serving the data — the methods — are fused together into a single unit so that access to each is available by default, and does not require explicit provisions for access or assignment in every case.

How does a method work? In its simplest form — consider the following code:

```
type
   Location =
      object
         x, y : integer;
      procedure SetLoc( PtX, PtY : integer );
         function GetX : integer;
         function GetY : integer;
      end;
```

What's happening here — a *procedure* and two *functions* being declared as if they were fields in a record structure?

That's exactly what's happening. The procedure SetLoc and the functions GetX and GetY have become part of the object type Location and are now a portion of the record.

OOPTest3 — Using Methods

The procedure SetLoc and the functions GetX and GetY still have to be defined:

```
procedure Location.SetLoc( PtX, PtY : integer );

begin

   x := PtX;

   y := PtY;

end;

function Location.GetX : integer;

begin

   GetX = x;

end;

function Location.GetY : integer;

begin

   GetY = y;

end;
```

For each of these, the object Location is referenced because, in other cases, there may be two or three or several SetLoc procedures along with any number of Get... functions, each referencing different object types and executing different tasks.

Finally, to use the SetLoc procedure. It is called as though it were merely a field of a record:

```
var

   TestPt : Location;

   . . .

   TestPt.SetLoc( 10, 20 );
```

What could be simpler? The SetLoc procedure, which is a method belonging to the object type Location, is called with two parameters which are then automatically assigned to the appropriate fields. Remember that the method SetLoc will also be inherited by all descendants of the object type Location. In like fashion, the functions GetX and GetY are called as *TestPt.GetX* or *TestPt.GetY* to return the specific values from TestPt.

Finally, the example OOPTest2 is revised, becoming OOPTest3, and using methods to assign and return values:

```
program OOPTest3;

    uses Crt;

    type

        Location =
            object
                x, y : integer;
                procedure SetLoc( PtX, PtY : integer );
                function GetX : integer;
                function GetY : integer;
            end;

        Point =
            object( Location )
                Color: integer;
                procedure SetColor( c : integer );
                function GetColor : integer;
            end;

        Circle =
            object( Point )
                radius : integer;
                procedure SetRadius( r : integer );
                function GetRadius : integer;
```

```
        end;
    var
        TestPt  : Location;
        ACircle : Circle;
```

Notice that seven different methods have been referenced as subse-quent generations were declared. Because each of these methods is a separate procedure or function, each must be defined. Granted, the definitions are simple in this example, but this will not always be the case in the future:

```
procedure Location.SetLoc( PtX, PtY : integer );
begin
    x := PtX;
    y := PtY;
end;
function Location.GetX : integer;
begin
    GetX = x;
end;
function Location.GetY : integer;
begin
    GetY = y;
end;

procedure Point.SetColor( c : integer );
begin
    Color := c;
end;
function Point.GetColor : integer;
```

```
begin

   GetColor = Color;

end;

procedure Circle.SetRadius( r : integer );

begin

   radius := r;

end;

function Circle.GetRadius : integer;

begin

   GetRadius = radius;

end;
```

Now that the procedures used for the methods are defined, the original six direct assignments used in OOPTest2 are replaced with four method calls:

```
begin

   TestPt.SetLoc( 10, 20 );

   ACircle.SetLoc( 30, 40 );

   ACircle.SetColor( 50 );

   ACircle.SetRadius( 60 );
```

Admittedly, the overall savings of two lines of code in the main procedure is certainly not enough to warrant the extra effort required to declare the method procedures, but the example here is a simple one. In more complex cases the savings will make a difference. To complete the example, the final portion of code uses the objects' functions to return the values:

```
   ClrScr;

   writeln(ACircle.GetX);

   writeln(ACircle.GetY);
```

```
    writeln(ACircle.GetColor);
    writeln(ACircle.GetRadius);
    writeln(TestPt.GetX);
    writeln(TestPt.GetY);
    writeln;
    write('Press ENTER to proceed'); readln;
end.
```

Encapsulation

Encapsulation is a term for the process of combining both code and data into an object; a process that was demonstrated in the examples in OOPTest3.

In some object-oriented languages, such as Smalltalk, encapsulation is strictly enforced and data elements belonging to an object are only accessible through the methods provided with the object. If no method is provided to read or write an object's data element (from outside the object), then the data cannot be directly accessed by the programmer.

In Turbo Pascal 5.5, however, encapsulation is provided and supported but is not enforced. As shown in OOPTest2, any object data element can be accessed directly either to read the data values or to change the data values.

The flexibility of Object Pascal — providing encapsulation without enforcing encapsulation — offers the programmer both broader opportunities and, at the same time, demands greater responsibility in exercising correct object-oriented programming practices.

In object-oriented programming (in theory) it should be unnecessary to ever access an object's internal data fields directly. The programmer should always provide methods to access objects' internal data fields, but what "should be" is not enforced and direct access is not prevented.

One of the capabilities of object-oriented programming is the ability to create libraries that extend Pascal's inherent capabilities, and these libraries can be distributed for use by other programmers. As a result, it is doubly important for proper access methods to be provided, for these methods to be documented and, since encapsulation is not enforced, for the data fields belonging to objects (and their identifiers) to also be documented.

The question of distributing object libraries is a topic of its own and will be covered later in detail. For the moment, however, please keep in mind that any object-oriented library can be distributed and that Turbo Pascal's open encapsulation standards impose greater demands than a more rigorously enforced encapsulation. Even if you develop objects only for your own use and never distribute the "raw" object libraries, the demands of proper encapsulation and proper methods should still be observed, simply for your own convenience. A few examples of the possible pitfalls in object-oriented programming will be shown in later examples.

Program Organization

A variant program organization is being used for the demo programs in this book; primarily for purposes of explanation and not because object-oriented programming requires any special variation in style. A general program structure appears in Figure 1-3.

Notice that the type declaration for each object is followed immediately by the method definitions that are created for the object. Only after all of the objects have been defined are the global variables, the non-object procedures and functions listed.

There is no firm rule requiring this organization; the program's global variables could appear at the beginning of the program listing, then the object declarations grouped together with the method definitions following or the global variables could follow the type declarations. The overall structure is generally unimportant and the organization shown is intended simply to group elements for your convenience in reference.

There is, however, a secondary reason. When defining methods for objects, the programmer should be particularly careful to ensure that all variables used are local to the method (i.e., local to the procedure or function), with the exception of those variables that belong specifically to the object.

For several reasons, global variables should never be referenced by an object's methods. First, it's difficult to ensure that a global variable is not being used for some purpose that may be incompatible with the object's use. Second, using a global variable directly or indirectly circumvents the concept of encapsulation. Third, any object using a global variable is not cleanly transportable (as with the Mouse and Button objects that will be created in Chapter 2, but transported for use in subsequent programs).

Figure 1-3: Demo Program Organization

```
Program header,
uses units, etc

type
    Point : object
    ...

type
    Circle : object( Point )
    ...

type
    Square : object( Circle)
    ...

var
    global variables, etc
other procedures, functions
main procedure
```

One method of ensuring that global variables are not accidentally utilized by methods is to have a program's global variable declarations follow the object and method definitions, as shown in the general program organization. If for any reason this organization or any of these guidelines prove impractical, exceptions will occur.

OOPTest4 — Using Polymorphism

The term **polymorphism** is taken from Greek, meaning "many shaped." It is a method of giving an action a single name that is shared throughout an object hierarchy, but accomplishes the named action in different fashions (as appropriate to the specific object referenced by the action). For example, in OOPTest4, three object types will be declared in order of descent; Point, Circle and Square — the object names should be essentially self-explanatory.

The object Point is the simplest screen image possible, a single pixel, and it is a duplication of a point in the video memory. Point is also an object and, in some respects, is more accessible than the video memory. It also has several methods that are not directly provided for video access. The object Point begins with three record values:

```
type

   Point = object

            x, y, Color : integer;
```

and provides seven methods for access:

```
      procedure Create( PtX, PtY,

                      C : integer );

      procedure Destroy;

      procedure Move( PtX, PtY : integer );

      procedure SetColor( C : integer );

      function  GetX : integer;

      function  GetY : integer;
```

```
     function  GetColor : integer;
end;
```

In brief, the method Create creates a point with the specified location and color, Destroy removes the point, Move changes the location and SetColor changes the color of the point. Finally, the last three methods return information about the referenced point. (The complete code for the object Point appears in the program listing at the end of this chapter.) The second object, Circle, is a descendant of Point and adds one new record, size. It also redeclares several of the methods that were inherited from Point — Create, SetColor and Destroy — as well as declaring a new method, GetSize.

```
Circle = object( Point )
           size : integer;
           procedure Create( PtX, PtY,
                               R, C : integer );
           procedure SetColor( C : integer );
           procedure Destroy;
           . . . .
           function  GetSize : integer;
         end;
```

The redeclaration of the Create, SetColor and Destroy methods are examples of polymorphism — the name of the method and its general function are inherited, but the specific implementation for each of these methods has been redefined in order to perform appropriately for the new object. The method GetSize is new because the object Point does not have a size.

Note: if you refer to the program listing at the end of this chapter, you will notice that several other methods, including Move and SetColor, are redefined for both Circle and Square. Three methods, however, are sufficient for illustration here.

The third object type, Square, is a descendant of Circle and does not declare any new variable records, but it does redeclare the methods Create, SetColor and Destroy; redefining each as appropriate for Square:

```
Square = object( Circle )
            procedure Create( PtX, PtY,
                                    R, C : integer );
            procedure SetColor( C : integer );
            procedure Destroy;

            . . . .

        end;
```

The method GetSize is neither redeclared nor redefined because the same GetSize method works for both Circle and Square. The methods GetX, GetY and GetColor — which are inherited from Point — are not redefined at all.

Polymorphing the Create Method

When the method Create is originally defined for the object point, only three arguments are required: the x and y coordinates and the color:

```
procedure Point.Create( PtX, PtY, C : integer );
begin
    x := PtX;
    y := PtY;
    Color := C;
    PutPixel( x, y, Color );
end;
```

Create ends by calling Turbo's PutPixel function with the values to set the screen pixel.

With Point's descendant, Circle, a fourth parameter, the radius, is required. The subsequent actions are also different because the Graph functions SetColor and Circle are called to execute the actual screen write:

```
procedure Circle.Create( PtX, PtY, R, C : integer );
begin
    x := PtX;
    y := PtY;
    color := C;
    size := R;
    Graph.SetColor( color );
    Graph.Circle( x, y, size );
end;
```

Also notice that the Graph functions are explicitly referenced (Graph.SetColor and Graph.Circle) to distinguish these from the object Circle and Circle's method, SetColor.

For the object Square, Create is redeclared. The arguments are the same as for Circle, but the execution is different.

```
procedure Square.Create( PtX, PtY, R, C : integer );
begin
    x := PtX;
    y := PtY;
    Color := C;
    size := R;
    Graph.SetColor( color );
    Graph.Rectangle( x-(size div 2), y+(size div 2),
                     x+(size div 2), y-(size div 2) );
end;
```

Since Circle is determined by a center point and a radius (size), Square has been defined in terms of the same three parameters with size being used as the square analog of the radius so that the total height and width of each square is twice the "radius." This is not necessarily the best way to program this object; simply the best for illustrating the subject.

The Polymorphic Destroy and SetColor Methods

The Destroy method is also redefined appropriately for each of the three objects. In all three cases, Destroy calls the Create method and uses GetBkColor to provide the background color value to redraw the pixel, circle or square to match the background:

```
procedure Point.Destroy;

begin

   Create( x, y, GetBkColor  );

end;

procedure Circle.Destroy;

begin

   Create( x, y, size, GetBkColor );

end;

procedure Square.Destroy;

begin

   Create( x, y, size, GetBkColor );

end;
```

Why has the Destroy method been redefined for each object type? This is neither accidental nor unique — take a look at the three redefinitions for the SetColor method:

```
procedure Point.SetColor( c : integer );

begin
```

```
    Create( x, y, Color );
end;

procedure Circle.SetColor( C : integer );
begin
    Create( x, y, size, C );
end;

procedure Square.SetColor( C : integer );
begin
    Create( x, y, size, C );
end;
```

Precisely the same thing is being done here — the coding is identical for Circle and Square, just as it was for the Destroy method(s). This has been illustrated for emphasis because it is a very important point!

The Destroy method(s) could have been defined:

```
procedure Point.Destroy;
begin
    Point.Create( x, y, GetBkColor  );
end;

procedure Circle.Destroy;
begin
    Circle.Create( x, y, size, GetBkColor );
end;

procedure Square.Destroy;
begin
    Square.Create( x, y, size, GetBkColor );
end;
```

to show the fact that each version of Destroy is calling the specific version of Create which is appropriate to Point, Circle and Square in each case. However, if the method Destroy had not been redefined for each generation of object, the results would have been very different.

Subtle Error #1

If the redefinition of Destroy was omitted from the object Square, an attempt to Destroy an object of type Square would actually erase a corresponding object of type Circle (the most recent ancestor type possessing the appropriate method).

In this case, the x and y coordinates and the size value used would belong to the referenced Square object, but the Destroy method would be calling Circle.Create, not Square.Create. This can be a very obvious error in some cases or a very subtle error in others. In the current example (with the pointillistic background provided by the program), the error should be relatively obvious and I recommend attempting the experiment of commenting out both the procedure declaration within the object definition and the procedure definition itself in the OOPTest4 program source code. In other cases, the error can be very difficult to find.

Subtle Error #2

In the OOPTest4 demo program, use Turbo Pascal's editor facilities to globally change the variable *MaxC* to *Color*. Note: if you are manually entering the program listing, be sure that it runs correctly before attempting this experiment. You might also use the Watch facility and type in the variable *Color* for tracking. After making this change, run the program again. Within a few moments you should get the message: *Fatal Error 200: division by zero.*

Turbo Pascal will indicate the error has occurred in the following block of code but, if you are using the Watch facility to track the value of *Color*, the value shown is not zero, so what's going on?

```
repeat

   for i := 1 to 32 do

      with ACircle[i] do
```

```
        SetColor( ( GetColor - 1 ) mod Color );
  until KeyPressed;
```

It's another very subtle error. The *Color* variable in the Watch facility is not the same *Color* variable that is causing a very real divide by zero error. The *Color* variable above is not the global variable *Color* which has the value returned by GetMaxColor, but is *ACircle[i].Color* which can reach a value of zero. This is one of the possible errors that can be caused by the lack of strictly enforced encapsulation (and also why I suggested typing in the variable name).

If you are aware of the possible pitfalls — and tread carefully — most of the errors are easily avoided.

Summary

In this chapter, a few aspects of object-programming have been demonstrated. In Chapter 2, object-oriented programming will be used to create an object-oriented mouse for both text and graphics applications.

OOPTest4 Program Listing

```
program OOPTest4;

uses Crt, Graph;

type

   Point = object
              x, y, Color : integer;
              procedure Create( PtX, PtY,
                                C : integer );
              procedure Destroy;
              procedure Move( PtX, PtY : integer );
              procedure SetColor( C : integer );
              function  GetColor : integer;
              function  GetX : integer;
```

```
              function  GetY : integer;
          end;

procedure Point.Create( PtX, PtY, C : integer );
begin
   x := PtX;
   y := PtY;
   Color := C;
   PutPixel( x, y, Color );
end;

procedure Point.Destroy;
begin
   Create( x, y, GetBkColor );
end;

procedure Point.Move( PtX, PtY : integer );
begin
   Destroy;
   x := PtX;
   y := PtY;
   Create( x, y, Color );
end;

procedure Point.SetColor( c : integer );
begin
   Create( x, y, c );
end;

function Point.GetColor;
```

```pascal
begin
   GetColor := Color;
end;

function Point.GetX;
begin
   GetX := x;
end;

function Point.GetY;
begin
   GetY := y;
end;

type
   Circle = object( Point )
               size : integer;
               procedure Create( PtX, PtY,
                                   R, C : integer );
               procedure SetColor( C : integer );
               procedure Destroy;
               procedure Move( PtX, PtY : integer );
               procedure SetSize( R : integer );
               function  GetSize : integer;
             end;

procedure Circle.Create( PtX, PtY, R, C : integer );
begin
   x := PtX;
```

```
   y := PtY;
   size := R;
   color := C;
   Graph.SetColor( color );
   Graph.Circle( x, y, size );
end;

procedure Circle.Destroy;
begin
   Create( x, y, size, GetBkColor );
end;

procedure Circle.SetColor( C : integer );
begin
   Create( x, y, size, C );
end;

procedure Circle.Move( PtX, PtY : integer );
begin
   Destroy;
   Create( PtX, PtY, size, color );
end;

procedure Circle.SetSize( R : integer );
begin
   Destroy;
   Create( x, y, R, color );
end;

function Circle.GetSize;
```

```
begin
   GetSize := size;
end;

type
   Square = object( Circle )
                  procedure Create( PtX, PtY,
                                         R, C : integer );
                  procedure SetColor( C : integer );
                  procedure Destroy;
                  procedure Move( PtX, PtY : integer );
                  procedure SetSize( R : integer );
              end;

procedure Square.Create( PtX, PtY, R, C : integer );
begin
   x := PtX;
   y := PtY;
   size := R;
   Color := C;
   Graph.SetColor( color );
   Graph.Rectangle( x-(size div 2), y+(size div 2),
                  x+(size div 2), y-(size div 2) );
end;

procedure Square.Destroy;
begin
   Create( x, y, size, GetBkColor );
```

```
end;

procedure Square.SetColor( C : integer );
begin
   Create( x, y, size, C );
end;

procedure Square.Move( PtX, PtY : integer );
begin
   Destroy;
   Create( PtX, PtY, side, Color );
end;

procedure Square.SetSize( R : integer );
begin
   Destroy;
   Create( x, y, R, color );
end;

{=========== end of object functions ============}

var
   TestPt  : Point;
   ACircle : array[1..32] of Circle;
   ASquare : array[1..32] of Square;
   i, MaxX, MaxY, MaxC, GDriver, GMode, GError,
   Cx, Cy, Size, TestColor : integer;
   Ch : char;

begin
```

```
    GDriver := Detect;

    InitGraph( GDriver, GMode, '\TP\BGI' );

    GError := GraphResult;

    if GError  grOk then

    begin

        writeln('Graphics error: ',GraphErrorMsg (GError));

        writeln('Program aborted...');

        halt(1);

    end;

{ create a background }

    ClearDevice;

    MaxC := GetMaxColor;

    for i := 1 to 10000 do

        TestPt.Create( random( GetMaxX ) + 1,

                       random( GetMaxY ) + 1,

                       random( MaxC ) + 1 );

{ draw receding circles }

    Cx := GetMaxX div 2;

    Cy := GetMaxY div 2;

    Size := GetMaxY div 2;

    for i := 1 to 32 do

    begin

        ACircle[i].Create( Cx, Cy, Size, i );

        dec( Size, 8 );

        dec( Cx, 10 );
```

```
     dec( Cy, 4 );
  end;

  repeat
     for i := 1 to 32 do
        with ACircle[i] do
           SetColor( ( GetColor - 1 ) mod MaxC );
  until KeyPressed;
  Ch := ReadKey;

  for i := 1 to 32 do ACircle[i].Destroy;

{ draw receding squares }

  Cx := 2 * GetMaxX div 3;
  Cy := GetMaxY div 2;
  Size := GetMaxY div 2;

  for i := 1 to 32 do
  begin
     ASquare[i].Create( Cx, Cy, Size, i );
     dec( Size, 6 );
     dec( Cx, 10 );
     dec( Cy, 4 );   }
  end;

  repeat
     for i := 1 to 32 do
        with ASquare[i] do
           SetColor( ( GetColor - 1 ) mod MaxC );
```

```
    until KeyPressed;

    Ch := ReadKey;

    for i := 1 to 32 do ASquare[i].Destroy;

    repeat until KeyPressed;
end.
```

CHAPTER 2

AN OBJECT-ORIENTED MOUSE

Most graphics programs use the mouse as a primary interface device. This book will, therefore, begin the graphics programming applications with an object-oriented mouse unit (MOUSE.PAS and MOUSE.TPU) and with a utility to create mouse cursor images (MOUSEPTR.PAS) that can be incorporated in the mouse unit or directly into your applications.

The programs in this chapter (and many of the later chapters) assume that your computer has a bus or serial mouse and mouse driver (Microsoft, Logitech or compatible) installed. The mouse unit created in this chapter is not itself a mouse driver, but an interface that uses the driver utility supplied with your mouse hardware.

When creating an object unit for use either by yourself or for distribution and use by other parties, it is helpful to provide descriptive documentation listing what functions are available via the unit, the parameters required to call these functions, and any data structures that are used by the object unit and are available to the calling program. For the MOUSE.TPU unit, sample documentation appears in Appendix B.

The Case of the Bashful Mouse

If you are using VGA or higher resolution graphics, and the mouse pointer does not appear in the graphics application, the problem may be in your mouse driver and can be cured by installing a newer driver package. The problem can be tested, however, by using Turbo Pascal's SetGraphMode command to select a lower-resolution graphics mode.

For example, using VGA graphics with a vertical resolution of 480 pixels, the graphics mouse cursor does not appear on screen, but when using the SetGraphMode(1) command to select medium resolution VGA graphics with a 350 vertical resolution, the mouse cursor does appear. If so, contact Microsoft, Logitech or your mouse supplier to obtain a new version mouse driver or purchase one of the new "HiRes" mice. With the Logitech mouse, mouse driver version 4.0 or later supports all VGA resolutions.

Creating an Object-Mouse Unit

The MOUSE.TPU unit (compiled from MOUSE.PAS) will be referenced by many of the programs in the book. If you are not familiar with the processes required to compile a unit, additional information can be found in Chapter 9 of the *Turbo Pascal Reference Guide*.

The program listing for a unit begins with the unit heading:

```
unit MOUSE;
```

which simply identifies the unit name that will be employed by other programs in the **uses** clause to refer to the unit. The unit name must be unique and the compiled unit must have the same filename and use the extension .TPU.

Following the unit declaration is the INTERFACE portion which declares constants, types, variables, procedures and functions that are **public**; they can be accessed by applications that use the unit:

```
INTERFACE
```

The type definitions declared by the unit are also available to the applications using the unit:

```
type
  Position = record
                btnStat,
                opCount,
                xPos, yPos  : integer;
            end;

  GCursor = record
                ScreenMask,
                CursorMask : array [0..15] of word;
                hotX, hotY : integer;
            end;
```

Two Buttons vs. Three

The mouse unit provides compatibility for both two- and three-button mice, principally by providing definitions for all three buttons:

```
ButtonL  = 0;

ButtonR  = 1;

ButtonM  = 2;
```

Note: if you have worked with OS/2–Presentation Manager, the mouse buttons are defined under OS/2 as 1-2-3, from left to right (with a system option to reverse the order for southpaws). Conventional mouse button ordering, however, began when computer mice had only two buttons — left and right — thus, the third (middle) button is out of order and is numbered 2. For two-button mice the third, middle, button is not available.

Four other constants are provided for general use. The constants **software** and **hardware** are used to set the text cursor and OFF and ON are for general use in Boolean applications as the equivalent of TRUE and FALSE:

```
Software = 0;

Hardware = 1;

OFF      = 0;

ON       = 1;
```

Graphics Mouse Cursors

Five graphics cursors are predefined in the mouse unit for use with graphics mouse applications. The **arrow** cursor is an angled arrow similar to the default graphics cursor. The **check** cursor is a check mark with the hot-spot at the base of the angle. The **cross** cursor is a circle with crosshairs marking a centered hot-spot. The **glove** cursor is a hand image with the hot-spot at the tip of the extended index finger and, last, the **ibeam** cursor duplicates the popular vertical bar marker used with graphics text applications. The hot-spot for the glove cursor is centered roughly on the vertical bar.

All of the graphics cursors are available to applications using the mouse unit and are defined as follows:

```
arrow : GCursor =
    ( ScreenMask : ( $1FFF, $0FFF, $07FF, $03FF,
                     $01FF, $00FF, $007F, $003F,
                     $001F, $003F, $01FF, $01FF,
                     $E0FF, $F0FF, $F8FF, $F8FF );
      CursorMask : ( $0000, $4000, $6000, $7000,
                     $7800, $7C00, $7E00, $7F00,
                     $7F80, $7C00, $4C00, $0600,
                     $0600, $0300, $0300, $0000 );
      hotX : $0001;  hotY : $0001 );
```

The MOUSEPTR program creates an ASCII text file following this same format and can be imported directly to any Turbo Pascal program listing or added to the MOUSE.PAS unit source listings.

The Object Definitions

The object definitions begin with a general mouse object type, GenMouse (GeneralMouse), which contains two record variables — the x- and y-axis position coordinates — and 12 functions and procedures belonging to the GenMouse object:

```
type

   GenMouse = object

      x, y : integer;

      Visible : Boolean;

      function  TestMouse: boolean;

      procedure SetAccel( threshold : integer );

      procedure Show( Option : Boolean );

      procedure GetPosition( var BtnStatus,

                               XPos, YPos : integer );

      procedure QueryBtnDn( button : integer;

                      var mouse : Position );

      procedure QueryBtnUp( button : integer;

                      var mouse : Position );

      procedure ReadMove( var XMove, YMove : integer );

      procedure Reset( var Status : Boolean;

                      var BtnCount : integer );

      procedure SetRatio( horPix, verPix : integer );

      procedure SetLimits( XMin, YMin,

                         XMax, YMax : integer );

      procedure SetPosition( XPos, YPos : integer );

   end;
```

The GenMouse object type is the base object type and contains functions and procedures that are common to all mouse objects. Four other object types, that will actually be used by applications, are declared. They begin with the GraphicMouse object type which adds three new procedures that are specific to graphics mouse applications;

```
GraphicMouse = object( GenMouse )

    procedure Initialize;

    procedure ConditionalHide( left, top, right,
                                    bottom : integer );

    procedure SetCursor( cursor : GCursor );

end;
```

The TextMouse object type is also a descendant of the GenMouse type, adding two text specific procedures:

```
TextMouse = object( GenMouse )

    procedure Initialize;

    procedure SetCursor( ctype, C1, C2 : word );

end;
```

The final two object types are descended, respectively, from the GraphicMouse object type and the TextMouse object type; each adding the LightPen procedure to support the rare, but still occasional, applications that require lightpen support for either graphics or text applications:

```
GraphicLightPen = object( GraphicMouse )

    procedure LightPen( Option : Boolean );

end;
```

```
TextLightPen = object( TextMouse )

    procedure LightPen( Option : Boolean );

end;
```

The Implementation Section

The IMPLEMENTATION section defines the body of the functions and procedures declared in the INTERFACE section. That is, the code specific to each procedure or function, and any types, constants, variables or local procedures or functions that are **private** — not directly available to the application using the unit:

```
IMPLEMENTATION

uses Crt, Dos, Graph;
```

The unit itself can, and often must, reference other units as above. Since this **uses** statement appears within the IMPLEMENTATION section, the referenced units are not automatically available to the calling application:

```
var

    Regs : registers;
```

The *Regs* variable is global to the procedures and functions in the unit, but it is not accessible to the application using the unit. Also, the two functions, Lower and Upper, are local functions and not accessible outside of the unit:

```
function Lower( n1, n2 : integer ) : integer;

    begin

        if n1 < n2 then Lower := n1

                    else Lower := n2;

    end;

function Upper( n1, n2 : integer ) : integer;

    begin

        if n1 > n2 then Upper := n1

                    else Upper := n2;

    end;
```

The GenMouse Implementation

The GenMouse implementations begin with the function TestMouse which executes a simple test to determine if a mouse driver is presently in the system. This is not a substitute for the Reset function, and should only be used if there is a question about whether a driver has already been loaded.

```
function GenMouse.TestMouse : Boolean;
   const
      iret = 207;
   var
      dOff, dSeg : integer;
   begin
      dOff := MemW[0000:0204];
      dSeg := MemW[0000:0206];
      if( ( dSeg = 0 ) or ( dOff = 0 ) )
         then TestMouse := FALSE
         else TestMouse := Mem[dSeg:dOff] <> iret;
   end;
```

The Reset Function

The Reset function calls the mouse driver, resetting the driver to default conditions and returning a mouse status argument in the AX register (–1 if mouse present, 0 if not available). The argument is tested to provide a Boolean response. The BX register returns the button count (2 or 3) for the mouse:

```
procedure GenMouse.Reset( var Status : Boolean;
                          var BtnCount : integer );
   begin
      regs.AX := $00;
```

```
    intr($33,regs);
    Status   := regs.AX <> 0;
    BtnCount := regs.BX;
  end;
```

The SetLimits Function

The SetLimits function establishes screen limits (in pixels) for the mouse movement. This is particularly important when using higher resolution graphics because the default limits may not include the entire screen and, if it does not, portions of the screen cannot be reached with the mouse.

The GraphicMouse.Initialize procedure calls SetLimits with the 0, 0, GetMaxX, GetMaxY arguments, to ensure that the entire screen is accessible to the mouse, but other applications may request smaller screen limits.

When restricting the mouse to a portion of the screen, if an application is using an exit button, as demonstrated in the MousePtr program, either ensure that an alternate exit procedure is supplied or that some method of reaching the exit button is always available:

```
procedure GenMouse.SetLimits( XMin, YMin,

                              XMax, YMax : integer );

  begin

    regs.AX := $07;               { horizontal limits }

    regs.CX := Lower(XMin,XMax);

    regs.DX := Upper(XMin,XMax);

    intr($33,regs);

    regs.AX := $08;               { vertical limits }

    regs.CX := Lower(YMin,YMax);

    regs.DX := Upper(YMin,YMax);

    intr($33,regs);

  end;
```

The Show Function

The Show function is used to turn the mouse cursor on and off by calling mouse functions 1 and 2, respectively.

Any time a screen update is being executed in an area that includes the mouse cursor, the mouse cursor should be turned off before repainting the screen and then restored afterwards. Otherwise, the effects can be surprising, but not desirable. If you would like to see examples caused by omission, comment out the body of this procedure and then run the MousePtr program (after recompiling the MOUSE.TPU unit):

```
procedure GenMouse.Show( Option : Boolean );

   begin

      if Option and not Visible then

      begin

         Visible := FALSE;

         regs.AX := $01          { show mouse cursor }

         intr($33,regs);

      end else

      if Visible and not Option then

         Visible := FALSE;

         regs.AX := $02;         { hide mouse cursor }

         intr($33,regs);

      end;

   end;
```

Conventional Mouse Functions Show and Hide

The mouse pointer (cursor) can be turned on or off multiple times but, for example, if the mouse pointer is hidden three times in succession, a corresponding sequence of show operations will be required to make it visible again. Both operations increment or decrement a status counter.

If the counter is zero or negative, the mouse cursor is hidden; if one or greater, the mouse cursor is visible.

Note that hiding the mouse cursor does not affect tracking or button operations — the mouse position is tracked even if the mouse is invisible.

The SetPosition Function

The SetPosition Function is used to move the mouse cursor to a specific location on the screen. The coordinates used are always absolute screen coordinates in pixels. In text modes, pixel coordinates are still used, but the coordinates are rounded off to position the cursor to the nearest character cell indicated by the pixel coordinates (for example with an 8x8 text display, x/y pixel coordinates of 80/25 would correspond to the 11th column and 4th row of the screen).

```
procedure GenMouse.SetPosition( XPos, YPos : integer );

    begin

        regs.AX := $04;

        regs.CX := XPos;

        regs.DX := YPos;

        intr($33,regs);

    end;
```

The GetPosition Function

The GetPosition function reports the mouse cursor position and the status of the mouse buttons. Position coordinates are always in pixels.

BtnStatus is an integer value with the three least-significant bits indicating the current status of the left, right and, if present, middle buttons. The corresponding bits in BtnStatus (starting with bit 0) will be set if the button is down or clear if the button is up:

```
procedure GenMouse.GetPosition( var BtnStatus,

                                XPos, YPos : integer );

    begin
```

```
      regs.AX := $03;

      intr($33,regs);

      BtnStatus := regs.BX;

      XPos      := regs.CX;

      YPos      := regs.DX;

   end;
```

The QueryBtnDn Function

The QueryBtnDn function reports the current status of all of the buttons,
a count of the number of times the requested button has been pressed
(since the last call to QueryBtnDn for this button), and the mouse
coordinates when the requested button was last pressed:

```
   procedure GenMouse.QueryBtnDn( button : integer;

                                   var mouse : Position );

   begin

      regs.AX := $05;

      regs.BX := button;

      intr($33,regs);

      mouse.btnStat := regs.AX;

      mouse.opCount := regs.BX;

      mouse.xPos    := regs.CX;

      mouse.yPos    := regs.DX;

   end;
```

The QueryBtnUp Function

The QueryBtnUp function is the equivalent of QueryBtnDn except for
reporting the number of times the requested button was released:

```
procedure GenMouse.QueryBtnUp( button : integer;
                                 var mouse : Position );

   begin

      regs.AX := $06;

      regs.BX := button;

      intr($33,regs);

      mouse.btnStat := regs.AX;

      mouse.opCount := regs.BX;

      mouse.xPos    := regs.CX;

      mouse.yPos    := regs.DX;

   end;
```

The ReadMove Function

The ReadMove function returns a total horizontal and vertical step count since the last call to the ReadMove function. For a normal mouse, the step count varies from a low of $^1/_{100}$ inch increments (100 mickeys/inch) for older mice to $^1/_{200}$ inch (200 mickeys/inch) for more modern mice and $^1/_{320}$ inch increments (320 mickeys/inch) for a HiRes mouse.

Movement step counts are always within the range $-32768..32767$, a positive value indicating a left to right motion horizontally or, vertically, a motion towards the user (assuming the cable is pointed away from the user). Both horizontal and vertical step counts are reset to zero after this call:

```
procedure GenMouse.ReadMove( var XMove,

                                 YMove : integer );

   begin

      regs.AX := $0B;

      intr($33,regs);

      XMove := regs.CX;
```

```
        YMove := regs.DX;

    end;
```

Since the mouse graphics or text cursors are updated automatically, the ReadMove function is not required to control the screen presentation, but may be used for special applications.

See also the SetRatio and SetAccel functions.

The SetRatio Function

The SetRatio function controls the ratio of physical mouse movement to screen cursor movement with the x- and y-axis arguments (*horPix* and *verPix*) expressed as the number of mickeys (units of mouse motion) required to cover eight pixels on the screen. Allowable values are 1 to 32767 mickeys, but the appropriate values are dependent on the number of mickeys per inch reported by the physical mouse: values which may be 100, 200 or 320 mickeys per inch depending on the mouse hardware.

Default values are 8 mickeys/8 pixels horizontal and 16 mickeys/8 pixels vertical. For a mouse reporting 200 mickeys/inch, this requires 3.2 inches horizontally and 2.0 inches vertically to cover a 640x200 pixel screen:

```
procedure GenMouse.SetRatio( horPix, verPix : integer );

    begin

        regs.AX := $0F;

        regs.CX := horPix;      { hor mickeys/pixel ratio }

        regs.DX := verPix;      { ver mickeys/pixel ratio }

        intr($33,regs);

    end;
```

The SetAccel Function

The SetAccel function establishes a threshold speed (in physical mouse velocity units, mickeys/second) above which the mouse driver adds an acceleration component, allowing fast movements with the mouse to move the cursor further than slow movements.

The acceleration component varies according to the mouse driver installed. For some drivers, acceleration is a constant multiplier — usually a factor of two — while other drivers, including the Logitech mouse, use variable acceleration with multiplier values increasing on an acceleration curve:

```
procedure GenMouse.SetAccel( threshold : integer );

    begin

        regs.AX := $13;

        regs.DX := threshold;

        intr($33,regs);

    end;
```

The threshold value can be any value in the range 0..7FFFh with an average value in the range of 300 mickeys/second. Acceleration can be disabled by setting a high threshold (7FFFh) or restored by setting a low or zero threshold.

The GraphicsMouse Implementation

The GraphicsMouse implementation adds three graphics-specific functions to the general mouse functions inherited from the GenMouse object type.

The SetCursor Function

The SetCursor function loads a new cursor screen and mask, making it the active graphics mouse pointer:

```
procedure GraphicMouse.SetCursor( cursor : GCursor );

    begin

        regs.AX := $09;

        regs.BX := cursor.hotX;
```

```
        regs.CX := cursor.hotY;

        regs.ES := Seg( cursor.ScreenMask );

        regs.DX := Ofs( cursor.ScreenMask );

        intr($33,regs);

    end;
```

The selected graphics cursor may be one of the predefined cursors supplied with the mouse unit (MOUSE.TPU) or may be a cursor defined by the application program.

The ConditionalHide Function

The ConditionalHide function designates part of a rectangular area of the screen where the mouse cursor will automatically be hidden and is used principally to guard an area of the screen that will be repainted:

```
procedure GraphicMouse.ConditionalHide(

        left, top, right, bottom : integer );

    begin

        regs.AX := $10;

        regs.CX := left;

        regs.DX := top;

        regs.SI := right;

        regs.DI := bottom;

        intr($33,regs);

    end;
```

The mouse cursor is automatically hidden if it is in or moves into the area designated, but the ConditionalHide function is temporary; functioning by decrementing the mouse counter in the same manner as a call to the Show(FALSE) function.

The area set by calling ConditionalHide will be cleared and the mouse cursor enabled over the entire screen by calling Show(TRUE).

The Initialize Function

The Initialize function is created as a convenience for setting up the graphics mouse operations and accomplishes four tasks: enabling the mouse to cover the entire graphics screen (recommended), setting the default mouse cursor (optional), centering the cursor on the screen (optional), and calling Show to make the mouse cursor visible:

```
procedure GraphicMouse.Initialize;

  begin

    Visible := FALSE;

    SetLimits( 0, 0, GetMaxX, GetMaxY );

    SetCursor( arrow );

    SetPosition( GetMaxX div 2, GetMaxY div 2 );

    Show( ON );

  end;
```

The TextMouse Implementation

While three functions were added to create a graphics mouse object descended from the general mouse object, to do the same for the text mouse, two procedures are provided. They parallel two of the graphic mouse procedures: Initialize, a function setting initial conditions for the text mouse and SetCursor, a function for setting the text cursor type.

While these two functions have the same names as the GraphicMouse functions, each is implemented in an entirely different manner. Strictly speaking, however, this is not an example of polymorphism because both the GraphicMouse and TextMouse are descended from GeneralMouse and not from each other (these are siblings, not descendants).

The Initialize Function

Like its GraphicMouse counterpart, the TextMouse.Initialize function begins by setting the Boolean variable *Visible* as FALSE.

To establish limits for the mouse movement, the SetLimits function is called with values retrieved from the Crt unit, containing the minimum and maximum window settings. Since WindMin and WindMax are word values and contain both x- and y-window (character) coordinates, the lo and hi functions are used to return individual values that are converted to pixel coordinates:

```
procedure TextMouse.Initialize;

   begin

      Visible := FALSE;

      SetLimits( lo(WindMin)*8, hi(WindMin)*8,

                 lo(WindMax)*8, hi(WindMax)*8 );

      SetCursor( Hardware, 6, 7 );

      SetPosition( 0,0 );

      Show( TRUE );

   end;
```

Finally, the text cursor is set to a hardware underline cursor and Show is called to make the cursor visible.

The SetCursor Function

The text version of the SetCursor function can be used to select either hardware or software cursor:

```
procedure TextMouse.SetCursor( cType, c1, c2 : word );

   begin

      regs.AX := $0A;

      regs.BX := cType;   {0 = software / 1 = hardware }

      regs.CX := c1;      { screen mask    or scan start }

      regs.DX := c2;      { cursor mask    or scan stop  }

      intr($33,regs);

   end;
```

The hardware cursor uses the video controller to create the cursor with the arguments (*c1* and *c2*) identifying the start and stop scan lines for the cursor. The number of scan lines in a character cell is determined by the hardware video controller (and monitor), but as a general rule, for monochrome systems the range is 0..7 and for CGA the range is 0..14, top to bottom.

In general, however, a start scan line of six and a stop scan line of seven will produce an underline cursor. A start scan line of two and a stop scan line of five or six produces a block cursor and works well even on high resolution VGA systems.

The software cursor is slightly more complicated. Using the software cursor, the *c1* and *c2* parameters create a character or character attributes which are, respectively, ANDed and XORed with the existing screen character.

The *c1* parameter (screen mask) is ANDed with the existing screen character and attributes at the mouse cursor location, determining which elements are preserved. Next, the *c2* parameter (cursor mask) is XORed with the results of the previous operation, determining which characteristics are changed.

In actual practice, a screen mask value of $7F00 might be used to preserve the color attributes, while a cursor mask value of $8018 would establish a blinking up-arrow cursor or $0018 for a non-blinking up arrow. In either case the existing foreground and background color attributes are preserved. In the same fashion, a screen mask of $0000 and a cursor mask of $FFFF will produce a flashing white block cursor. See Table 2-1 for more information.

As a general rule, the eight least-significant bits of the screen mask should be either $..00 or $..FF; with the former preferred.

Table 2-1: Software Cursor Parameter Format

BIT	DESCRIPTION
0..7	Extended ASCII character code
8..10	Foreground color
11	Intensity: 1 = high, 0 = medium
12..14	Background color

Table 2-1: Software Cursor Parameter Format

BIT	DESCRIPTION
15	Blinking (1) or non-blinking (0)

The LightPen Implementation

While lightpens are relatively scarce, a few applications do continue to use these, and the mouse driver package offers a pair of functions supporting lightpen emulation.

Because these are rarely needed, two descendant object types have been created — one descended from the TextMouse and the other from the GraphicMouse object types. Both implement the lightpen functions in exactly the same manner:

```
procedure TextLightPen.LightPen( Option : Boolean );

   begin

      if Option then regs.AX := $0D     { turn pen on  }
                else regs.AX := $0E;     { turn pen off }

      intr($33,regs);

   end;

procedure GraphicLightPen.LightPen( Option : Boolean );

   begin

      if Option then regs.AX := $0D     { turn pen on  }
                else regs.AX := $0E;     { turn pen off }

      intr($33,regs);

   end;
```

Lightpen emulation is turned off by default. When enabled, simultaneous down states of both the right and left buttons emulate the pen-down state and release of both buttons emulates the pen-up state.

The Mouse Pointer Utility

A mouse cursor editor (MOUSEPTR.PAS) is the second example in this chapter (see Figure 2-1); a program providing both a useful utility to create mouse cursor images and a means of demonstrating the use of the mouse unit.

While MOUSEPTR could have been created as an object-oriented program, this utility is written largely in conventional Pascal format, aside from calls to the object-oriented mouse unit. This is done for two reasons: first, to avoid complicating the utility itself and, second, because portions of the code used in this program will serve to contrast the object-oriented graphics button structures to be created in Chapter 3.

You are, however, welcome and invited to practice object-oriented programming by revising the MOUSEPTR program using the object-oriented button utilities that will be presented shortly.

Figure 2-1: The Mouse Cursor Editor

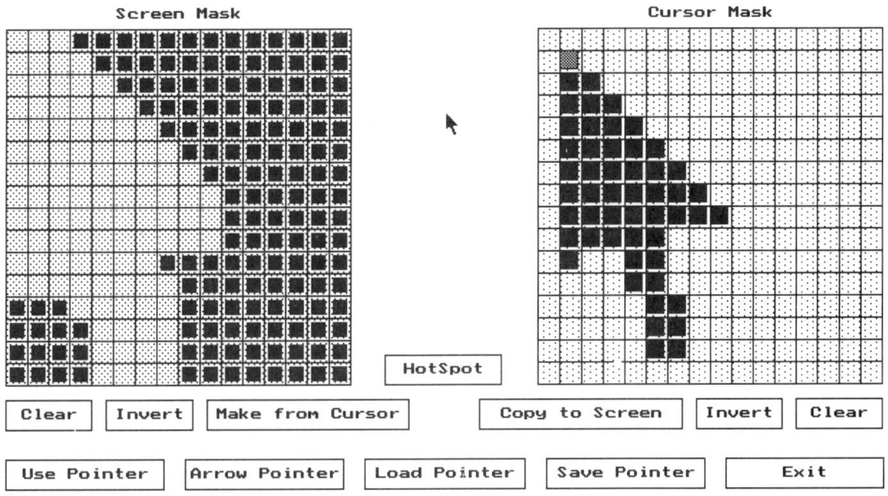

The MOUSEPTR program is generally self-explanatory and provides two grid structures for editing the screen and cursor masks to create a mouse pointer image. Naturally, editing is accomplished using the mouse to toggle squares in the grids or to select the option buttons below the grids. In brief, the options listed in Tables 2-2 and 2-3 are provided:

Table 2-2: Option Buttons

CURSOR MASK OPTIONS	DESCRIPTION
Clear	Reset all bits in the cursor mask grid to FALSE (zero).
Invert	Reverse all bits in the cursor mask grid.
Copy to Screen	Copies the cursor mask grid to the screen mask grid.

Table 2-3: Screen Mask Options

SCREEN MASK OPTIONS	DESCRIPTION
Clear	Reset all bits in the screen mask grid to FALSE (zero).
Invert	Reverse all bits in the screen mask grid.
Make room Cursor	Creates a screen mask grid image from the cursor mask grid — for each point in the screen mask grid, if the corresponding point in the cursor mask grid or any adjacent point in the cursor mask grid is TRUE, the screen mask grid point is FALSE.
Hot Spot	The next point selected in either the screen or cursor mask grids will be the hot-spot for the mouse cursor and will appear in red on both grids. Any existing hot-spot is cleared.
Use Pointer	Makes the edited cursor image the active mouse pointer on the screen.
Arrow Pointer	Restores the arrow mouse pointer.
Load Pointer	Requests a filename to load a saved cursor image. Must be an ASCII file in the same general format as created by this program. The extension .CUR and current directory are assumed.
Save Pointer	Saves the current screen and cursor grid images to an ASCII file using hexadecimal format. The output file can be imported directly for use by any Turbo Pascal program. The current directory is used and the filename extension .CUR is automatically supplied.

Table 2-3: Screen Mask Options

SCREEN MASK OPTIONS	DESCRIPTION
Clear	Reset all bits in the screen mask grid to FALSE (zero).
Exit	Exits from the program — no safety features are supplied to prevent accidental exits.

The control options affect both the screen and cursor masks.

The .CUR File Format

The mouse cursor image is saved in an ASCII format that is suitable for direct inclusion in any program. It is included by using the MOUSE.TPU unit:

```
const
    arrow : GCursor =
    (   ScreenMask : ( $1FFF, $0FFF, $07FF, $03FF,
                       $01FF, $00FF, $007F, $003F,
                       $003F, $003F, $01FF, $00FF,
                       $E0FF, $F0FF, $F0FF, $F0FF );
        CursorMask : ( $0000, $4000, $6000, $7000,
                       $7800, $7C00, $7E00, $7F00,
                       $7F80, $7C00, $4C00, $0C00,
                       $0600, $0600, $0600, $0000 );
        hotX : $0001;  hotY : $0001 );
```

All values are written in hexadecimal format, simplifying any manual editing or revising that might be desired. The *hotX* and *hotY* values are written as word values though these are actually only integer values (and never exceed $000F). Conversion is handled automatically by Turbo Pascal.

Conventional Style Button Operations

The MOUSEPTR utility is operated by the series of button controls listed previously, but these are buttons only in a limited sense. An outline and label are written to the screen with a separate function arbitrarily matching the mouse pointer location coordinates at the time that a mouse button is pressed to the corresponding screen images. The screen and cursor grids are treated in a similar fashion.

In Chapter 3, this dichotomy will be resolved in an object type named Button. Also, image, screen positions and control responses will be merged into a single control object.

The Button object type could be used to replace a large part of the programming instructions in the MOUSEPTR utility program, replacing not only the screen, cursor and general control buttons, but also replacing the screen and cursor grids with arrays of blank buttons.

For the moment, however, the topic is the conventional or non-object-oriented control structure that begins by using the GMouse object (type GraphicMouse) to enable graphics mouse operations:

```
GMouse.Reset( mStatus, Buttons );

if mStatus then

begin

   SetWriteMode( CopyPut );

   GMouse.Initialize;

   with GMouse do

   repeat
```

Instead of specifying the GMouse object for every operation within the repeat loop, the instruction with GMouse *do* simplifies the programmer's task. Within the loop, only the left mouse button is used and the loop begins by calling QueryBtnDn to test for a left button pressed event:

```
QueryBtnDn( ButtonL, mButton );

if mButton.opCount > 0 then

begin
```

If the returned opCount is not zero, the next step is to decide where the mouse cursor was located when the button was pressed. This is accomplished with nested case statements.

```
                    case mButton.yPos of
                  30..270 :    { screen or cursor grids }
                  case mButton.xPos of
{ screen mask }          15..255 : ScreenSet( mButton );
{ set hot-spot }        279..359 : if mButton.yPos >= 250
                                       then SetHotSpot;
{ cursor mask }         384..624 : CursorSet( mButton );
                  end; { case mButton.xPos }
              280..300 : { screen or cursor commands }
              case mButton.xPos of
                        { screen mask items }
                  15..75:  ClearScreen;      {Clear}
                  85..145: InvertScreen;     {Invert}
                 155..295: ScreenFromCursor; {Make}
                        { cursor mask items }
                 364..484: CursorToScreen; { Copy }
                 494..554: InvertCursor;  { Invert }
                 564..624: ClearCursor;     { Clear }
              end; { case mButton.XPos }
            320..340 :    { general command options }
            case mButton.xPos of
                 15..125: UseNewCursor;    { Use  }
                140..250: SetCursor( arrow );
                265..375: LoadPointer;     { Load }
```

```
              390..500: SavePointer;      { Save }
              515..625: Exit := TRUE;
            end; { case mButton.xPos }
          end; { case mButton.yPos }
      end;
    until Exit;
```

While this response structure does work well it has a serious deficiency. A popular adage holds that "if it works, don't fix it!" But sometimes what works in one situation does not work in all situations. The coding used in this example is a case in point. For an EGA or higher resolution graphics system, the MOUSEPTR program works just fine, but, for a CGA video, extensive conversions would have to be made before the image grids and the control buttons could fit within a 200-pixel vertical resolution.

While it would be possible to write formulas to provide adaptation to different vertical (and horizontal) resolutions for the screen images, it would also be necessary to have a series of variables associated with each of these screen elements and to assign screen coordinate values to each corresponding to the video resolution in use. In conventional programming, however, this is awkward and unwieldy. This is also one point where object-oriented programming provides tremendous advantages, see Chapter 3.

The remainder of the MOUSEPTR.PAS program is generally self-explanatory and appears in the listings at the end of this chapter.

Summary

In this chapter, an object-mouse was created to be compiled as a unit — MOUSE.TPU — and will be used in examples to provide general mouse control. Before proceeding further, you should have a working mouse unit, containing both the graphics and text mouse object methods, compiled and ready for use.

Either the MOUSEPTR program or the demo programs in Chapter 3 can be used to test the object-mouse unit:

```
{ MOUSE.PAS — Creates MOUSE.TPU Unit  }

unit MOUSE;
INTERFACE

type
   Position = record
                  btnStat,
                  opCount,
                  xPos, yPos : integer;
              end;
   GCursor =  record
                  ScreenMask,
                  CursorMask : array [0..15] of word;
                  hotX, hotY : integer;
              end;
const
   ButtonL  = 0;
   ButtonR  = 1;
   ButtonM  = 2;
   Software = 0;
   Hardware = 1;

       {=======================================}
       { five graphics cursors are predefined  }
       {        for use with GraphicMouse       }
       {=======================================}

   arrow : GCursor =           { default graphics cursor }
       (  ScreenMask : ( $1FFF, $0FFF, $07FF, $03FF,
```

```
                                $01FF, $00FF, $007F, $003F,

                                $001F, $003F, $01FF, $01FF,

                                $E0FF, $F0FF, $F8FF, $F8FF );

            CursorMask : ( $0000, $4000, $6000, $7000,

                           $7800, $7C00, $7E00, $7F00,

                           $7F80, $7C00, $4C00, $0600,

                           $0600, $0300, $0300, $0000 );

     hotX : $0001;  hotY : $0001 );

check : GCursor =        { check mark graphics cursor }
   ( ScreenMask : ( $FFF0, $FFE0, $FFC0, $FF81,

                     $FF03, $0607, $000F, $001F,

                     $803F, $C07F, $E0FF, $F1FF,

                     $FFFF, $FFFF, $FFFF, $FFFF );

            CursorMask : ( $0000, $0006, $000C, $0018,

                           $0030, $0060, $70C0, $3980,

                           $1F00, $0E00, $0400, $0000,

                           $0000, $0000, $0000, $0000 );

     hotX : $0005;  hotY : $0010 );

cross : GCursor =         { circle with cross hairs }
   ( ScreenMask : ( $F01F, $E00F, $C007, $8003,

                     $0441, $0C61, $0381, $0381,

                     $0381, $0C61, $0441, $8003,

                     $C007, $E00F, $F01F, $FFFF );

            CursorMask : ( $0000, $07C0, $0920, $1110,

                           $2108, $4004, $4004, $783C,

                           $4004, $4004, $2108, $1110,
```

```
                             $0920, $07C0, $0000, $0000 );
         hotX : $0007;  hotY : $0007 );

  glove : GCursor =          { glove or hand image cursor }
    (  ScreenMask : ( $F3FF, $E1FF, $E1FF, $E1FF,
                      $E1FF, $E049, $E000, $8000,
                      $0000, $0000, $07FC, $07F8,
                      $9FF9, $8FF1, $C003, $E007 );
       CursorMask : ( $0C00, $1200, $1200, $1200,
                      $1200, $13B6, $1249, $7249,
                      $9249, $9001, $9001, $8001,
                      $4002, $4002, $2004, $1FF8 );
         hotX : $0004;  hotY : $0000 );

  ibeam : GCursor =
             { I-beam cursor, popular for graphics text }
    (  ScreenMask : ( $F3FF, $E1FF, $E1FF, $E1FF,
                      $E1FF, $E049, $E000, $8000,
                      $0000, $0000, $07FC, $07F8,
                      $9FF9, $8FF1, $C003, $E007 );
       CursorMask : ( $0C30, $0240, $0180, $0180,
                      $0180, $0180, $0180, $0180,
                      $0180, $0180, $0180, $0180,
                      $0180, $0180, $0240, $0C30 );
         hotX : $0007;  hotY : $0007 );

type
  GenMouse = object
    x, y : integer;
```

```pascal
        visible : Boolean;
        function  TestMouse: boolean;
        procedure SetAccel( threshold : integer );
        procedure Show( Option : Boolean );
        procedure GetPosition( var BtnStatus,
                                XPos, YPos : integer );
        procedure QueryBtnDn( button : integer;
                               var mouse : Position );
        procedure QueryBtnUp( button : integer;
                               var mouse : Position );
        procedure ReadMove( var XMove, YMove : integer );
        procedure Reset( var Status : Boolean;
                         var BtnCount : integer );
        procedure SetRatio( horPix, verPix : integer );
        procedure SetLimits( XPosMin, YPosMin,
                            XPosMax, YPosMax : integer );
        procedure SetPosition( XPos, YPos : integer );
                      end;
  GraphicMouse = object( GenMouse )
    procedure Initialize;
    procedure ConditionalHide( left, top,
                              right, bottom : integer );
    procedure SetCursor( cursor : GCursor );
end;

TextMouse = object( GenMouse )
    procedure Initialize;
```

```
    procedure SetCursor( ctype, C1, C2 : word );
  end;

  GraphicLightPen = object( GraphicMouse )
    procedure LightPen( Option : Boolean );
  end;

  TextLightPen = object( TextMouse )
    procedure LightPen( Option : Boolean );
  end;

IMPLEMENTATION

uses Crt, Graph, Dos;

var
  Regs : registers;

function Lower( n1, n2 : integer ) : integer;
  begin                              { local function }
    if n1 < n2 then Lower := n1
              else Lower := n2;
  end;

function Upper( n1, n2 : integer ) : integer;
  begin                              { local function }
    if n1 > n2 then Upper := n1
              else Upper := n2;
  end;
```

```
{=========================================}
{ implementation methods for GeneralMouse }
{=========================================}
function GenMouse.TestMouse : Boolean;
   const
      iret = 207;
   var
      dOff, dSeg : integer;
   begin
      dOff := MemW[0000:0204];
      dSeg := MemW[0000:0206];
      if( ( dSeg = 0 ) or ( dOff = 0 ) )
         then TestMouse := FALSE
         else TestMouse := Mem[dSeg:dOff] <> iret;
   end;

procedure GenMouse.Reset( var Status : Boolean;
                          var BtnCount : integer );
   begin
      regs.AX := $00;    { reset to default conditions }
      intr( $33, regs );
      Status   := regs.AX <> 0;        { mouse present }
      BtnCount := regs.BX;             { button count  }
   end;

procedure GenMouse.SetAccel( threshold : integer );
   begin
      regs.AX := $13;
```

```
        regs.DX := threshold;

        intr( $33, regs );

    end;

procedure GenMouse.Show( Option : Boolean );

    begin

        if Option and not Visible then

        begin

            regs.AX := $01;              { show mouse cursor }

            Visible := TRUE;

            intr( $33, regs );

        end else

        if Visible and not Option then

        begin

            regs.AX := $02;              { hide mouse cursor }

            Visible := FALSE;

            intr( $33, regs );

        end;

    end;

procedure GenMouse.GetPosition( var BtnStatus,

                                XPos, YPos : integer );

    begin                                { function 03h }

        regs.AX := $03;

        intr( $33, regs );

        BtnStatus := regs.BX;

        XPos      := regs.CX;

        YPos      := regs.DX;
```

```pascal
        end;

    procedure GenMouse.SetPosition( XPos, YPos : integer );
        begin
            regs.AX := $04;
            regs.CX := XPos;
            regs.DX := YPos;
            intr( $33, regs );
        end;

    procedure GenMouse.SetRatio( horPix, verPix : integer );
        begin
            regs.AX := $0F;
            regs.CX := horPix;     { horizontal mickeys/pixel }
            regs.DX := verPix;     { vertical   mickeys/pixel }
            intr( $33, regs );
        end;

    procedure GenMouse.QueryBtnDn( button : integer;
                                   var mouse : Position );
        begin
            regs.AX := $05;                      { function 05h }
            regs.BX := button;
            intr( $33, regs );
            mouse.btnStat := regs.AX;
            mouse.opCount := regs.BX;
            mouse.xPos    := regs.CX;
            mouse.yPos    := regs.DX;
        end;
```

```
procedure GenMouse.QueryBtnUp( button : integer;
                               var mouse : Position );
   begin
      regs.AX := $06;
      regs.BX := button;
      intr( $33, regs );
      mouse.btnStat := regs.AX;
      mouse.opCount := regs.BX;
      mouse.xPos    := regs.CX;
      mouse.yPos    := regs.DX;
   end;

procedure GenMouse.SetLimits( XPosMin, YPosMin,
                              XPosMax, YPosMax : integer );
   begin
      regs.AX := $07;                { horizontal limits }
      regs.CX := Lower( XPosMin, XPosMax );
      regs.DX := Upper( XPosMin, XPosMax );
      intr( $33, regs );
      regs.AX := $08;                { vertical limits }
      regs.CX := Lower( YPosMin, YPosMax );
      regs.DX := Upper( YPosMin, YPosMax );
      intr( $33, regs );
   end;

procedure GenMouse.ReadMove( var XMove,
                             YMove : integer );
```

```pascal
begin
   regs.AX := $0B;
   intr( $33, regs );
   XMove := regs.CX;
   YMove := regs.DX;
end;


{=========================================}
{ implementation method for GraphicsMouse }
{=========================================}
procedure GraphicMouse.SetCursor( cursor : GCursor );
   begin
      regs.AX := $09;
      regs.BX := cursor.hotX;
      regs.CX := cursor.hotY;
      regs.DX := Ofs( cursor.ScreenMask );
      regs.ES := Seg( cursor.ScreenMask );
      intr( $33, regs );
   end;

procedure GraphicMouse.ConditionalHide( left, top,
                          right, bottom : integer );
   begin
      regs.AX := $0A;                    { function 0Ah }
      regs.CX := left;
      regs.DX := top;
      regs.SI := right;
      regs.DI := bottom;
```

```
      intr( $33, regs );

   end;

procedure GraphicMouse.Initialize;

   begin

      Visible := FALSE;

      SetLimits( 0, 0, GetMaxX, GetMaxY );

      SetCursor( arrow );

      SetPosition( GetMaxX div 2, GetMaxY div 2 );

      Show( TRUE );

   end;

         {=====================================}
         { implementation method for TextMouse }
         {=====================================}

procedure TextMouse.Initialize;

   begin

      Visible := FALSE;

      SetLimits( lo( WindMin ) * 8, hi( WindMin ) * 8,
                 lo( WindMax ) * 8, hi( WindMax ) * 8 );

      SetCursor( Hardware, 6, 7 );

      SetPosition( 0,0 );

      Show( TRUE );

   end;


procedure TextMouse.SetCursor( cType, c1, c2 : word );

   begin

      regs.AX := $0A;                        { function 10h }
```

```pascal
    regs.BX := cType;  { 0 = software / 1 = hardware }
    regs.CX := c1; { screen mask or scan start line }
    regs.DX := c2; { cursor mask or scan stop line  }
    intr( $33, regs );
  end;

  {========================================}
  { implementation method for TextLightPen }
  {========================================}
procedure TextLightPen.LightPen( Option : Boolean );
  begin
    if Option then regs.AX := $0D     { turn pen on  }
              else regs.AX := $0E;    { turn pen off }
    intr( $33, regs );
  end;

  {===========================================}
  { implementation method for GraphicsLightPen }
  {===========================================}
procedure GraphicLightPen.LightPen( Option : Boolean );
  begin
    if Option then regs.AX := $0D     { turn pen on  }
              else regs.AX := $0E;    { turn pen off }
    intr( $33, regs );
  end;

end.
```

MOUSEPTR.PAS

```
{====================================}
{    Demo program for Mouse Object    }
{ and utility to create mouse cursor }
{====================================}
program MOUSE_POINTER;

uses Crt, Graph, Mouse;
type

    Str20 = string[20];

var

    GMouse    : GraphicMouse;
    TMouse    : TextMouse;
    mButton   : Position;
    NewCursor : GCursor;
    GDriver, GMode, GError, i, j, Buttons,
       XIndex, YIndex, HotSpotX, HotSpotY : integer;
    Exit, HotSpotSelect, MStatus : Boolean;
    outline : array[1..5] of pointtype;
    Screen, Cursor : array[0..15,0..15] of Boolean;
    Ch : char;

procedure BoxItem( x, y, w, h : integer; text : str20 );
    begin
       SetTextJustify( CenterText, CenterText );
       Rectangle( x, y, x+w, y+h );
       OutTextXY( x+(w div 2), y+(h div 2), text );
    end;
```

```pascal
procedure FillSquare( x1, y1, x2, y2,
                      FillStyle, Color : integer );
   var
      outline : array[1..5] of PointType;
   begin
      outline[1].x := x1;  outline[1].y := y1;
      outline[2].x := x2;  outline[2].y := y1;
      outline[3].x := x2;  outline[3].y := y2;
      outline[4].x := x1;  outline[4].y := y2;
      outline[5] := outline[1];
      SetFillStyle( FillStyle, Color );
      FillPoly( sizeof( outline ) div
                sizeof( PointType ), outline );
   end;

procedure EraseSquare( x1, y1, x2, y2 : integer );
   var
      i, j : integer;
   begin
      FillSquare( x1, y1, x2, y2, SolidFill, BLACK );
   end;

procedure Beep;
   begin
      Sound( 220 ); delay( 100 ); NoSound;
                    delay(  50 );
      Sound( 440 ); delay( 100 ); NoSound;
   end;
```

```pascal
function StrToHex( WorkStr: string ): word;
   var
      TempVal : word;
   begin
      TempVal := $0000;
      for i := 1 to length(WorkStr) do
      begin
         TempVal := TempVal shl 4;
         case WorkStr[i] of
            '1' : inc(TempVal, 1);
            '2' : inc(TempVal, 2);
            '3' : inc(TempVal, 3);
            '4' : inc(TempVal, 4);
            '5' : inc(TempVal, 5);
            '6' : inc(TempVal, 6);
            '7' : inc(TempVal, 7);
            '8' : inc(TempVal, 8);
            '9' : inc(TempVal, 9);
            'A' : inc(TempVal,10);
            'B' : inc(TempVal,11);
            'C' : inc(TempVal,12);
            'D' : inc(TempVal,13);
            'E' : inc(TempVal,14);
            'F' : inc(TempVal,15);
         end; {case}
      end;
```

```pascal
    StrToHex := TempVal;
  end;

function HexToStr( NumVal : word ): string;
  var
    Temp : string[4];
    CVal : byte;
      i : integer;
  begin
    Temp := '';
    for i := 1 to 4 do
    begin
      CVal := NumVal and $000F;
      NumVal := NumVal shr 4;
      case CVal of
          0 : Temp := '0' + Temp;
          1 : Temp := '1' + Temp;
          2 : Temp := '2' + Temp;
          3 : Temp := '3' + Temp;
          4 : Temp := '4' + Temp;
          5 : Temp := '5' + Temp;
          6 : Temp := '6' + Temp;
          7 : Temp := '7' + Temp;
          8 : Temp := '8' + Temp;
          9 : Temp := '9' + Temp;
         10 : Temp := 'A' + Temp;
         11 : Temp := 'B' + Temp;
```

```
          12 : Temp := 'C' + Temp;
          13 : Temp := 'D' + Temp;
          14 : Temp := 'E' + Temp;
          15 : Temp := 'F' + Temp;
        end; {case}
    end;
    HexToStr := Temp;
  end;

procedure MakeCursor;
  var
      i, j : integer;
      TBit : word;
  begin
      with NewCursor do
      begin
        hotX := HotSpotX;
        hotY := HotSpotY;
        for i := 0 to 15 do
        begin
           ScreenMask[i] := $0000;
           CursorMask[i] := $0000;
        end;
        for i := 0 to 15 do
        begin
           TBit := $0001;
           for j := 0 to 15 do
```

```pascal
            begin
                CursorMask[i] := CursorMask[i] shl 1;
                if Cursor[j,i] then inc(CursorMask[i]);
                ScreenMask[i] := ScreenMask[i] shl 1;
                if Screen[j,i] then inc(ScreenMask[i]);
            end;
        end;
    end;
end;

procedure UseNewCursor;
    begin
        MakeCursor;
        GMouse.Show( FALSE );
        GMouse.SetCursor( NewCursor );
        GMouse.Show( TRUE );
    end;

procedure PaintScreen( X, Y : integer );
    var
        Color : integer;
    begin
        if ( X = HotSpotX ) and ( Y = HotSpotY )
            then Color := LIGHTRED
            else Color := WHITE;
        GMouse.Show( FALSE );
        if Screen[X,Y] then
            FillSquare( (X+1) * 15 + 3, (Y+2) * 15 + 3,
```

```
                              (X+2) * 15 - 3, (Y+3) * 15 - 3,
                              SolidFill, Color )
         else
             FillSquare( (X+1) * 15, (Y+2) * 15,
                         (X+2) * 15, (Y+3) * 15,
                         CloseDotFill, WHITE );
         GMouse.Show( TRUE );
         SetColor( WHITE );
      end;

procedure PaintCursor( X, Y : integer );
   var
      Color : integer;
   begin
      if ( X = HotSpotX ) and ( Y = HotSpotY )
         then Color := LIGHTRED
         else Color := WHITE;
      GMouse.Show( FALSE );
      if Cursor[X,Y] then
         FillSquare( (X+1) * 15 + 369, (Y+2) * 15,
                     (X+2) * 15 + 366, (Y+3) * 15 - 3,
                     SolidFill, Color )
      else
         FillSquare( (X+1) * 15 + 369, (Y+2) * 15,
                     (X+2) * 15 + 369, (Y+3) * 15,
                     WideDotFill, Color );
      GMouse.Show( TRUE );
```

```pascal
        SetColor( WHITE );
    end;

  procedure HotSpotComplete;
    var
        X, Y : integer;
    begin
        X := HotSpotX;
        Y := HotSpotY;
        PaintCursor( X, Y );
        PaintScreen( X, Y );
        GMouse.Show( FALSE );
        HotSpotSelect := FALSE;
        SetColor( WHITE );
        SetTextJustify( CenterText, CenterText );
        BoxItem(   279, 250, 80, 20, 'HotSpot' );
        GMouse.Show( TRUE );
    end;

  procedure SetHotSpot;
    var
        X, Y : integer;
    begin
        X := HotSpotX;
        Y := HotSpotY;
        HotSpotX := -1;
        HotSpotY := -1;
        PaintCursor( X, Y );
```

```
        PaintScreen( X, Y );

        GMouse.Show( FALSE );

        HotSpotSelect := TRUE;

        SetColor( RED );

        SetTextJustify( CenterText, CenterText );

        BoxItem(   279, 250, 80, 20, 'HotSpot' );

        SetColor( WHITE );

        GMouse.Show( TRUE );

    end;

procedure ScreenLayout;

    var

        j : integer;

    begin

        j := GetMaxX;

        SetTextJustify( CenterText, CenterText );

        OutTextXY( 135, 20, 'Screen Mask' );

        OutTextXY( 504, 20, 'Cursor Mask' );

        HotSpotComplete;
                    { screen mask items }
        BoxItem(  15, 280,  60, 20, 'Clear' );

        BoxItem(  85, 280,  60, 20, 'Invert' );

        BoxItem( 155, 280, 140, 20, 'Make from Cursor' );
                    { cursor mask items }
        BoxItem( 564, 280,  60, 20, 'Clear' );

        BoxItem( 494, 280,  60, 20, 'Invert' );

        BoxItem( 344, 280, 140, 20, 'Copy to Screen' );
```

```
                    { control options }
      BoxItem(  15, 320, 110, 20, 'Use Pointer' );
      BoxItem( 140, 320, 110, 20, 'Arrow Pointer' );
      BoxItem( 265, 320, 110, 20, 'Load Pointer' );
      BoxItem( 390, 320, 110, 20, 'Save Pointer' );
      BoxItem( 515, 320, 110, 20, 'Exit' );
   end;

procedure ClearScreen;
   var
      i, j : integer;
   begin
     for i := 0 to 15 do
        for j := 0 to 15 do
           if Screen[i,j] then
           begin
              Screen[i,j] := FALSE;
              PaintScreen( i, j );
   end;      end;

procedure ClearCursor;
   var
      i, j : integer;
   begin
     for i := 0 to 15 do
        for j := 0 to 15 do
           if Cursor[i,j] then
           begin
```

```
                Cursor[i,j] := FALSE;
                PaintCursor( i, j );
   end;      end;

procedure InvertScreen;
   var
      i, j : integer;
   begin
      for i := 0 to 15 do
         for j := 0 to 15 do
         begin
            Screen[i,j] := not Screen[i,j];
            PaintScreen( i, j );
   end;   end;

procedure InvertCursor;
   var
      i, j : integer;
   begin
      for i := 0 to 15 do
         for j := 0 to 15 do
         begin
            Cursor[i,j] := not Cursor[i,j];
            PaintCursor( i, j );
   end;   end;

procedure ScreenSet( mButton : Position );
   var
```

```pascal
    x, y : integer;
begin
    x := mButton.xPos div 15 - 1;
    y := mButton.yPos div 15 - 2;
    if HotSpotSelect then
    begin
       HotSpotX := x;
       HotSpotY := y;
       HotSpotComplete;
    end else
    begin
       Screen[x,y] := not Screen[x,y];
       PaintScreen( x, y );
    end;
end;

procedure CursorSet( mButton : Position );
    var
    x, y : integer;
begin
    x := ( mButton.xPos - 384 ) div 15;
    y := mButton.yPos div 15 - 2;
    if HotSpotSelect then
    begin
       HotSpotX := x;
       HotSpotY := y;
       HotSpotComplete;
```

```
        end else Cursor[x,y] := not Cursor[x,y];
        PaintCursor( x, y );
    end;

procedure CursorToScreen;
    var
        i, j : integer;
    begin
        for i := 0 to 15 do
            for j := 0 to 15 do
            begin
                Screen[i,j] := Cursor[i,j];
                PaintScreen( i, j );
    end;   end;

procedure ScreenFromCursor;
    var
        i, j, x, y : integer;
        Test : boolean;
    begin
        for i := 0 to 15 do
            for j := 0 to 15 do
            begin
                Test := TRUE;
                for x := -1 to 1 do
                    for y := -1 to 1 do
                        if( i + x in [0..15] ) and
                           ( j + y in [0..15] ) and
```

```pascal
                    Cursor[ i + x, j + y] then
                        Test := FALSE;
              Screen[ i , j ] := Test;
              PaintScreen( i, j );
    end;   end;

procedure SavePointer;
    var
        i, j, k : integer;
        Ch : char;
        CF : text;
        Done : Boolean;
        FileName : string[12];
    begin
        i := 0;
        Done := FALSE;
        FileName := '........';
        SetViewPort( 269, 0, 369, 42, TRUE );
        SetTextJustify( CenterText, CenterText );
        GMouse.SetCursor( ibeam );
        repeat
            inc(i);
            GMouse.Show( FALSE );
            ClearViewPort;
            SetColor( LightRed );
            Rectangle( 0, 0, 100, 40 );
            OutTextXY( 50, 10, 'Save As');
```

```
    OutTextXY( 50, 20, 'File Name?' );
    OutTextXY( 50, 30, FileName);
    GMouse.Show( TRUE );
    GMouse.SetPosition( 285+i*8,30 );
    repeat until KeyPressed;
    Ch := ReadKey;
    case Ch of
        #$0D : Done := TRUE;
        #$08 : if( i > 1 ) then dec( i,2 );
      '0'..'9',
            ' ',
      'A'..'Z',
      'a'..'z': if( i > 8 ) then
                begin
                    Beep;
                    dec(i,1);
            end else FileName[i] := UpCase(Ch);
    end; {case}
until Done;
GMouse.SetCursor( arrow );
GMouse.Show( FALSE );
ClearViewPort;
GMouse.Show( TRUE );
for i := 8 downto 1 do
   if( FileName[i] = '.' ) or
     ( FileName[i] = ' ' ) then
```

```pascal
        FileName[0] := chr( i-1 );
FileName := FileName + '.CUR';
SetViewPort( 0, 0, GetMaxX, GetMaxY, TRUE );
MakeCursor;
if FileName <> '' then
begin
   Assign( CF, FileName );
   Rewrite( CF );
   writeln( CF, 'const');
   write   ( CF, '    ' +
       copy( FileName, 1, length(FileName)-4 ) );
   writeln( CF, ' : GCursor =');
   with NewCursor do
   begin
      writeln( CF, '   (  ScreenMask : ( $',
                HexToStr(ScreenMask[0]), ', $',
                HexToStr(ScreenMask[1]), ', $',
                HexToStr(ScreenMask[2]), ', $',
                HexToStr(ScreenMask[3]), ',' );
      for i := 1 to 3 do
      begin
         write( CF, '                        $',
             HexToStr(ScreenMask[i*4  ]), ', $',
             HexToStr(ScreenMask[i*4+1]), ', $',
             HexToStr(ScreenMask[i*4+2]), ', $',
             HexToStr(ScreenMask[i*4+3]) );
```

```
          if i < 3 then writeln( CF, ',' )
                  else writeln( CF, ' ); ' );
      end;
      writeln( CF, '        CursorMask : ( $',
              HexToStr(CursorMask[0]), ', $',
              HexToStr(CursorMask[1]), ', $',
              HexToStr(CursorMask[2]), ', $',
              HexToStr(CursorMask[3]), ',' );
      for i := 1 to 3 do
      begin
        write( CF, '                    $',
            HexToStr(CursorMask[i*4  ]), ', $',
            HexToStr(CursorMask[i*4+1]), ', $',
            HexToStr(CursorMask[i*4+2]), ', $',
            HexToStr(CursorMask[i*4+3]) );
        if i < 3 then writeln( CF, ',' )
                  else writeln( CF, ' ); ' );
      end;
      writeln( CF, '        hotX : $',
              HexToStr(hotX), ';   hotY : $',
              HexToStr(hotY), ' );' );
    end;
    writeln( CF );
    Close( CF );
  end else Beep;
end;
```

```pascal
procedure LoadPointer;
  var
      i, j, k : integer;
      Ch : char;
      CF : text;
      Done : Boolean;
      FileName : string[12];
      WorkText : string;
      TempVal  : word;
  begin
      i := 0;
      Done := FALSE;
      FileName := '........';
      SetViewPort( 269, 0, 369, 42, TRUE );
      SetTextJustify( CenterText, CenterText );
      GMouse.SetCursor( ibeam );
      repeat
         inc(i);
         GMouse.Show( FALSE );
         ClearViewPort;
         SetColor( LightRed );
         Rectangle( 0, 0, 100, 40 );
         OutTextXY( 50, 10, 'Load From');
         OutTextXY( 50, 20, 'File Name?' );
         OutTextXY( 50, 30, FileName);
         GMouse.Show( TRUE );
```

```
      GMouse.SetPosition( 285+i*8,30 );
      repeat until KeyPressed;
      Ch := ReadKey;
      case Ch of
          #$0D : Done := TRUE;
          #$08 : if( i > 1 ) then dec( i,2 );
        '0'..'9',
             ' ',
        'A'..'Z',
        'a'..'z': if( i > 8 ) then
                    begin
                       Beep;
                       dec(i,1);
                    end else FileName[i] := UpCase(Ch);
      end; {case}
   until Done;
   GMouse.SetCursor( arrow );
   SetColor( White );
   GMouse.Show( FALSE );
   ClearViewPort;
   SetViewPort( 0, 0, GetMaxX, GetMaxY, TRUE );
   GMouse.Show( TRUE );
   for i := 8 downto 1 do
      if( FileName[i] = '.' ) or
        ( FileName[i] = ' ' ) then
          FileName[0] := chr(i-1);
```

```
if FileName <> '' then
begin
    FileName := FileName+'.CUR';
    Assign( CF, FileName );
    {$I-} Reset( CF ); {$I+}
    if( IOresult = 0 ) then
    begin
        ClearScreen;
        ClearCursor;
        i := 0;
        repeat
            readln( CF, WorkText );
            if Pos('$',WorkText) > 0 then
            for j := 1 to 4 do
            begin
                while WorkText[1] <> '$' do
                    delete(WorkText,1,1);
                delete(WorkText,1,1);
                TempVal :=
                    StrToHex(copy(WorkText,1,4));
                case i of
                    0..15: for k := 0 to 15 do
                        begin
                            if ( TempVal and $8000 ) <> 0
                            then begin
                                Screen[k,i] := TRUE;
```

```
            PaintScreen(k,i);
        end;
        TempVal := TempVal shl 1;
      end;
  16..31: for k := 0 to 15 do
    begin
      if ( TempVal and $8000 ) <> 0
        then Cursor[k,i-16] := TRUE;
        PaintCursor(k,i-16);
        TempVal := TempVal shl 1;
    end;
    32: HotSpotX := TempVal;
    33: begin
            HotSpotY := TempVal;
            PaintCursor( HotSpotX,
                          HotSpotY );
            PaintScreen( HotSpotX,
            HotSpotY );
            j := 4;
              { break out of loop }
          end;
    end; {case}
    inc( i );
  end;
  until i > 33;
  Close( CF );
end else Beep;
```

```pascal
        end else Beep;
    end;

begin
    GDriver := Detect;
    InitGraph( GDriver, GMode, '\TP\BGI' );
    GError := GraphResult;
    if GError <> grOk then
    begin
        writeln('Graphics error: ',GraphErrorMsg(GError));
        writeln('Program aborted...');
        halt(1);
    end;
    ClearDevice;
    Exit := FALSE;
    ScreenLayout;
    for i := 0 to 15 do
        for j := 0 to 15 do
        begin
            Screen[i,j] := TRUE;
            Cursor[i,j] := TRUE;
        end;
    ClearCursor;
    ClearScreen;
    GMouse.Reset( mStatus, Buttons );
    if mStatus then
    begin
```

```
SetWriteMode( CopyPut );
GMouse.Initialize;
with GMouse do
repeat
    QueryBtnDn( ButtonL, mButton );
    if mButton.opCount > 0 then
    begin
        case mButton.yPos of
            30..270 :    { screen or cursor grids }
                case mButton.xPos of
{ screen mask grid }  15..255 : ScreenSet( mButton );
{ set hot spot }     279..359 : if mButton.yPos >= 250
                                    then SetHotSpot;
{ cursor mask grid } 384..624 : CursorSet( mButton );
                end; { case mButton.xPos }
            280..300 : { screen or cursor commands }
                case mButton.xPos of
                { screen mask items }
                    15..75:  ClearScreen;
                    85..145: InvertScreen;
                    155..295: ScreenFromCursor;
                { cursor mask items }
                    364..484: CursorToScreen;
                    494..554: InvertCursor;
                    564..624: ClearCursor;
                end; { case mButton.XPos }
            320..340 :    { general command options }
```

```pascal
                    case mButton.xPos of
                        15..125: UseNewCursor;
                       140..250: SetCursor( arrow );
                       265..375: LoadPointer;
                       390..500: SavePointer;
                       515..625: Exit := TRUE;
                    end; { case mButton.xPos }
                end; { case mButton.yPos }
            end;
        until Exit;
    end;
    TMouse.Reset( mStatus, Buttons );
    TMouse.SetCursor( hardware, 11, 12 );
    Beep;
end.
```

CHAPTER 3

OBJECT BUTTON CONTROLS

By itself, the object mouse created in Chapter 2 is interesting, but useless until applied to a practical task. The next step is, therefore, to create two types of control objects, BUTTONS and TBOXES, that respond to mouse hit events; and to create a simple demo program, BTNTEST, to show how these control objects work. Before going into details on the creation of these two object types, I'll begin with an overview of the operations of each.

Graphics and Text Button Operations

While the graphics and text button operations are provided as independent units, there are similarities between the two object types. Examples of the text button objects appear in Figure 3-1 and the graphics button objects appear in Figure 3-2.

For both object types, several elements are assigned when each object instance is created. For the text buttons, the parameters include the outline type, size, position, color and text label. For text buttons, the box outline is created using the extended ASCII character set and may be a single, double or blank outline. For graphic buttons, the button style may be Square, Rounded or ThreeD.

For text buttons, only the horizontal size (in columns) is selected, with the vertical size fixed at three rows. For graphics buttons, both vertical and horizontal sizes are set (in pixels) and, if the vertical size is greater than the horizontal, the text orientation is set as vertical.

Figure 3-1: Text Button Images

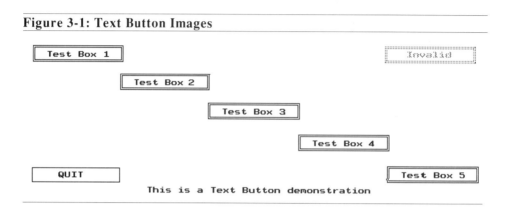

This is a Text Button demonstration

Both the text and graphics buttons accept string arguments for the text label, but the handling is slightly different in each case. For the text button, the label is truncated if it will not fit within the button outline. For the graphics button, labels are also truncated if necessary, but first, the typeface is sized and reduced as necessary to find the best fit for the label within the button. As you can see in Figure 3-2, even after selecting a smaller font size, the label has still been truncated in some instances.

Position arguments are accepted by both button types. For the text buttons the coordinates are row/column positions and, for the graphic buttons they are pixel positions; both setting the upper left corner positions.

Text Button States and Colors

Foreground and background colors are also assigned when each instance of the object is created. In this implementation, however, the assigned background color is used immediately, but the foreground color is used only when the text button's state is set as Select. Initially, each text button is set as Off and must be explicitly changed to Select — either by the program or by mouse-selection — before the assigned color will be used for highlighting. In the default Off state, the button is drawn using the LightGray color.

Figure 3-2: Graphic Button Images

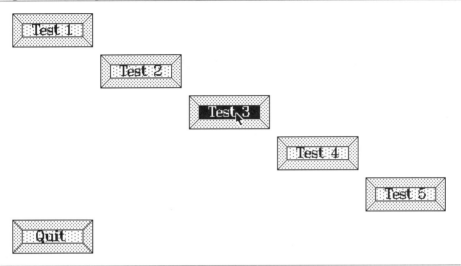

A third text button state, Invalid (shown in Figure 3-1), is also provided. This causes the button to be drawn using the DarkGray color. This particular provision is often useful when an option should be shown but is not, in the present circumstances, selectable.

Graphic Button States and Colors

For the graphics button objects, only two states are provided — TRUE or FALSE — and no Invalid state is implemented. As before, a default state of FALSE is assigned when the button is created and must be explicitly changed.

The graphic buttons differ from the text buttons in another respect: the graphic button images are always drawn using the assigned color and, for highlighting to show selection, the background and foreground colors are swapped (button 3 in Figure 3-2) and the buttons are redrawn.

Button Mouse Selection

Both the text (TBoxes) and graphic (Buttons) button objects have provisions to recognize mouse hits, but in the current programs, neither object type tests the mouse position or interrogates mouse button events directly. Instead, the application program must watch for mouse button events, passing the event coordinates to each instance of the object for testing.

When the object detects a mouse hit, by comparing the event coordinates with its own position and size, a boolean hit result is returned to the application program. Either the text or graphics object button automatically changes its own state and redisplays itself accordingly.

In the present demo, the tests and responses are limited. The only mouse button tested is a left-button down event and, when the left button is pressed, the first response is to test all of the text or graphic buttons. If any are set as Select then the button's Invert procedure is called to turn it off. After all screen buttons have been reset, a second loop polls each of the screen buttons for a mouse hit. If the mouse button event did coincide with a screen button, the screen button turns itself on and the application program responds with an audible prompt.

If a text button with the Invalid state set is mouse-selected, the only result is an audio prompt generated by the button object — not by the application.

The TBoxes Unit

The TBoxes unit is the first control object created. This provides a text-oriented object type displaying a box outline and text label (see Figure 3-1). TBoxes begins by declaring the two data types:

```
type

    BoxState = ( Off, Select, Invalid );

    BoxType = ( None, Single, Double );
```

In this case, the object type Box is not created as a descendant of any other object type:

```
Box = object
    x, y, Color, BackColor, SizeX : integer;
    Exist    : boolean;
    State    : BoxState;
    ThisBox  : BoxType;
    BtnTxt   : STR40;
```

The Box object has several variables shown, most are self-explanatory.
The Boolean variable, *Exist*, however, deserves a few comments and a
few cautions.

The Exist Variable

In the demo program, BTNTEST, two arrays of objects are declared as:

```
GButton : array[1..10] of Button;
TButton : array[1..10] of Box;
```

Because these are object-type variables, they are often expected to
carry out semi-independent operations, but if the variable has not been
initialized, the operations executed can be surprising at best and, at
worst, may cause a system hang-up.

In the demo programs used in this book, there is little chance for a
declared, but uninitialized object to be called. I prefer to err on the side
of safety. In the application programs, after declaring an array of object,
the *Exist* variables for all elements in the array are declared as FALSE
by calling the Initialize method:

```
for i := 1 to 10 do
begin
    GButton[i].Initialize;
    TButton[i].Initialize;
end;
```

Many of the critical methods in the object do not execute unless the *Exist* variable has been set to TRUE. This is done when the Create method is called for each object type.

If you examine the source code for each of these objects, you will note that more than the *Exist* flag is affected by the Initialize method. Also, the Box.Initialize method is more elaborate than the Button.Initialize method. In either case, the *Exist* flag setting which is the primary objective of the Initialize method, while the remaining method code is either optionally redundant or might be handled equally well by the object's Create method.

To return to the purpose, using the graphic button object as an example, suppose that a nonexistent button is called by any of several instructions, resulting in the Draw method being called. If the button size has not been assigned by a call to the Create method, it could result in an extremely long wait while graphics operations are attempted over an indeterminate area or, in other cases, a system hang-up may be the result (see Table 3-1).

Table 3-1: Random Results Returned by Ten Uncreated Buttons

WIDTH		HEIGHT		EXIST	
Width =	1024	Height =	0	Exist =	TRUE
Width =	191	Height =	7680	Exist =	TRUE
Width =	-24240	Height =	0	Exist =	FALSE
Width =	232	Height =	-30464	Exist =	TRUE
Width =	30464	Height =	24044	Exist =	TRUE
Width =	-442	Height =	-4983	Exist =	TRUE
Width =	0	Height =	17923	Exist =	TRUE
Width =	154	Height =	0	Exist =	TRUE
Width =	-30463	Height =	3590	Exist =	FALSE
Width =	1654	Height =	-6130	Exist =	TRUE

In the worst case the size of the button object is 30,464 by 24,044 — a total of 732,476,416 pixels; over 3,000 times the size of the average screen. Drawing or erasing an image of this size can take a bit longer than expected, or worse, operations may extend to critical memory locations, disrupting the system. Another method of preventing such accidents; using constructor and destructor calls and dynamic allocation, will be demonstrated later.

Box Object Methods

Nineteen methods are declared for the object-type Box, most are self-explanatory. A few of these, however, deserve at least a brief mention.

The Create method for the text button, accepts arguments setting the initial position, size, foreground and background colors, and text label for a text button object. The Create procedure sets *Exist* as TRUE for the current instance, ensures that the text string will fit within the declared size and finally, calls the Draw method to create a text button on the screen. No position tests are provided, but if they are desired, they would be better implemented in the Draw method than here in the Create method.

The Initialize method requires no arguments, but resets all variables to zeros or to FALSE, clearing the object instance for further use. No screen operations are executed.

The DrawBox method is the heart of the Box object, writing the text button screen image:

```
procedure Box.DrawBox;

   var

      BoxStr : string[6];

      i, XPos, YPos : integer;

      OldAttr : word;

   begin

      XPos := WhereX;

      YPos := WhereY;

      OldAttr := TextAttr;
```

Since the text buttons are intended for use with applications that will have other text material on screen, before a button is created, the current screen attributes and cursor position are saved and will be restored before the DrawBox method is completed.

The current text color is determined by the button's State and the button's assigned background color:

```
case State of
       Off : TextColor( LightGray );
    Select : TextColor( Color );
   Invalid : TextColor( DarkGray );
end; {case}

TextBackground( BackColor );
```

Next, the local variable, *BoxStr*, is given the characters appropriate to the assigned box style:

```
case ThisBox of
    None: BoxStr := '        ';
    Single: BoxStr := #$DA+#$BF+#$C0+#$D9+#$C4+#$B3;
    Double: BoxStr := #$C9+#$BB+#$C8+#$BC+#$CD+#$BA;
end; { case }
```

At this point, all that's left is to write the screen image:

```
gotoxy( x, y );                              { top of box }
write( BoxStr[1] );
for i := 2 to SizeX-1 do write( BoxStr[5] );
write( BoxStr[2]);
gotoxy( x, y+1 );                            { center of box }
write( BoxStr[6] );
for i := 2 to SizeX-1 do write(' ');
write( BoxStr[6] );
```

The interior of the box is written as spaces to clear anything that might already appear on the screen, then the new label is written, centered.

```
gotoxy( x + ( SizeX-ord(BtnTxt[0]) ) div 2, y+1 );

write( BtnTxt );

gotoxy( x, y+2 );                              { bottom of box }

write( BoxStr[3] );

for i := 2 to SizeX-1 do write( BoxStr[5] );

write( BoxStr[4] );
```

Finally, the saved cursor position and screen attributes are restored, leaving the system ready for other operations.

```
    TextAttr := OldAttr;               { restore colors }

    gotoxy( XPos, YPos );            { restore position }

end;
```

One more method deserves explanation. The BoxHit method which is called by the application with two parameters that give the coordinates of a mouse button event and returning a boolean result:

```
function Box.BoxHit( MouseX, MouseY: integer ): boolean;

    var

        Result : boolean;

    begin

        MouseX := MouseX div 8 + 1;

        MouseY := MouseY div 8 + 1;
```

Because the coordinates reported by the mouse event are in pixel units, the *MouseX* and *MouseY* parameters are converted to character positions (row/column units) before testing:

```
Result := FALSE;
```

```
if ( MouseX >= x ) and ( MouseX < x+SizeX ) and
   ( MouseY >= y ) and ( MouseY <= y+2 ) then
      Result := TRUE;
```

If the reported coordinates fall within the button object's parameters (i.e., Result is TRUE), then the BoxHit method calls the Invert method to show that the button has been hit; finally returning Result to the calling application:

```
if Result then Invert;

BoxHit := Result;
end;
```

The remaining 15 methods used by the Box object can be found in the program listings at the end of this chapter. Quite a few methods are provided but not utilized by the demo program. Remember, any methods that are not used by an application are not included by Turbo Pascal in the compiled program. Nothing is saved by being skimpy about declaring methods.

The Buttons Unit

The Buttons unit is the graphics parallel of the TBoxes unit; providing graphic button images that can be tested for mouse event hits, responding with a visual queue as well as returning a boolean result.

Note, however, that the methods provided for the text and graphic button features are only approximately parallel and the graphic buttons differ from the text buttons in two principal respects: buttons may be any size (within the limits of the screen or window) and the button caption may be oriented vertically instead of horizontally.

A variety of graphic button examples appear in Figure 3-3, in varying sizes, styles and orientations with button #5 (ThreeD-style) showing the selected state.

Notice also that buttons #1 and #2 are actually too small to properly display labels, but which attempt to do so anyway. The demo generating the illustration in Figure 3-3 used Borland's TriplexFont that is sometimes too large for many applications. The SmallFont (LITT.CHR) provides an alternate stroked character font that is approximately half the size of the triplex font and, in general, more useful for small button labels. For more details on Borland's fonts and sizing examples, refer to *Graphics Programming In Turbo C 2.0*, Addison-Wesley Publishing Company, 1988.

Depending on your application, you may prefer to modify the Buttons unit to use this smaller font, or to adapt the label sizing algorithm to switch fonts for smaller labels.

Figure 3-3: Assorted Graphics Buttons

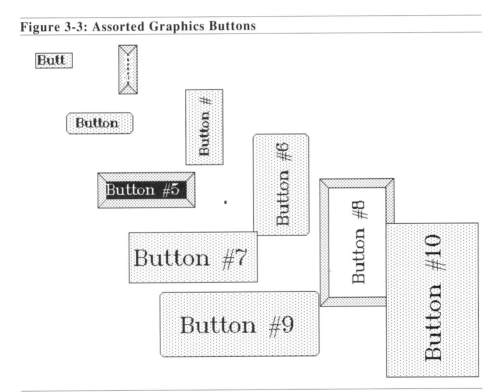

As can be seen in Figure 3-3, button labels are oriented vertically any time the button image is taller (in pixel units) than it is wide. This is an optional feature, and the graphics button unit could be redesigned for closer similarities to the text buttons, but if the vertical orientation is eliminated, the revision should probably include restrictions on button height.

Like the text version, the graphic buttons are established by calling the Create method but the parameter list is different in one respect: Button.Create is called as:

```
procedure Create( PtX, PtY,

                  Width, Height, C : integer;

                  Text : STR40 );
```

Unlike the text version, no explicit background color is assigned, but a width parameter is required.

Like the text button version, the Create method is primarily concerned with assigning values derived from the calling parameters before calling the Draw method to execute the actual screen operations. One difference, however, is the boolean *Rotate* variable that is set by testing the width against the height:

```
begin

    SetViewPort( 0, 0, GetMaxX, GetMaxY, ClipOn );

    SetTextJustify( CenterText, CenterText );

    x := PtX;

    y := PtY;

    SizeX := Width;

    SizeY := Height;

    if SizeX < 20 then SizeX := 20;

    if SizeY < 20 then SizeY := 20;

    if( SizeY > SizeX ) then Rotate := TRUE
                        else Rotate := FALSE;

    Color := C;

    State := FALSE;
```

```
Exist   := TRUE;
BtnTxt := Text;
Draw;
end;
```

The Draw method for the graphics buttons is somewhat more complicated than the text counterpart. It begins with two constants, *radius* and
offset, that are used for the rounded corners and in order to control the
fill area:

```
procedure Button.Draw;
const
    radius = 6;
    offset = 3;
```

The *RectArr* variable is an array of PointType (coordinate pairs) used
to fill a rectangular outline:

```
var
    RectArr : RectOutline;
    AlignX, AlignY, TempSize, TextLen,
    i, BtnWd, BtnHt, TextDir : integer;
begin
```

The Draw method begins by setting a viewport (a graphics window)
to the button size and further graphics drawing operations will be restricted to the viewport limits:

```
SetViewPort( x, y, x+SizeX, y+SizeY, ClipOn );
Graph.SetColor( color );
```

A case statement that uses the *Style* variable, selects the appropriate
drawing routines. It begins with the simplest case of the Square style:

```
case Style of
Square:
  begin
      Graph.Rectangle( 0,   0,   SizeX, SizeY );
      BtnWd := SizeX - 10;
      BtnHt := SizeY - 10;
  end;
```

For the Square style, the local variables, *BtnWd* and *BtnHt*, are set 10 pixels smaller than the button outline for later use in sizing the text label.

The ThreeD style is next and begins by drawing the outer rectangle and filling the entire rectangle with using the CloseDotFill pattern:

```
ThreeD:
  begin
      Graph.Rectangle( 0, 0, SizeX, SizeY );
      SetOutline( RectArr, 1, 1, SizeX-1, SizeY-1);
      SetFillStyle( CloseDotFill, color );
      SetLineStyle( UserBitLn, 0, NormWidth );
      FillPoly( sizeof(RectArr) div
               sizeof(PointType), RectArr );
```

On top of the dot-filled rectangle, the next step is drawing the inner rectangle and the four diagonal lines defining the sloped corner edges of the button:

```
SetLineStyle( SolidLn, 0, NormWidth );
Graph.Rectangle( 2*radius, 2*radius,
            SizeX-2*radius, SizeY-2*radius );
Line( 0, 0, 2*radius, 2*radius );
Line( 0, SizeY, 2*radius, SizeY-2*radius );
```

```
    Line( SizeX, 0, SizeX-2*radius, 2*radius );

    Line( SizeX, SizeY,

            SizeX-2*radius, SizeY-2*radius );

    BtnWd := SizeX-4*radius;

    BtnHt := SizeY-4*radius;

  end;
```

Finally, the *BtnWd* and *BtnHt* variables are sized smaller than the outer rectangle, again for use in later sizing the text label.

If you are running the demo program BTNTEST.PAS while reading this text, you may wish to change line 25 in BTNTEST.PAS from *SetButtonType(ThreeD)* to *SetButtonType(Rounded)* to view this button style.

The default style, Rounded, is the most complex of the three button styles and begins by drawing three quarter-circle arcs at the corner positions for the button image:

```
  else

    begin

      Style := Rounded;

      Graph.Arc( SizeX-radius, radius,

                 0,  90, radius );

      Graph.Arc( radius, radius,

                 90, 180, radius );

      Graph.Arc( radius, SizeY-radius,

                 180, 270, radius );

      Graph.Arc( SizeX-radius, SizeY-radius,

                 270, 360, radius );
```

After the corners are drawn, the straight sides are drawn connecting the ends of the arcs:

```
       Graph.Line( radius, 0, SizeX-radius, 0 );
       Graph.Line( radius, SizeY,
                   SizeX-radius, SizeY   );
       Graph.Line( 0, radius, 0, SizeY-radius );
       Graph.Line( SizeX,  radius,
                   SizeX, SizeY-radius );
       BtnWd := SizeX-2*radius;
       BtnHt := SizeY-2*radius;
     end;
   end; { case }
```

Again, the final step is defining the *BtnWd* and *BtnHt* variables to later size the text label.

The SetOutline subprocedure is provided to simplify assigning coordinate points to the RectArr structure with slightly different coordinates used for the Square or Rounded and ThreeD styles:

```
case Style of
    Square,
    Rounded:
        SetOutline( RectArr, offset, offset,
                    SizeX-offset, SizeY-offset );
    ThreeD:
        SetOutline( RectArr, 2*radius+1, 2*radius+1,
                    SizeX-2*radius-1,SizeY-2*radius);
  end; { case }
```

After the RectArr structure is set, a fill style is selected to show the button state, using a solid fill for a selected button or a wide dot pattern for a button that is off:

```
if State then SetFillStyle( SolidFill, color )
        else SetFillStyle( WideDotFill, color );
SetLineStyle( UserBitLn, 0, NormWidth );
FillPoly( sizeof(RectArr) div sizeof(PointType),
        RectArr );
```

Finally, the RectArr structure is passed to the FillPoly procedure to fill the interior of the button with the selected pattern.

Now, the text label needs to be written, but first, the font size and string length have to be adjusted to fit the available space:

```
SetLineStyle( SolidLn, 0, NormWidth );

        { adjust fonts and string to fit }
TempSize := FontSize;

TextDir := HorizDir;

if Rotate then

begin                          { vertical text display }

    TextDir := VertDir;

    TextLen := BtnWd;

    BtnWd := BtnHt;

    BtnHt := TextLen;

end;

SetTextStyle( TypeFace, TextDir, TempSize );
```

Before changing the type size or truncating the string, the Rotate flag is tested and, if necessary, the label width and height are swapped (using *TextLen* as a convenient temporary variable). Finally, the text style is set as vertical or horizontal.

Now, the font size — which begins large — is reduced until it either fits the vertical character space (*BtnHt*) or the size multiplier reaches one:

```
for i := FontSize downto 1 do
   if( TextWidth(BtnTxt) > BtnWd )
      then SetTextStyle( TypeFace, TextDir, i )
   else
      if( TextHeight(BtnTxt) > BtnHt )
         then SetTextStyle( TypeFace, TextDir, i );
```

As long as the text size for *BtnTxt* is too large, each time the loop
cycles, a new font size is set and tested on the next loop. The final loop,
when the font multiplier reaches one, is not tested. If the text is still too
large, the label is written anyway (see Button 2 in Figure 3-3).

Finally, the text length is tested for fit and the string is truncated if
necessary. Since the text will be displayed with centered alignment, any
trail space is also truncated:

```
TextLen := ord( BtnTxt[0] );

while( TextWidth(copy(BtnTxt,1,TextLen))>BtnWd ) do

   dec( TextLen );

if BtnTxt[TextLen] = ' ' then dec( TextLen );

if State then Graph.SetColor( GetBkColor );
```

If the button State is TRUE — the button has been written as a solid
field; the background color is selected before drawing the text.

Required Unit References

If the instruction, *if State then Graph.SetColor(...,* is written without the
explicit reference to the Graph unit, a conflict will occur and, instead of
the graphic SetColor procedure being called, the object's own SetColor
method will be called. In turn, it will recursively call the Draw method,
which will call the SetColor method, which, will result in a closed loop
hang-up.

In this case, the conflict could have been prevented by not giving the
object method a name that conflicts with an existing procedure in the
Graph unit. Instead, the Button.SetColor method might have been better

named as SetButtonColor. This conflict has been left in place, however, to illustrate a potential problem.

There is also hope for such an error because omitting the explicit unit identification (Graph.xxx) will produce a stack overload (after about two minutes — depending on your CPU clock) and this will break you out of the loop. For purposes of instruction, the experiment is highly recommended.

Warnings aside, the remaining step is to draw the text label. Afterwards, if necessary, the drawing color is reset and the viewport is reset to the full screen:

```
OutTextXY( AlignX, AlignY, copy(BtnTxt,1,TextLen));

if State then Graph.SetColor( color );

SetViewPort( 0, 0, GetMaxX, GetMaxY, ClipOn );
end;
```

The remaining methods provided for the Buttons unit are largely self-explanatory, providing inquiries for various button parameters or options to change parameters for an existing button without having to explicitly erase one button and create another.

The Button Test Program

The button test program (BTNTEST.PAS) is a simple demo utility that creates first a text and then a graphic button display (see Figures 3-1 and 3-2), using the mouse unit created in Chapter 2 as the control I/O. If your system lacks a mouse, a keyboard mouse emulator can be created as a substitute.

Five Pascal units are required: Crt, Graph, Mouse, Buttons and TBoxes; of which the latter three must be compiled to disk before the button test demo can be executed.

The button test demo begins with the graphics buttons display, but, if when you execute the program, the graphics mouse cursor does not appear, you may have a problem that was mentioned in Chapter 2 — a high resolution monitor and a low resolution mouse driver. If so, a one line revision (shown below) should reset the graphics driver to a resolution that is compatible with the mouse driver:

```
GDriver := Detect;
InitGraph( GDriver, GMode, '\TP\BGI' );
SetGraphMode( 1 );   { for low-res mouse drivers }
GError := GraphResult;
```

For a long term solution, the mouse driver may be upgraded — with or without purchasing a Hi-Res Mouse (hardware). Contact Microsoft, Logitech or your mouse manufacturer for more details. If this does not work, you might simply comment out the graphics portion of the demonstration and proceed directly with the text button demo.

The BTNTEST program itself should require no special explanations.

Summary

With the mouse object unit created in the previous chapter, the basics of control button operations were demonstrated using the text and graphics button objects. At the same time, a couple of potential problems were mentioned: uninitiated objects and duplicate method/procedure names.

The first potential problem was the case of calling an uninitiated object. In many cases, depending on the object type defined, this may be no problem at all. In other cases, this can be only an annoyance or possibly a disaster. In either case, it is bad programming practice. As an alternative, the practice of providing a boolean flag for each object type was suggested, with the flags for all elements of an array of object initialized as false until each instance of the object has been assigned values for any critical variables.

The second potential problem was the conflict of duplicate method/procedure names where both an object's method and a procedure external to the object were given the same name and calling parameter arrangement — with a relatively safe experiment suggested to demonstrate one aspect of such a conflict.

BUTTONS.PAS — creates BUTTONS.TPU

```
unit Buttons;
```

```
INTERFACE

type
   STR40 = string[40];

   Point = object
      x, y, Color : integer;
      procedure Move( PtX, PtY : integer );
      procedure Create( PtX, PtY, C : integer );
      procedure SetColor( c : integer );
      function  GetColor : integer;
      function  GetX : integer;
      function  GetY : integer;
   end;

   ButtonType = ( Rounded, Square, ThreeD );
   Button = object( Point )
      Exist, State, Rotate : boolean;
      FontSize, TypeFace, SizeX, SizeY : integer;
      Style : ButtonType;
      BtnTxt : STR40;
      procedure Draw;
      procedure Create( PtX, PtY,
                        Width, Height, C : integer;
                        Text : STR40 );
      procedure Initialize;
      procedure Erase;
      procedure Invert;
```

```pascal
        procedure Move( PtX, PtY : integer );
        procedure SetColor( C : integer );
        procedure SetState( BState : boolean );
        procedure SetLabel( Text : STR40 );
        procedure SetButtonType( WhatType : ButtonType );
        procedure SetTypeSize( TxtSize : integer );
        procedure SetTypeFace( TxtFont : integer );
        function  GetWidth : integer;
        function  GetHeight : integer;
        function  GetState : boolean;
        function  GetTextSize : integer;
        function  GetType : ButtonType;
        function  ButtonHit( MouseX,
                    MouseY: integer ): boolean;
    end;

IMPLEMENTATION

uses Crt, Graph;

type
    RectOutline = array[1..5] of PointType;

    {==========================================}
    { local procedure used by Button functions }
    {==========================================}

procedure SetOutline( var RectArr: RectOutline;
                        x1, y1, x2, y2 : integer );
    begin
```

```
        RectArr[1].x := x1;    RectArr[1].y := y1;
        RectArr[2].x := x1;    RectArr[2].y := y2;
        RectArr[3].x := x2;    RectArr[3].y := y2;
        RectArr[4].x := x2;    RectArr[4].y := y1;
        RectArr[5]  := RectArr[1];
     end;


        {=====================================}
        { implementation for object type Point }
        {=====================================}
procedure Point.Create( PtX, PtY, C : integer );
     begin
        x := PtX;
        y := PtY;
        Color := C;
        PutPixel( x, y, Color );
     end;

procedure Point.Move( PtX, PtY : integer );
     begin
        Create( PtX, PtY, Color );
     end;

procedure Point.SetColor( c : integer );
     begin
        Create( x, y, c );
     end;

function  Point.GetColor;
```

```pascal
   begin
      GetColor := Color;
   end;

function  Point.GetX;
   begin
      GetX := x;
   end;

function  Point.GetY;
   begin
      GetY := y;
   end;

      {======================================}
      { implementation for object type Button }
      {======================================}

procedure Button.Initialize;
   begin
      Exist := FALSE;
      SetTypeSize( 10 );
      SetTypeFace( TriplexFont );
   end;

procedure Button.Draw;
   const
      radius = 6;                              { radius }
      offset = 3;                      { offset for fill }
   var
```

```
    RectArr : RectOutline;
    AlignX, AlignY, TempSize, TextLen,
    i, BtnWd, BtnHt, TextDir : integer;
begin
    SetViewPort( x, y, x+SizeX, y+SizeY, ClipOn );
    Graph.SetColor( color );
    case Style of
    Square:
        begin
            Graph.Rectangle( 0,  0,  SizeX, SizeY );
            BtnWd := SizeX - 10;
            BtnHt := SizeY - 10;
        end;
    ThreeD:                           { ThreeD Outline }
        begin
            Graph.Rectangle( 0, 0, SizeX, SizeY );
            SetOutline( RectArr, 1, 1, SizeX-1, SizeY-1);
            SetFillStyle( CloseDotFill, color );
            SetLineStyle( UserBitLn, 0, NormWidth );
            FillPoly( sizeof(RectArr) div
                    sizeof(PointType), RectArr );
            SetLineStyle( SolidLn, 0, NormWidth );
            Graph.Rectangle( 2*radius, 2*radius,
                    SizeX-2*radius, SizeY-2*radius );
            Line( 0, 0, 2*radius, 2*radius );
            Line( 0, SizeY, 2*radius, SizeY-2*radius );
```

```
      Line( SizeX, 0, SizeX-2*radius, 2*radius );
      Line( SizeX, SizeY,
            SizeX-2*radius, SizeY-2*radius );
      BtnWd := SizeX-4*radius;
      BtnHt := SizeY-4*radius;
   end;
else                                   { default case }
   begin
      Style := Rounded;               { default }
            { draw corners }
      Graph.Arc( SizeX-radius, radius,
                 0,  90, radius );
      Graph.Arc( radius, radius,
                 90, 180, radius );
      Graph.Arc( radius, SizeY-radius,
                 180, 270, radius );
      Graph.Arc( SizeX-radius, SizeY-radius,
                 270, 360, radius );
            { draw sides }
      Graph.Line( radius, 0, SizeX-radius, 0 );
      Graph.Line( radius, SizeY,
                  SizeX-radius, SizeY   );
      Graph.Line( 0, radius, 0, SizeY-radius );
      Graph.Line( SizeX,   radius,
                  SizeX, SizeY-radius );
      BtnWd := SizeX-2*radius;
      BtnHt := SizeY-2*radius;
```

```
      end;
end; { case }

case Style of                         { fill button }
   Square,
   Rounded:
      SetOutline( RectArr, offset, offset,
                  SizeX-offset, SizeY-offset );
   ThreeD:
      SetOutline( RectArr, 2*radius+1, 2*radius+1,
                  SizeX-2*radius-1,SizeY-2*radius);
end; { case }
            { show State }
if State then SetFillStyle( SolidFill, color )
         else SetFillStyle( WideDotFill, color );
SetLineStyle( UserBitLn, 0, NormWidth );
FillPoly( sizeof(RectArr) div sizeof(PointType),
          RectArr );
SetLineStyle( SolidLn, 0, NormWidth );
   { adjust fonts and string to fit }
TempSize := FontSize;
TextDir := HorizDir;   { horizontal text display }
if Rotate then
begin                     { vertical text display }
   TextDir := VertDir;
   TextLen := BtnWd;      { swap width and height }
   BtnWd := BtnHt;
   BtnHt := TextLen;
```

```pascal
        end;
    SetTextStyle( TypeFace, TextDir, TempSize );
    for i := FontSize downto 1 do
        if( TextWidth(BtnTxt) > BtnWd )
            then SetTextStyle( TypeFace, TextDir, i )
        else
            if( TextHeight(BtnTxt) > BtnHt )
                then SetTextStyle( TypeFace, TextDir, i );
    TextLen := ord( BtnTxt[0] );
    while( TextWidth(copy(BtnTxt,1,TextLen))>BtnWd ) do
        dec( TextLen );
    AlignX := SizeX div 2 - 3; { fine tune position }
    AlignY := SizeY div 2 - 3;
    if BtnTxt[TextLen] = ' ' then dec( TextLen );
    if State then Graph.SetColor( GetBkColor );

                { add label }
    OutTextXY( AlignX, AlignY, copy(BtnTxt,1,TextLen));
    if State then Graph.SetColor( color );
    SetViewPort( 0, 0, GetMaxX, GetMaxY, ClipOn );
  end;

procedure Button.Create( PtX, PtY,
                         Width, Height, C : integer;
                         Text : STR40 );
  begin
    SetViewPort( 0, 0, GetMaxX, GetMaxY, ClipOn );
    SetTextJustify( CenterText, CenterText );
```

```
        x := PtX;

        y := PtY;

        SizeX := Width;

        SizeY := Height;

        if SizeX < 20 then SizeX := 20;

        if SizeY < 20 then SizeY := 20;

        if( SizeY > SizeX ) then Rotate := TRUE

                             else Rotate := FALSE;

        Color  := C;

        State  := FALSE;

        Exist  := TRUE;

        BtnTxt := Text;

        Draw;

    end;

procedure Button.Erase;
    var

        OldColor : integer;

    begin

        if Exist then

        begin

            SetViewPort( x, y, x+SizeX, y+SizeY, ClipOn );

            ClearViewPort;

            Exist := FALSE;

        end;

    end;

procedure Button.Move( PtX, PtY : integer );
```

```pascal
    begin
        Erase;
        x := PtX;
        y := PtY;
        Draw;
    end;

procedure Button.SetLabel( Text : STR40 );
    begin
        BtnTxt := Text;
        Draw;
    end;

procedure Button.SetColor( C : integer );
    begin
        Color := C;
        Draw;
    end;

procedure Button.SetState( BState : boolean );
    begin
        if( State <> BState ) then Invert;
    end;

procedure Button.SetTypeSize( TxtSize : integer );
    begin
        FontSize := TxtSize;
    end;

procedure Button.SetTypeFace( TxtFont : integer );
```

```
   begin

      TypeFace := TxtFont;

   end;

procedure Button.SetButtonType( WhatType : ButtonType );

   begin

      Style := WhatType;

   end;

procedure Button.Invert;

   begin

      State := not State;

      Draw;

   end;

function Button.GetWidth;

   begin

      GetWidth := SizeX;

   end;

function Button.GetHeight;

   begin

      GetHeight := SizeY;

   end;

function Button.GetState;

   begin

      GetState := State;

   end;
```

```pascal
function Button.GetTextSize;

   begin

      GetTextSize := FontSize;

   end;

function Button.GetType;

   begin

      GetType := Style;

   end;

function Button.ButtonHit( MouseX, MouseY: integer ): boolean;
   var

      Result : boolean;

   begin

      Result := FALSE;

      if ( MouseX >= x ) and ( MouseX <= x+SizeX ) and

         ( MouseY >= y ) and ( MouseY <= y+SizeY ) then

            Result := TRUE;

      if Result then Invert;

      ButtonHit := Result;

   end;

{ =========== end of methods ============= }

end.
```

TBOXES.PAS — creates TBOXES.TPU

```
unit TBoxes;

INTERFACE

type
   STR40 = string[40];
   BoxState = ( Off, Select, Invalid );
   BoxType = ( None, Single, Double );

   Box = object
      x, y, Color, BackColor, SizeX : integer;
      Exist    : boolean;
      State    : BoxState;
      ThisBox  : BoxType;
      BtnTxt   : STR40;
      procedure Move( PtX, PtY : integer );
      procedure DrawBox;
      procedure Create( PtX, PtY,
                        Width, C1, C2 : integer;
                        Text : STR40 );
      procedure Initialize;
      procedure Erase;
      procedure Invert;
      procedure SetColor( C : integer );
      procedure SetBackColor( C : integer );
      procedure SetState( BState : BoxState );
      procedure SetLabel( Text : STR40 );
```

```
    procedure SetBoxType( WhatType : BoxType );
    function  GetColor : integer;
    function  GetBackColor : integer;
    function  GetX : integer;
    function  GetY : integer;
    function  GetWidth : integer;
    function  GetState : BoxState;
    function  GetType : BoxType;
    function  BoxHit( MouseX,

                      MouseY: integer ): boolean;
  end;

IMPLEMENTATION

uses Crt;

    {=====================================}
    { implementation for object type Box }
    {=====================================}

procedure Box.Initialize;
  begin
    State := Off;
    Exist := FALSE;
    x := 0;
    y := 0;
    SizeX := 0;
    Color := 0;
    BackColor := 0;
    BtnTxt := '';
```

```
    end;

procedure Box.DrawBox;
    var
        BoxStr : string[6];
        i, XPos, YPos : integer;
        OldAttr : word;
    begin
        XPos := WhereX;
        YPos := WhereY;
        OldAttr := TextAttr;
        case State of
                Off : TextColor( LightGray );
              Select : TextColor( Color );
             Invalid : TextColor( DarkGray );
        end; {case}
        TextBackground( BackColor );
        case ThisBox of
            None: BoxStr := '      ';
          Single: BoxStr := #$DA+#$BF+#$C0+#$D9+#$C4+#$B3;
          Double: BoxStr := #$C9+#$BB+#$C8+#$BC+#$CD+#$BA;
        end; { case }
        gotoxy( x, y );                         { top of box }
        write( BoxStr[1] );
        for i := 2 to SizeX-1 do write( BoxStr[5] );
        write( BoxStr[2]);
        gotoxy( x, y+1 );                       { center of box }
```

```pascal
    write( BoxStr[6] );
    for i := 2 to SizeX-1 do write(' ');
    write( BoxStr[6] );
    gotoxy( x + ( SizeX-ord(BtnTxt[0]) ) div 2, y+1 );
    write( BtnTxt );
    gotoxy( x, y+2 );                       { bottom of box }
    write( BoxStr[3] );
    for i := 2 to SizeX-1 do write( BoxStr[5] );
    write( BoxStr[4] );
    TextAttr := OldAttr;            { restore colors }
    gotoxy( XPos, YPos );           { restore position }
  end;

procedure Box.Create( PtX, PtY, Width, C1, C2 : integer;
                      Text : STR40 );
  begin
    x := PtX;
    y := PtY;
    SizeX := Width;
    Color := C1;
    BackColor := C2;
    State := Off;
    Exist := TRUE;
    BtnTxt := Text;
    while ord(BtnTxt[0]) > SizeX-2 do
       dec( BtnTxt[0] );
    DrawBox;
```

```
    end;

procedure Box.Erase;
    var
        i, j, XPos, YPos : integer;
        OldAttr : word;
    begin
        XPos := WhereX;
        YPos := WhereY;
        if Exist then
        begin
            OldAttr := TextAttr;
            TextColor( 0 );
            for j := 0 to 2 do
            begin
                gotoxy( x, y+j );
                for i := 1 to SizeX do write(' ');
            end;
            TextAttr := OldAttr;
        end;
        gotoxy( XPos, YPos );
    end;

procedure Box.Move( PtX, PtY : integer );
    begin
        Erase;
        x := PtX;
        y := PtY;
```

```
        DrawBox;
    end;

procedure Box.SetLabel( Text : STR40 );
    begin
        BtnTxt := Text;
        DrawBox;
    end;

procedure Box.SetColor( C : integer );
    begin
        Color := C;
        DrawBox;
    end;

procedure Box.SetBackColor( C : integer );
    begin
        BackColor := C;
        DrawBox;
    end;

procedure Box.SetState( BState : BoxState );
    begin
        if( State <> BState ) then
        begin
            State := BState;
            DrawBox;
        end;
    end;
```

```
procedure Box.SetBoxType( WhatType : BoxType );
   begin
      ThisBox := WhatType;
   end;

procedure Box.Invert;
   begin
      case State of
            Off : SetState( Select );
         Select : SetState( Off );
        Invalid : begin
                     Sound( 440 );
                     delay( 200 );
                     NoSound;
                  end;
      end; {case}
   end;

function  Box.GetColor;
   begin
      GetColor := Color;
   end;

function  Box.GetBackColor;
   begin
      GetBackColor := BackColor;
   end;

function  Box.GetX;
```

```
   begin
      GetX := x;
   end;

function  Box.GetY;
   begin
      GetY := y;
   end;

function Box.GetWidth;
   begin
      GetWidth := SizeX;
   end;

function Box.GetState;
   begin
      GetState := State;
   end;

function Box.GetType;
   begin
      GetType := ThisBox;
   end;

function Box.BoxHit( MouseX,
                    MouseY: integer ): boolean;
   var
      Result : boolean;

   begin
```

```pascal
    MouseX := MouseX div 8 + 1;
    MouseY := MouseY div 8 + 1;
    Result := FALSE;
    if ( MouseX >= x ) and ( MouseX < x+SizeX ) and
       ( MouseY >= y ) and ( MouseY <= y+2 ) then
          Result := TRUE;
    if Result then Invert;
    BoxHit := Result;
  end;


  { =========== end of methods ============= }
end.
```

BTNTEST.PAS

```pascal
program Button_Test;

uses Crt, Graph, Mouse, Buttons, TBoxes;

var
    GMouse   : GraphicMouse;
    TMouse   : TextMouse;
    mButton  : Position;
    GButton  : array[1..10] of Button;
    TButton  : array[1..10] of Box;
    Exit, Status : Boolean;
    GDriver, GMode, GError, i, j, SButtons, BtnCount : integer;

procedure Create_Buttons;
```

```
var
   i : integer;
   TempStr : string[2];
begin
   for i := 1 to 5 do
      with GButton[i] do
      begin
         str( i:2, TempStr );
         Initialize;
         SetButtonType( ThreeD );
         Create( (i-1)*110+10, (i-1)*50+10,
                 100, 40, i+8, ' Test'+TempStr );
      end;
      with GButton[6] do
      begin
         SetButtonType( ThreeD );
         Initialize;
         Create( 10, 260, 100, 40, White, 'Quit' );
   end;  end;

procedure Create_TButtons;
   var
      i : integer;
      TempStr : string[2];
   begin
      for i := 1 to 5 do
         with TButton[i] do
```

```
        begin
            str( i:2, TempStr );
            Initialize;
            SetBoxType( Double );
            Create( (i-1)*15+1, (i-1)*5+1,
                    15, i+8, 0, ' Test'+TempStr );
        end;
    with TButton[6] do
    begin
        SetBoxType( Single );
        Initialize;
        Create( 1, 21, 15, White, 0, 'Quit' );
    end;
    with TButton[7] do
    begin
        SetBoxType( Double );
        Initialize;
        Create( 61, 1, 15, White, 0, 'Invalid' );
        SetState( Invalid );
    end;
  end;

begin
  for i := 1 to 10 do
  begin
    GButton[i].Initialize;
    TButton[i].Initialize;
```

```
    end;
    GDriver := Detect;
    InitGraph( GDriver, GMode, '\TP\BGI' );
{                      }{ if you have a low res mouse  }
{ SetGraphMode( 1 ); }{ and a high res video, then    }
{                      }{ you may need to include this }
    GError := GraphResult;
    if GError <> grOk then
    begin
        writeln('Graphics error: ',GraphErrorMsg(GError));
        writeln('Program aborted...');
        halt(1);
    end;
    ClearDevice;
    Create_Buttons;
    GMouse.Reset( Status, BtnCount );
    Exit := FALSE;
    if Status then
    begin
        GMouse.Initialize;
        repeat
            GMouse.QueryBtnDn( ButtonL, mButton );
            if mButton.opCount > 0 then
            begin
                GMouse.Show( FALSE );
                with GButton[i] do
```

```
      begin
          for i := 1 to 6 do
             if State then Invert;
          for i := 1 to 6 do
          if ButtonHit( mButton.XPos,
                        mButton.YPos ) then
          begin
              GMouse.Show( TRUE );
             Sound( i*220 ); delay( 100 ); NoSound;
                             delay( 100 );
             Sound( i*110 ); delay( 100 ); NoSound;
              if i = 6 then Exit := TRUE;
            end;
        end;
        GMouse.Show( TRUE );
    end;
until Exit;
CloseGraph;          { close graphics and restore }
TMouse.Initialize; { text mouse operation         }
Exit := FALSE;
ClrScr;
  { set up for text button operation }
gotoxy( 20, 24);
write('This is a Text Button test routine');
Create_TButtons;
repeat
   TMouse.QueryBtnDn( ButtonL, mButton );
```

```pascal
        if mButton.opCount > 0 then
      begin
          TMouse.Show( FALSE );
          for i := 1 to 6 do
             if( TButton[i].State = Select ) then
                TButton[i].Invert;
          for i := 1 to 7 do
             if TButton[i].BoxHit( mButton.XPos,
                                   mButton.YPos ) then
             begin
                TMouse.Show( TRUE );
                Sound( i*220 ); delay( 100 ); NoSound;
                                delay( 100 );
                Sound( i*110 ); delay( 100 ); NoSound;
                 if i = 6 then Exit := TRUE;
             end;
          TMouse.Show( TRUE );
      end;
   until Exit;
   delay(500);
  end;
end.
```

CHAPTER 4

INTRODUCTION TO
OBJECT-ORIENTED PASCAL

The basic principles of object-oriented programming shown thus far are applicable to all object types. In simple forms, you have seen how an object can be created and then extended to form a new object type. Also in previous examples, some degree of data abstraction has been used.

In this chapter, the theory of data abstraction will be brought up again, along with the theory and practice of extending objects and the potential problems and opportunities inherent in doing so.

Object Data Abstraction

While the theory and principles of data abstraction were explained earlier (See the Encapsulation section in Chapter 1), this topic will recur periodically. Now that you have seen how an object can be referenced indirectly though methods, rather than calling its values directly, and how an object can be prevented from relying on global variables, I will again emphasize the importance of providing complete object methods.

In the example objects presented in Chapters 2 and 3, a complete series of methods were provided for all conceivable accesses required — even though the demo programs themselves did not require all of them. Furthermore, while the units created contain quite a few unreferenced object methods (since the Turbo Pascal linker does not include any methods that are not actually used by the program), there is no penalty — in terms of the compiled program size or performance of the program — for being thorough.

There is a big advantage in designing the object with complete access methods because the object itself can later be redesigned internally — as long as the original access methods are retained. This can be done without requiring any applications using the object to be rewritten, they only need to be recompiled in order to include the revised object.

Later, if it becomes necessary to add a new access method or to expand the performance of the object, since only hindsight is 20/20, it can be done with complete freedom as long as the object's original methods are still supported.

The degree of freedom afforded by providing complete access methods is virtually unlimited. Since none of the object's internal variables are accessed directly by name, all of them can be renamed or restructured as necessary, their internal handling rewritten entirely or any manner of alteration performed as long as it does not affect the manner in which the object responds to the calling application.

Remember, this freedom of revision is not totally unlimited. There is one caution to keep in mind: *any descendants of an altered object will be affected by the revisions.*

Of course, the degree to which revisions will require updating descendant objects depends on the parent and child objects and the nature of the revisions. In general, renaming internal variables will require revision of child objects, but rewriting the procedures used internally should not require revisions of child procedures as long as the same inputs are used and the same objective result is achieved.

For the same reason, the example objects previously created used internal method calls wherever possible (for example, the implementation of an object method may call another method belonging to the same object rather than using duplicate code). As a secondary benefit, this also produces economy both in the source code and compiled program and is good practice in any type of programming — not merely object-oriented programming.

Other aspects of methods provisions will be discussed later in this chapter.

Extending Objects

Objects are extended by defining a new object type as a descendant of an existing object — a technique shown in Chapter 1 and again in Chapter 3 — but extending objects can take many different forms.

In standard Pascal, a few procedures such as Write and WriteLn can accept a variable number of parameters and varying parameter types, for example:

```
Write('A string message');

WriteLn('The cursor is at: ', X:2, ' : ', Y:2 );
```

Unfortunately, however, Pascal does not allow programmers to create equally flexible procedures of their own and even the graphics analogues of the Write and WriteLn procedures, OutText and OutTextXY, lack the originals' convenience and will accept only a single string argument for output.

Object-oriented programming does restore a portion of this desired flexibility through inheritance: each descendant object type inherits the methods and data fields of its ancestor type, but can add whatever new methods and data fields are necessary for a specific application. It does so without having to totally recreate the parent object.

Also, the parent object's methods may be overwritten — replaced with new methods applicable to the specific requirements of the new object.

Static Method Inheritance and Overrides

Axiomatically, each descendant object inherits all of the methods belonging to the parent object, but this does not mean that the descendant object is bound to perform exactly like the parent. Instead, any inherited method which is inappropriate to the new object's purpose can either be ignored or overwritten — the latter being the more appropriate choice.

As an example, in Chapter 3, the Button object was created as a descendant of the Point object type and it then inherited the Move, Create, SetColor, GetColor, GetX and GetY methods defined for Point.

But, for the Button object, the Move, Create and SetColor methods were overwritten by defining new methods, using the same names but not always with the same calling parameters.

For the Point object, the three methods in question were defined as:

```
procedure Move( PtX, PtY : integer );

procedure Create( PtX, PtY, C : integer );

procedure SetColor( C : integer );
```

And for the Button object, the same three method names were defined as:

```
procedure Move( PtX, PtY : integer );

procedure Create( PtX, PtY,

                  Width, Height, C : integer;

                  Text : STR40 );

procedure SetColor( C : integer );
```

Now, the changes in the Create method are obvious: three new parameters, two integers and one string, which did not appear in the Point method have been added, thus requiring a new method for handling.

What about the Move and SetColor methods? These do not appear to have changed. However, if you examine their implementations, the differences become more apparent:

```
procedure Point.Move;

   begin

      Create( PtX, PtY, Color );

   end;

procedure Button.Move;

   begin

      Erase;

      x := PtX;
```

```
      y := PtY;

      Draw;

   end;

procedure Point.SetColor( C : integer );

   begin

      Create( X, Y, C );

   end;

procedure Button.SetColor( C : integer );

   begin

      Color := C;

      Draw;

   end;
```

In actual fact, the differences are misleading. As created, the Point object type, which has not been used for real applications except to serve as a convenient parent for other object types, is relatively unsophisticated. As it stands, the Point.Move method simply creates a new point on the screen but does nothing to erase the earlier screen image — a programming flaw provided to point out one type of possible error.

At the same time, the Button object type has been provided with the mechanisms necessary (in the Move method), to erase an existing button before recreating a new image at a new position. In turn, the Button.Set-Color method uses the provisions originally made for the Move method.

Now, suppose that the Point object was given the same sophistication as the Button object: the ability to erase an existing point in response to a Move. If this were done, the two pairs of procedures could look like this:

```
procedure Point.Move( PtX, PtY : integer );

   begin

      Erase;
```

```
        x := PtX;

        y := PtY;

        Draw;

    end;

procedure Button.Move( PtX, PtY : integer );

    begin

        Erase;

        x := PtX;

        y := PtY;

        Draw;

    end;

procedure Point.SetColor( Color : integer );

    begin

        Color := C;

        Draw;

    end;

procedure Button.SetColor( Color : integer );

    begin

        Color := C;

        Draw;

    end;
```

The two paired methods are now identical.

Is there any further reason for redefining the Move and SetColor methods for the Button object?

Static Method Inheritance

Obviously, the previous question is intended as a trap. If the answer No sprang to mind, consider yourself snared because it is vitally important for the Move and SetColor methods to be redefined. The reasons are not always obvious.

The object methods appearing here are called **static methods** as opposed to **virtual methods.** The conflicts discussed in this section are specific to static methods. Virtual methods, which provide a second solution to these problems, will be discussed later.

Using static methods, the flaw in not redefining the Move method for the Button object is simply that the Point.Move method calls the Point.Erase and Point.Draw methods, not the Button.Erase and Button.Draw methods (see also the Compiler Operations section). Since the Point.Erase and Point.Draw methods have very little to do except to erase and draw a single screen pixel, they have virtually no relevance to the Button object. The same is true of the two SetColor methods that call two separate, and far from identical, Draw methods.

On the other hand, the GetColor, GetX and GetY methods defined for the Point object do not need to be redefined for the Button object and can be used as is with perfect accuracy. Thus, which methods must be redefined for child objects depends entirely on the parent and child objects and the tasks that must be implemented by the methods.

Dot Referencing

Dot referencing was introduced in Chapter 3, in the Button object implementation, when it was used to explicitly call the Graph.SetColor procedure, avoiding a conflict with the Button.SetColor procedure. This is not, however, the only reason for using dot referencing.

In general, any inherited method can be explicitly referenced using the form, Ancestor.Method. For example, assume that the Point object has been rewritten as previously suggested and now includes a method titled SetLoc which is defined as:

```
procedure SetLoc( PtX, PtY : integer );

   begin
```

```
        x = PtX;
        y = PtY;
    end;
```

With the SetLoc method provided, the Point.Move method can be simplified:

```
procedure Point.Move( PtX, PtY : integer );
    begin
        Erase;
        SetLoc( PtX, PtY );
        Draw;
    end;
```

Since the SetLoc method belongs to the Point object, no dot reference is required here. In like fashion, the Button.Move method can be rewritten to also call the parent method SetLoc:

```
procedure Button.Move( PtX, PtY : integer );
    begin
        Erase;
        Point.SetLoc( PtX, PtY );
        Draw;
    end;
```

Now, in this particular case, the dot reference is redundant because the Button object has not redefined the inherited SetLoc method; thus, the call automatically goes to the Point object's method.

Suppose, however, that the Button object has its own version of SetLoc:

```
procedure Button.SetLoc( PtX, PtY : integer );
    begin
```

```
      ... Button specific handling provisions ...

      Point.SetLoc( PtX, PtY );

      ... Button specific handling provisions ...
   end;
```

In this case, the Point.SetLoc dot reference would be absolutely necessary both here, to prevent a recursive loop, and in the Button.Move method (unless, of course, Button.Move was intended to call Button.SetLoc). In conclusion, dot referencing may be used for three purposes:

1. To resolve conflicts between object methods and external routines that have the same name.

2. To allow child methods to explicitly call ancestor methods that have been overwritten in the child object.

3. To allow a child method to call an explicit ancestor method where several generations of objects have redefined the method two or more times.

Global Variables

Global variables should not be referenced or required by objects! Having stated this, I will proceed to qualify the statement in several fashions.

First, all variables declared within an object definition are global to the object and its methods. Therefore, while these are global variables, this is true in a more limited sense than usual, but within the object the variables may be treated in the same fashion as variables declared for a procedure are global to the procedure's subprocedures. (The variables declared within the object's methods are valid only within the method.)

The second qualification is broader because there can be cases where a true global variable is simply the best solution to a program's needs. For example, an editor utility might be written as an object using dynamic memory allocation to store text data, such that the data is available to the calling application with the object returning pointers to the data's location in memory.

For simplicity, a variety of memory pointers might be global both to the object and to the application; if so, the declaration of the pointer variables should be made within the object unit — not by the calling application (I am assuming that an object of this type would be compiled as a referenced unit and not included within the main program's source code).

Third, predefined constants and flag values (or even flag variables) are more convenient if declared globally, however, these should always be declared within the object unit, not by the calling application. For those of you who wish to quibble that global constants are not global variables: you are correct, but remember that the computer is a worse quibbler than thee.

Last, the original statement stands as rephrased: no object should reference nor require externally declared global variables. Attempting to do so will limit the portability (from application to application of the object), will prevent the object (and its descendants) from being compiled as program units and, finally, is bad programming practice.

Inheriting Data Fields

Data fields, as well as methods, are inherited by child objects, but unlike inherited methods, inherited data fields cannot be overwritten or redefined. If necessary, however, inherited data fields can be ignored or used for purposes not originally intended. You cannot define a new data field with the same identifier as an inherited data field or change the structure of an inherited data field.

Compiler Operations for Static Methods

The inheritance problems described above are a product of the Pascal compiler/linker operations specific to static methods. Virtual methods are handled in a different fashion, but before the solution is explained, it helps to understand the problem.

The source of the problem is the means by which the compiler resolves method calls (or procedure or function calls in conventional Pascal). When the compiler encounters the Point.Move method, the Erase, SetLoc and Draw methods already have addresses within code segment. Later, when another method or the main program makes a call to the Move method:

```
Move( PtX, PtY );
```

becomes the equivalent of:

```
Erase;                        { Point.Erase address   }

SetLoc( PtX, PtY );           { Point.SetLoc address }

Draw;                         { Point.Draw address    }
```

This is also the reason that forward declarations are used — to provide addresses to procedures and functions for the compiler's use before the actual code is encountered. (Note: this also reduces the need for the multiple passes required by some compiler languages.)

Now, assume that the Erase and Draw methods are also reimplemented for the Button object, but the Move method has not been reimplemented. When a Button object calls the Move method, the result is still a series of calls to the Point methods, not the Button methods.

When the compiler encounters the reference Button.Move, it looks first in the Button method definitions, but if no Move has been defined for the Button method, the compiler moves up to the immediate ancestor of the current object type, continuing to regress until the method referenced is found. Of course, if no such method is encountered, the compiler terminates, issuing an error message that the method named is not defined.

Even though the Button object has its own Erase and SetLoc methods, the Move method called is Point.Move and — with static methods — the reference addresses of the Erase and Draw methods refer only to the Point implementations, not the Button implementations.

When the Button.Move method is implemented (see Figure 4-1), then the compiled result correctly becomes:

```
Erase;                        { Button.Erase address }

SetLoc( PtX, PtY );           { Point.SetLoc address }

Draw;                         { Button.Draw address   }
```

The SetLoc method, which simply assigns the calling parameters to the x- and y-axis location variables, is not redefined for the Button object.

Remember: when the inherited methods are static methods, the method called is the method precisely as it was defined and compiled for the ancestor type. If the ancestor type calls other methods, the addresses of the subsequent methods called will be those of the ancestor type — even when the descendant object has defined methods overriding the ancestor methods.

Figure 4-1: Static-Linked Object Method Calls

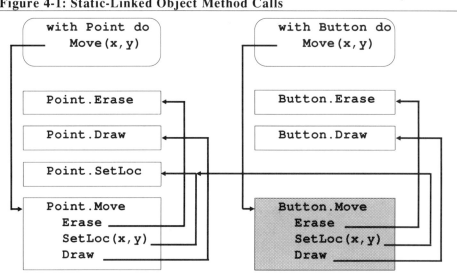

"In otherwords, to bind a method to a message (that is, a function call), the compiler must look at the type of the object involved and select the appropriate method for the message." — *HyperGuide to Turbo Pascal 5.5* by Brian Flamig.

HyperGuide to Turbo Pascal 5.5 is a public-domain utility available on CompuServe in the BPROGA forum.

Static vs. Virtual Methods

While static methods work, they do not provide the optimum flexibility that we desire for object-oriented programming, however, they still should be considered the basic tools for OOP. Note that there are more versatile tools available and virtual methods offer an alternative in which the structure and programming demands are not so rigid.

The main difference between a static and a virtual method lies in the point at which the methods are linked or bound. Static methods, as shown, are subject to a process called **early binding** with their links determined at the time a program (or unit) is compiled; this is shown in Figure 4-1.

Alternatively, **late binding** — used with virtual methods — does not create any fixed links between methods and calling procedures. Instead, at compile time, a binding mechanism is installed which will link the method and the calling process at the time the call is actually executed.

How virtual methods are created and how the mechanisms for virtual methods work will be shown, beginning in Chapter 5.

Summary

This chapter has reviewed the basic elements of object-oriented programming using static object methods and, at the same time, suggested a number of revisions for the Point and Button object types originally created in Chapter 3.

In Chapter 5, virtual methods will be the topic and the Point and Button objects will modified once again, this time with previously static methods becoming virtual methods. The suggested revisions appear in the following listings.

BUTTON2.PAS — creates BUTTON2.TPU

```
unit Button2;

INTERFACE

type
   STR40 = string[40];

   Point = object
      x, y, Color : integer;
```

```pascal
    procedure Move( PtX, PtY : integer );
    procedure Draw;                                 { new }
    procedure Create( PtX, PtY, C : integer );
    procedure SetColor( c : integer );
    procedure SetLoc( PtX, PtY : integer );    { new }
    procedure Erase;                                { new }
    function  GetColor : integer;
    function  GetX : integer;
    function  GetY : integer;
  end;

  ButtonType = ( Rounded, Square, ThreeD );
  Button = object( Point )
    Exist, State, Rotate : boolean;
    FontSize, TypeFace, SizeX, SizeY : integer;
    Style : ButtonType;
    BtnTxt : STR40;
    procedure Draw;
    procedure Create( PtX, PtY,
                      Width, Height, C : integer;
                      Text : STR40 );
    procedure Initialize;
    procedure Erase;
    procedure Invert;
    procedure Move( PtX, PtY : integer );
    procedure SetColor( C : integer );
    procedure SetState( BState : boolean );
```

```
     procedure SetLabel( Text : STR40 );

     procedure SetButtonType( WhatType : ButtonType );

     procedure SetTypeSize( TxtSize : integer );

     procedure SetTypeFace( TxtFont : integer );

     function  GetWidth : integer;

     function  GetHeight : integer;

     function  GetState : boolean;

     function  GetTextSize : integer;

     function  GetType : ButtonType;

     function  ButtonHit( MouseX,

                          MouseY: integer ): boolean;

  end;

IMPLEMENTATION

uses Crt, Graph;

type

   RectOutline = array[1..5] of PointType;


     {=========================================}
     { local procedure used by Button functions }
     {=========================================}

procedure SetOutline;                          { no changes }


     {======================================}
     { implementation for object type Point }
     {======================================}

procedure Point.SetLoc;                          { new }

   begin
```

```
      x := PtX;
      y := PtY;
   end;

procedure Point.Draw;                              { new }
   begin
      PutPixel( x, y, Color );
   end;

procedure Point.Create;                            { revised }
   begin
      SetLoc( PtX, PtY );
      Color := C;
      Draw;
   end;

procedure Point.Erase;                             { new }
   var
      Temp : integer;
   begin
      Temp := Color;
      Color := GetBkColor;
      Draw;
      Color := Temp;
   end;

procedure Point.Move;                              { revised }
   begin
      Erase;
```

```
      SetLoc( PtX, PtY );
      Draw;
   end;

procedure Point.SetColor;                    { revised }
   begin
      Color := C;
      Draw;
   end;


function  Point.GetColor;              { no changes }
function  Point.GetX;                  { no changes }
function  Point.GetY;                  { no changes }


      {=====================================}
      { implementation for object type Button }
      {=====================================}

procedure Button.Initialize;           { no changes }
procedure Button.Draw;                 { no changes }
procedure Button.Create;                   { revised }
   begin
      SetViewPort( 0, 0, GetMaxX, GetMaxY, ClipOn );
      SetTextJustify( CenterText, CenterText );
      SetLoc( PtX, PtY );
      if Width < 20 then SizeX := 20
                  else SizeX := Width;
      if Height < 20 then SizeY := 20
                  else SizeY := Height;
```

```
        if( SizeY > SizeX ) then Rotate := TRUE
                          else Rotate := FALSE;

      Color  := C;
      State  := FALSE;
      Exist  := TRUE;
      BtnTxt := Text;
      Draw;
   end;
procedure Button.Erase;                    { no changes }
procedure Button.Move;                       { revised }
   begin
      Erase;
      SetLoc( PtX, PtY );
      Draw;
   end;

procedure Button.SetLabel;              { no changes }
procedure Button.SetColor;              { no changes }
procedure Button.SetState;              { no changes }
procedure Button.SetTypeSize;           { no changes }
procedure Button.SetTypeFace;           { no changes }
procedure Button.SetButtonType;         { no changes }
procedure Button.Invert;                { no changes }
function Button.GetWidth;               { no changes }
function Button.GetHeight;              { no changes }
function Button.GetState;               { no changes }
function Button.GetTextSize;            { no changes }
```

```
function Button.GetType;                         { no changes }
function Button.ButtonHit;                        { no changes }
(* =========== end of methods ============= *)
end.
```

The BtnTest demo program requires one change to use the revised unit,
BUTTON2.TPU, thus:

BTNTEST2.PAS

```
program Button_Test_2;

uses Crt, Graph, Mouse, Button2, TBoxes;

                              { no further changes required }
```

CHAPTER 5

VIRTUAL OBJECT METHODS

While static methods are addressed and resolved at compile time and use fixed references, virtual methods are dynamically referenced. At compile time, virtual methods are compiled, but references calling the virtual methods or references within one virtual method calling another virtual method, are not resolved (i.e., the references are not replaced by link addresses at this time).

For example, assume that the Point and Button objects previously demonstrated are recreated with the Erase and Draw methods changed from static to virtual methods. In this case, instead of addresses replacing the method references in Move, virtual references are made which will be resolved later — at run time instead of at compile time.

If method addresses are not resolved at compile time, how can they be resolved at run time?

The Virtual Method Table

Instead of replacing method calls with method addresses, the compiler creates a new element for each virtual object type: the Virtual Method

Table or VMT which becomes part of the data segment of each object type definition.

Each VMT contains a variety of information including the object type's size and, for each of the virtual methods belonging to the object type, a pointer to the virtual method's implementation code. These pointers to the implementation codes for the methods are used at run time to resolve the method calls, linking each to the appropriate implementation.

Figure 4-1 shows a partial diagram for the Point and Button object methods and the Virtual Method Tables created for each, compare this figure with the static implementation links shown in Figure 5-1.

In the static version shown previously, even though both versions were defined identically, the Move method was still redefined for the Button object so that Button's version would call Button.Erase and Button.Draw instead of Point.Erase and Point.Draw.

Figure 5-1: Methods Using VMT References

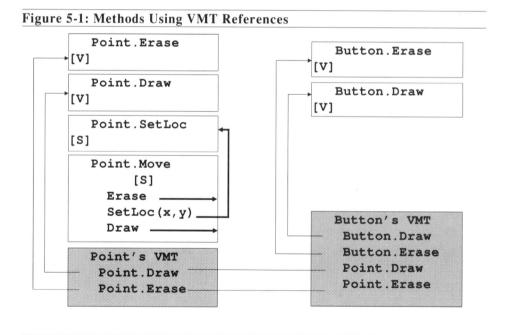

Instead, for the virtual methods version, notice that while Point.Move is still static, no Button.Move method is defined. The Point.Move method has unresolved references to the virtual Erase and Draw methods. The SetLoc method, which also remains static and is not redeclared by the Button object, is still referenced directly by its implementation address.

To satisfy the unresolved references, Point's VMT contains implementation addresses for Point's Draw and Erase methods, while Button's VMT inherits Point's method addresses, but adds its own Draw and Erase addresses. In this fashion at run time (see Figures 5-2 and 5-3), a Button instance calling Point's Move method still uses the Button.Erase and Button.Draw methods while a Point instance calling Move uses Point.Erase and Point.Draw methods.

This is precisely what virtual methods are for! By using virtual methods, when a new descendant of either Point or Button is created, the Move method does not need to be redefined, not even when the new object has its own versions of Erase or Draw because they will be used automatically.

Suppose that a descendant object, titled ScrollBar, defines a new version of SetLoc? So far, the SetLoc method has been statically linked. What happens now?

Two possibilities occur here, depending on whether the new ScrollBar.SetLoc method is created as a static or virtual method, but in either case the solution is the same.

The Move method will need to be redefined (as ScrollBar.Move for the descendant object type) before the ScrollBar.SetLoc method will be used. This is because the Point.Move method is still statically linked to Point.SetLoc.

Second, it is preferable, when ScrollBar redefines SetLoc, to make SetLoc a virtual method so that future revisions and/or descendants will not need to further redefine the Move method which, itself, is already a virtual method. Keep this in mind, it will be important later.

Assuming that only these two redefinitions are required (SetLoc redefined as a virtual method; Move redefined, but still static; and the Erase and Draw methods remain unchanged), an instance of ScrollBar calling the Move method appears in Figure 5-4.

This time, the Point.Move method is not referenced at all. Instead, the ScrollBar.Move method is linked by virtual reference to the Button.Erase, ScrollBar.SetLoc and Button.Draw methods. Any descendant objects of ScrollBar will not need to redefine the Move method, even if they redefine the Erase, SetLoc or Draw methods. What about the Move method itself? Should it have been a virtual method from the start? Or should ScrollBar.Move be declared as a virtual method?

Figure 5-2: A Point Instance Calling the Move Method

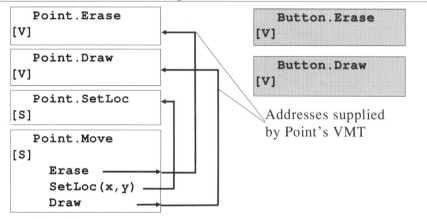

Figure 5-3: A Button Instance Calling the Move Method

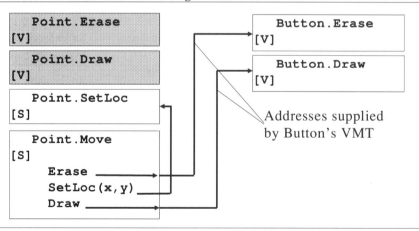

Figure 5-4:   A ScrollBar Instance Calling the Move Method

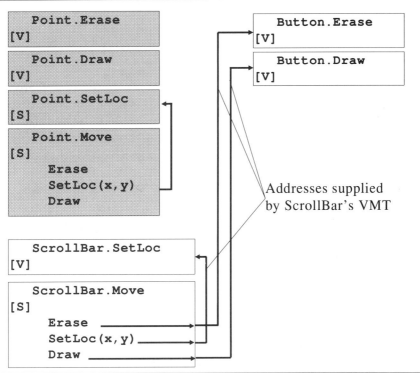

So far, nothing has been done that actually requires either of the Move methods to be virtual and, even if both were virtual methods, their effective execution would not be affected in any way. Instead, it is the fact that the methods called by the two Move methods are virtual; that accomplishes the principal task.

On the other hand, if the Point.SetLoc method had originally been defined as a virtual rather than a static method, only the original Point.Move method would be needed and no redefinition of the ScrollBar.Move method would be required. So why not declare all methods virtual and simply be done with it?

It could be done, but with two small flaws. First, each virtual method requires an entry in the object's Virtual Methods Table — which requires a small, but real amount of space. Second, execution of the program would be slightly slower with each instance of an object requiring a small slice of time for the instance's constructor to consult the VMT and link the virtual method calls to the appropriate addresses.

Static vs. Virtual

As a general rule, static methods are used to optimize for speed and memory efficiency, while virtual methods provide extensibility.

As a rule of thumb, if any method is likely to be redefined by a descendant object and the redefined method should be accessible to the ancestor, then the method should be created as virtual rather than static.

But, if an object has any virtual methods, a VMT is created for that object type in the data segment and every instance of the object will possess a link to the VMT. Every call to a virtual method references the VMT, while static methods are called directly by the address.

While the VMT is efficient, the static method calls remain slightly faster than virtual calls and, if no VMT is required or created, then a small savings in code size is realized.

In the end, one of the points of object-oriented programming is **extensibility**, allowing the extension of existing code without recompiling the source code; this is achieved, in part, by using virtual methods. Don't forget the possibility that later users of your object types will probably think of ways of employing the object type which were not anticipated when the object type was created. This, in the final analysis, is what extensibility is all about!

Static Methods Redefined as Virtual

Despite the preceding cautions, static methods are not necessarily dead-ends and, instead of all methods being initially and unnecessarily declared as virtual, any descendant object type can redeclare a static method as a virtual method.

If you refer back to Figures 5-1, 5-2 and 5-3, you should notice that both Point.Erase and Button.Erase, and Point.Draw and Button.Draw are indicated as virtual methods (indicated in the diagrams by the shorthand notation [V]). Once any method is defined as a virtual method, all descendant redefinitions of the method must also be virtual.

The drawback, of course, in redeclaring a static method as a virtual method, is that complete information about the original declaration is required in order to redefine the complete method, while an initial virtual declaration permits extensibility without revealing the original method's source. Also remember, static to virtual redefinition is a one-way street and a method which was previously virtual, cannot be redefined as static!

Creating Virtual Methods

Having talked about the theoretical how and why of virtual methods, it's time to move on to the practical aspects, beginning with how a virtual method is declared.

Virtual methods are declared simply by appending the reserved word *virtual* to the method declaration. Beginning with the Point object declaration in the Buttons unit, the changes appear as follows:

```
Point = object
    x, y, Color : integer;
    constructor Init;                              { new }
    procedure Create( PtX, PtY, C : integer );
    procedure Move( PtX, PtY : integer );
    procedure Draw; virtual;                     { revised }
    procedure SetColor( c : integer );
    procedure SetLoc( PtX, PtY : integer ); virtual;
                                                 { revised }
    procedure Erase; virtual;                    { revised }
    function  GetColor : integer;
    function  GetX : integer;
    function  GetY : integer;
  end;
```

In addition to the keyword *virtual* being appended to the SetLoc, Draw and Erase methods, you should also notice that a new method, titled Init, has been declared using the reserved word *constructor*. A **constructor** is a special type of procedure provided to handle some of the initial setup work required for virtual methods. They will be discussed in a moment. For the present, simply remember that the object's constructor method must be called before any virtual methods are used. Otherwise, if a virtual method is called before the object constructor, a system hang-up will occur.

Note also that the compiler does not normally test the order in which methods are called and cannot tell you if an object's constructor method is not called correctly — see the Range Checking and Virtual Method Calls section.

For the Button object, the Draw and Erase methods are redefined, but are again defined as virtual — not static — methods. Remember, once a method has been defined as virtual, all descendant methods must also be defined as virtual. The remaining virtual method defined in the Point object, SetLoc, is not redefined in the Button object.

The Initialize method defined in previous versions has now become the constructor method, Init. The name change has been made for compatibility with the identifier suggested in the Turbo Pascal OOP Guide, though the tasks executed by the Button.Init method have not been changed:

```
Button = object( Point )
    Exist, State, Rotate : boolean;
    FontSize, TypeFace, SizeX, SizeY : integer;
    ThisButton : ButtonType;
    BtnTxt : STR40;
    constructor Init;                              { revised }
    procedure Draw; virtual;                       { revised }
    procedure Create( PtX, PtY,
                   Width, Height, C : integer;
                   Text : STR40 );
    procedure Erase; virtual;                      { revised }
```

```
        { no further declaration changes }
end;
```

Aside from these three changes in the declarations, the remainder of the methods are declared exactly as they appeared in the previous versions of the Button unit. But there are a couple of additional other revisions. First, the Point.Init method is new and has to be defined in the IMPLEMENTATION section of the Button unit:

```
constructor Point.Init;

    begin

    end;
```

Please note: the preceding code is not an error. The fact that the Point.Init method implementation does not contain any instruction is perfectly correct because, in this case, nothing is required except the constructor call itself.

Alternatively, the Point.Create method could have become the constructor, but this particular version is used to illustrate the importance of the constructor call, irrespective of any secondary tasks accomplished by the constructor method.

Constructor Methods

The constructor method is vital to objects using virtual methods because it is the constructor call that establishes the link between an object instance and the object type's Virtual Method Table. Without this link, any call to a virtual method simply leads to some never-never-land where it can not be resolved, and the result is a hang up that can only be corrected by resetting the computer.

Each object type using virtual methods has a single VMT, but the individual instances of an object type do not contain copies of the VMT itself. The only way that an object instance can access the VMT is through the link created by the constructor call.

Obviously, the constructor method cannot be a virtual method; because the constructor implementation could not be called by the object until after the constructor had supplied the link to the VMT. The link identifies the address of the constructor implementation which is only done in response to the constructor call. While recursion is permitted, this type of circular bootstrap recursion is not. The constructor method; therefore, is always static.

Each individual instance of a method — whether the method instance is static or dynamic (see Chapter 7) — must be initialized by its own constructor call. Thus, one instance of a method cannot be initialized and then subsequently assigned to other instances because only the first, initialized method instance will contain a correct link to the VMT and the remaining instances — if virtual methods are called — will produce a system hang-up.

The constructor method also has wide applicability and it is not necessary for every method to have a constructor method. For example, the Button object in the Button3 demo does not require redefinition of a constructor method, but can simply inherit the Point.Init constructor which will correctly initialize each Button instance's link to the Button VMT, not to the Point VMT.

At the same time, since the constructor method is always static, descendant objects are free to overwrite inherited constructor methods without the constraints imposed by virtual methods (i.e., a descendant's constructor method is not required to match the calling format of the ancestor's constructor).

Range Checking and Virtual Method Calls

Turbo Pascal 5.5 has provided a "safety net" feature in the form of the *$R* compiler directive. In the active state (*$R+*), before compiling any virtual method call, the compiler tests the initialization state of the instance placing the call, issuing a range check run-time error if the instance calling the virtual method has not been initialized (by first calling the constructor method).

After a program has been debugged, execution can be speeded by setting the *$R* toggle to inactive (*$R-*), but uninitialized virtual method calls will no longer be trapped and an error of this type will probably cause a system hang up.

Obviously, when virtual methods are used, each object definition must contain at least one constructor method and the *$R* toggle can be used to test, indirectly, for the omission of a constructor call.

There is, however, a second possible error that cannot be trapped quite so easily — the presence of a redundant, duplicate constructor declaration within an object's definition or both an inherited constructor call and a newly declared constructor call. This second error is not fatal and will not prevent a program from executing correctly, but it does add a small amount of unnecessary overhead to the unit or the .EXE program. (A brief test using the Button3 unit, declaring the Button3.Create method a second constructor, added 32 bytes to the .TPU unit and 48 bytes to the .EXE program, but otherwise executed correctly.)

Summary

This chapter has provided an introduction to virtual methods, discussing the theory behind virtual methods, the reasons for using virtual methods instead of static methods, and some of the trade-offs involved. The constructor method type has also been introduced and explained, together with the *$R* toggle used to test object instance initialization. Finally, the Button unit has appeared in a third revision using virtual methods (listings showing all necessary changes for the Button3 unit and BtnTest3.PAS follow).

Next, the ScrollBar object, cited as an example in the current chapter, will finally be created as a descendant (however unlikely) of the Button type. This will be accomplished using the Button4.TPU unit (a slight modification of the Button3 unit), rather than adding to the source code — to show how object extensibility actually works.

BUTTON3.PAS — creates BUTTON3.TPU

```
unit Button3;

        (*===================================*)
        (* this version uses virtual methods *)
        (*===================================*)

INTERFACE
```

```
type
   STR40 = string[40];

   Point = object
      x, y, Color : integer;
      constructor Init;                              { new }
      procedure Create( PtX, PtY, C : integer );
      procedure Move( PtX, PtY : integer );
      procedure Draw; virtual;                       { revised }
      procedure SetColor( c : integer );
      procedure SetLoc( PtX, PtY : integer ); virtual;
                                                     { revised }
      procedure Erase; virtual;                      { revised }
      function  GetColor : integer;
      function  GetX : integer;
      function  GetY : integer;
   end;

   ButtonType = ( Rounded, Square, ThreeD );
   Button = object( Point )
      Exist, State, Rotate : boolean;
      FontSize, TypeFace, SizeX, SizeY : integer;
      ThisButton : ButtonType;
      BtnTxt : STR40;
      constructor Init;                              { revised }
      procedure Draw; virtual;                       { revised }
      procedure Create( PtX, PtY, Width, Height, C : integer;
                        Text : STR40 );
```

```
    procedure Erase; virtual;                  { revised }

    procedure Invert;

    procedure Move( PtX, PtY : integer );

    procedure SetColor( C : integer );

    procedure SetState( BState : boolean );

    procedure SetLabel( Text : STR40 );

    procedure SetButtonType( WhatType : ButtonType );

    procedure SetTypeSize( TxtSize : integer );

    procedure SetTypeFace( TxtFont : integer );

    function  GetWidth : integer;

    function  GetHeight : integer;

    function  GetState : boolean;

    function  GetTextSize : integer;

    function  GetType : ButtonType;

    function  ButtonHit( MouseX, MouseY: integer ): boolean;
  end;

IMPLEMENTATION

uses Crt, Graph;

type
   RectOutline = array[1..5] of PointType;

   {=========================================}
   { local procedure used by Button functions }
   {=========================================}

procedure SetOutline( ... );                 { no change }
```

```
        {=======================================}
        { implementation for object type Point }
        {=======================================}
constructor Point.Init;                              { new }
   begin                          { no instructions required }
   end;                           { for this method ...      }

procedure Point.SetLoc;                          { no change }
procedure Point.Draw;                            { no change }
procedure Point.Create;                          { no change }
procedure Point.Erase;                           { no change }
procedure Point.Move;                            { no change }
procedure Point.SetColor;                        { no change }
function  Point.GetColor;                        { no change }
function  Point.GetX;                            { no change }
function  Point.GetY;                            { no change }

        {========================================}
        { implementation for object type Button }
        {========================================}
constructor Button.Init;                         { revised }
   begin
      Exist := FALSE;
      SetTypeSize( 10 );
      SetTypeFace( TriplexFont );
   end;

procedure Button.Draw;                           { no change }
procedure Button.Create;                         { no change }
```

```
procedure Button.Erase;                    { no change }

procedure Button.Move;                      { no change }

procedure Button.SetLabel;                  { no change }

procedure Button.SetColor;                  { no change }

procedure Button.SetState;                  { no change }

procedure Button.SetTypeSize;               { no change }

procedure Button.SetTypeFace;               { no change }

procedure Button.SetButtonType;             { no change }

procedure Button.Invert;                    { no change }

function Button.GetWidth;                    { no change }

function Button.GetHeight;                   { no change }

function Button.GetState;                    { no change }

function Button.GetTextSize;                 { no change }

function Button.GetType;                      { no change }

function Button.ButtonHit;                   { no change }

(* =========== end of methods ============= *)

end.
```

BTNTEST3.PAS

```
program Button_Test_3; { BTNTEST3.PAS }

uses Crt, Graph, Mouse, Button3, TBoxes;

var
   ...                                       { no changes }

procedure Init_Buttons;
   var
```

```
          i : integer;
          TempStr : string[2];
      begin
          for i := 1 to 5 do
             with GButton[i] do
             begin
                str( i:2, TempStr );
                Init;                              { revised }
                SetButtonType( ThreeD );
                Create( (i-1)*110+10, (i-1)*50+10,
                        100, 40, i+8, ' Test'+TempStr );
             end;
          GButton[6].Init;                         { revised }
          GButton[6].SetButtonType( ThreeD );
          GButton[6].Create( 10, 260, 100, 40,
                             White, 'Quit' );
      end;

  procedure Init_TBox;
  begin
      ...                                          { no changes }
  end;

  begin
      GDriver := Detect;
      InitGraph( GDriver, GMode, '\TP\BGI' );
      GError := GraphResult;
```

```
    if GError   grOk then
    begin
       writeln('Graphics error: ',
                 GraphErrorMsg(GError));
       writeln('Program aborted...');
       halt(1);
    end;
    ClearDevice;
    Init_Buttons;
    GMouse.Reset( Status, BtnCount );
    Exit := FALSE;
    for i := 1 to 10 do
    begin
       GButton[i].Init;                      { revised }
       TBox[i].Initialize;
    end;
    ...                                       { no further changes }
end.
```

CHAPTER 6

SCROLLBARS AND OBJECT EXTENSIBILITY

In this chapter, object extensibility with be the principal topic. To demonstrate extensibility, the ScrollBar object will be developed as a descendant of the Button object type.

Previously, examples have been created by building on existing source code or by modifying an existing object type. But correctly demonstrating extensibility, even when the ancestor source code is readily available, requires creating a descendant object type from an already compiled ancestor. Before developing the ScrollBar object, a few modifications will be made to the Button object unit to improve its own extensibility.

First, however, a review of the what and why of extensibility is in order.

Object Extensibility

Object extensibility is one of the principal advantages of object-oriented programming. Using extensibility, toolbox units can be created and distributed to users in linkable .TPU form as modifiable sources for use in creating their own applications.

For distribution purposes, the source code of an object-oriented unit can remain the property of the developer, while the distributed unit does not require release of any more documentation than the INTERFACE portion of the unit. Additional documentation, however, is suggested for clarity and the user's convenience.

Because the source code itself is not distributed, programmers are able to maintain a proprietary interest in their software development and, at the same time, can develop new versions of distributed packages without sacrificing compatibility with previous versions.

Extensibility is simply a method of distributing programming toolboxes because toolbox units can conveniently be used, modified and extended by their original developers without the necessity of recompiling the original source codes.

Extensibility is derived from two elements: **object inheritance** and **late binding**. Object inheritance allows a descendant object to possess everything the ancestor object owned. Late binding permits new and old object methods to meld together so that extensions of existing objects and methods are created without imposing performance penalties beyond a brief reference to the Virtual Method Table.

Programming for Extensibility

The Button and Point objects have been created and subsequently modified to demonstrate different aspects of object-oriented programming. At the same time, any considerations that were not immediately relevant to the topic of discussion were ignored and a few programming elements were written in the simplest possible fashion to avoid digressive explanations. Some topics however, can only be differed so long. The time has come, as the Walrus said, to speak of many things.

Programming for extensibility requires two parts advance planning and one part hindsight and revision. While it is both impossible and impractical for a programmer to anticipate every descendant object type that will later be created from a unit, there are a few guidelines which can be applied.

Please realize: these are not hard, fast rules — defining absolute rules would be even harder than anticipating all possible descendant object types, but these are suggestions which will reduce the amount of hindsight and revision required.

Tool Declarations

Any tools that will be required to implement a unit should, if at all practical, be declared within the unit's INTERFACE section and not depend on the application program for declaration or inclusion.

For example, in the previous versions of the Button unit, the Mouse unit did not appear in the **uses** declaration. Instead, the three demo programs called on the Mouse unit and defined the graphic mouse instance which was used to operate the object Button instances. In this final revision of the Buttons unit (titled BUTTON4.PAS), however, the Mouse unit is declared within the unit:

```
INTERFACE

uses Crt, Graph, Mouse;
```

An instance of the GraphicMouse object, GMouse — which was previously left to the application to provide — is also declared as a variable in the INTERFACE unit:

```
var

    GMouse : GraphicMouse;
```

In this fashion, the *GMouse* instance is available both to the object methods in the unit and to any application using the unit, but it is also available to any descendant objects. Reasons for this will be demonstrated soon.

Procedure and Function Availability

Any procedures or functions used by an ancestor object will probably be needed by a descendant object. Obvious, right?

The obvious is the easily overlooked and in Buttons, Button2 and Button3, there is one very useful procedure that is not available to any descendants created by extensibility, which means that the extensibility of the unit is limited.

The procedure in question is the SetOutline procedure which, beginning with the original Buttons unit in Chapter 3, appears in the IMPLEMENTATION section of the unit.

Because the SetOutline method was not intended for general use (i.e., was not intended to be called directly by any application using the unit) SetOutline was not created as a method. Still, the SetOutline procedure was available to the Buttons methods and would also be available to any other object methods within the same unit, so what's wrong?

What's wrong is that the SetOutline method is not — as created — available to any descendant object defined outside of the Buttons unit. Extensibility, therefore, suffers.

To repair this omission, two changes are required. First, the RectOutline type definition is moved from the IMPLEMENTATION section of the unit to the INTERFACE section:

```
type
    STR40 = string[40];
    RectOutline = array[1..5] of PointType;
```

This change makes the RectOutline type definition valid not just for the current unit methods, but also to any applications using the unit and, more importantly, to any descendant object types created outside the current unit.

But, the type definition is only one aspect and the procedure itself also needs to be available to descendant objects. As previously defined, it is not.

Instead, to make the SetOutline procedure inheritable, it has to become a method and, since it hardly belongs to the Point object type, it is now added to the Button object definition as:

```
Button = object( Point )

    . . .

    procedure SetOutline( var RectArr: RectOutline;
                          x1, y1, x2, y2 : integer );

    . . .

end;
```

The body of the SetOutline procedure is not changed except to modify its header, making it a Button method, and moving it — purely for organizational reasons — in with the rest of the Button methods:

```
procedure Button.SetOutline;

   begin

      RectArr[1].x := x1;    RectArr[1].y := y1;

      RectArr[2].x := x1;    RectArr[2].y := y2;

      RectArr[3].x := x2;    RectArr[3].y := y2;

      RectArr[4].x := x2;    RectArr[4].y := y1;

      RectArr[5] := RectArr[1];

   end;
```

The remaining Point and Button method definitions are unchanged and the Button4 unit is otherwise the same as Button3 from Chapter 5. The revisions discussed here appear in the listings at the end of this chapter.

The ScrollBar Object

The ScrollBar object type is probably a familiar feature. It appears in a variety of graphics-based applications ranging from drawing and design utilities to Windows and OS/2 Presentation Manager applications. Even if you haven't yet encountered scrollbar controls, their operation should be self-explanatory.

In this case, the ScrollBar objects were chosen for two purposes: to demonstrate extensibility, as well as to create a second useful graphics control feature.

Despite the fact that Buttons and ScrollBars have relatively little in common, the ScrollBar object is defined as a descendant of the Button object type, inheriting the Button data and method elements, but also defining new methods and elements peculiar to the ScrollBar object type.

Two instances of the ScrollBar object type appear in Figure 6-1.

Figure 6-1: ScrollBar Control Objects

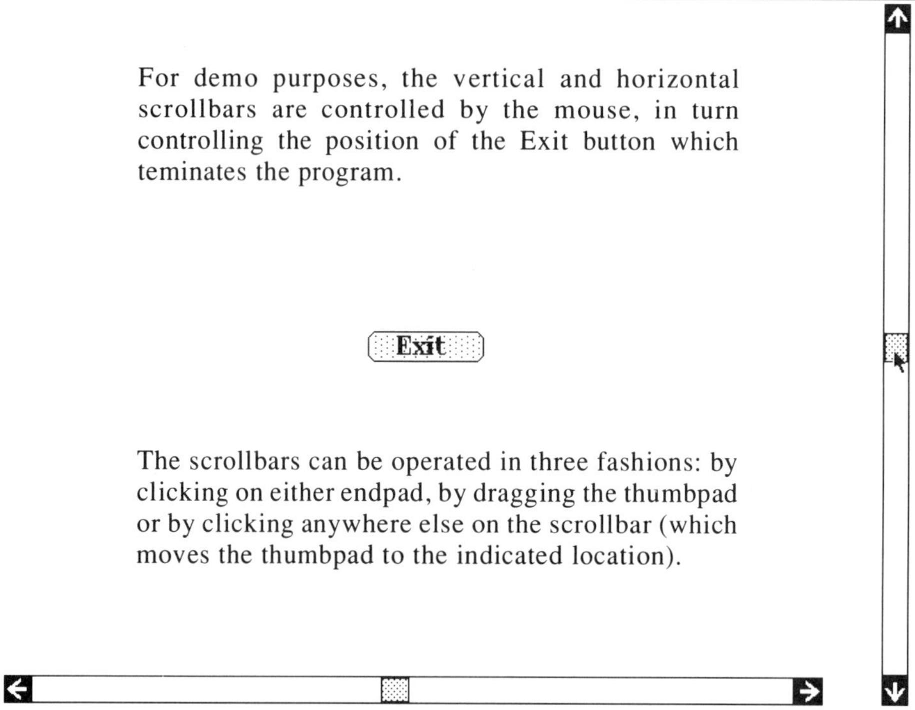

For demo purposes, the vertical and horizontal scrollbars are controlled by the mouse, in turn controlling the position of the Exit button which teminates the program.

> Exit

The scrollbars can be operated in three fashions: by clicking on either endpad, by dragging the thumbpad or by clicking anywhere else on the scrollbar (which moves the thumbpad to the indicated location).

Creating the ScrollBar Object

The primary difference between previous examples and the ScrollBar object and the ScrlBar unit is that these are created as an extension of the Button4 unit; therefore, ScrlBar.PAS begins with a uses statement:

```
unit ScrlBar;   { SCRLBAR.PAS / SCRLBAR.TPU }

INTERFACE

uses Button4, Graph;
```

The Button4 unit is referenced because the current object will be defined as a descendant of the Button object type. While the Graph unit was referenced by the Button4 unit, this earlier reference does not carry forward to the current unit and, therefore, must be repeated here to validate the variable declaration to the ViewPortType — which is defined in the Graph unit — as well as later calls to procedures in this unit.

Two data types are defined, beginning with HitType which is used by the ScrollHit method both as an internal flag and to report scrollbar selection events to the calling application. The second data type, Direction, is used to select a horizontal or vertical scrollbar:

```
type

    HitType = ( NONE, RIGHT, UP, HBAR, VBAR, LEFT, DOWN );

    Direction = ( Vertical, Horizontal );
```

The ScrollBar object begins by declaring itself a descendant of the Button object type from the Button4 unit, and then adds four new variables:

```
ScrollBar = object ( Button )

    ScrollMove : Direction;

    LineColor, SPos, Step : integer;

    VRef : ViewPortType;
```

The *ScrollMove* variable, of course, is the orientation of the ScrollBar. Since two color specifications are needed for ScrollBar object, the *LineColor* variable supplements the original *Color* variable inherited from the Button object type. Of the remaining new variables, *SPos* is used to track the thumbpad (slider pad) position for the scrollbar and Step is a local variable controlling the movement increment of the thumbpad.

Since the ScrollBar object is likely to be used with a graphics window, the *VRef* variable is used to retrieve and store the current viewport (window) settings.

Previously, in the Button3 unit, the method's Init constructor did little or nothing (Point.Init was defined as an empty procedure) aside from providing the constructor call to create a link to the object type's VMT:

```
constructor Init( PtX, PtY, Size, C1, C2 : integer;
                  Orientation : Direction );
```

This time, for the ScrollBar object, the Init method assumes the functions which, for the Button and Point objects, were assigned to the Create method so that initialization and creation of the object instance are now accomplished by a single method call. In most cases, this will be the preferred form for an Init method and you may wish to rewrite the original Button object type to follow it.

The SetLoc method will be redefined for the ScrollBar object type and, at this time, is made a virtual method in recognition of the possibility (and probability) that future descendants may require further variations of the SetLoc method:

```
procedure SetLoc( PtX, PtY : integer ); virtual;

procedure Draw; virtual;
```

The Draw method has already been declared as a virtual method, but the ScrollBar object requires very different drawing instructions from the Button method and therefore, is also redefined.

The SetThumbPad and EraseThumbPad methods are designed primarily for use by the Draw and ScrollHit methods and do not require any parameters aside from the object instance's own variables. Likewise, the RestoreViewPort method is used to restore the graphics window settings after a viewport change is used to create a graphics screen element. While none of these three methods is intended for direct use by an application, any method may be called directly if desired:

```
    procedure SetThumbPad;

    procedure EraseThumbPad;

    procedure RestoreViewPort;

    function  GetPosition: integer;

    function  GetDirection: Direction;

    function  ScrollHit: HitType;
end;
```

Of the remaining methods, the GetPosition method reports the thumbpad (slider pad) position relative to the scrollbar — not the screen — while the GetDirection method simply reports the scrollbar orientation as horizontal or vertical.

The final ScrollBar method, ScrollHit, is the workhorse method of the ScrollBar object. As you can readily discern from the method declaration, the ScrollHit method does not require any parameters, but does return an argument reporting the scrollbar hit type. This indicates either no scrollbar hit (NONE), horizontal or vertical endpad hits (RIGHT, UP, LEFT or DOWN), or a mouse hit somewhere within the body of the scrollbar (HBAR or VBAR). The HitType returned by the ScrollHit method can be used by the calling application to decide what action should be taken in response to the event.

This is not by any means all that ScrollHit accomplishes (which is one good example of why units should have more documentation than simply the INTERFACE section of the object code).

Unlike the Button object that required the calling application to pass mouse coordinate parameters to determine a button hit event, the Scroll-Hit method is able to retrieve mouse coordinates directly — a much simpler procedure.

But this is also why the Mouse unit is added to the Button4 uses declaration and the *GMouse* variable is declared within the Button4 unit instead of relying on the calling application to define a mouse handle or to provide mouse button event information. These two revisions could have been made in the ScrlBar unit instead of the Button4 unit — since neither is currently required by the Button or Point objects. But, after seeing how the mouse is called by the ScrollBar.ScrollHit method, you may well prefer to revise the ButtonHit method for similar handling, in which case, the revisions will be necessary in the Button*X* unit and would be redundant in the ScrlBar unit.

After retrieving the mouse coordinates, the ScrollHit method determines the mouse pointer position relative to the scrollbar coordinates and decides on the HitType, as well as adjusting the thumbpad position within the scrollbar. In addition to retrieving mouse coordinates, the ScrollHit method turns off (hides) the mouse pointer before updating the scrollbar image and then restores the mouse pointer image when done. All of this is smoother and faster than relying on the calling application to prevent graphics conflicts with the mouse pointer.

The ScrollBar Constructor

The ScrollBar.Init method, which is also ScrollBar's constructor, is called with parameters setting the scrollbar's position, outline and fill colors and orientation (horizontal or vertical) and begins by setting minimums, constants and initial values for the object instance.

Since the ScrollBar is designed and intended for use with application windows, the Init method begins by retrieving the current viewport settings. The viewport settings are used for two purposes: first, to restore the original window settings after a graphics drawing routine has changed viewport settings and; second, because the window origin offset is necessary to translate mouse positions from absolute screen coordinates to window (viewport) coordinates:

```
constructor ScrollBar.Init;

   begin

      GetViewSettings( VRef );

      if Size < 100 then Size := 100;

      ScrollMove := Orientation;

      Step := Size div 100;
```

The Init method also sets a minimum width (or height if vertical) of 100 pixels and establishes the Step increment by dividing the overall size by 100. Both values, of course are optional — see the section titled Omissions.

Of course, the *SizeX* and *SizeY* parameters — which were inherited from the Button object type — have to be set according to the ScrollMove orientation:

```
case ScrollMove of

     Vertical : begin  SizeX := 20;

                       SizeY := Size;   end;
```

```
  Horizontal : begin  SizeX := Size;
                       SizeY := 20;     end;
end; {case}
SPos := 21;
```

An arbitrary thickness of 20 pixels is also set and the initial position of the thumbpad is established at the left or top of the scrollbar. Last, the *PtX* and *PtY* parameters are passed on to the SetLoc method, the two color parameters are assigned, the *Exist* variable is turned on and the Draw method is called to create the scrollbar image:

```
  SetLoc( PtX, PtY );
  LineColor := C1;
  Color := C2;
  Exist := TRUE;
  Draw;
end;
```

The RestoreViewPort Method

The RestoreViewPort method is a convenience provided to restore the original graphic window settings. It uses the *VRef* (ViewPortType) variable which was set when the object instance was initialized:

```
procedure ScrollBar.RestoreViewPort;
  begin
    with VRef do
        SetViewPort( X1, Y1, X2, Y2, Clip );
  end;
```

The SetLoc Method

The SetLoc method originally defined in the Point object is redefined here, making the coordinates relative and, at the same time, adjusting the

SizeX and *SizeY* parameters to ensure that the object does not exceed the window limits:

```
procedure ScrollBar.SetLoc;
  begin
    with VRef do
    begin
      X := X1 + PtX;
      Y := Y1 + PtY;
      while( SizeX + X > X2 ) do dec( SizeX );
      while( SizeY + Y > Y2 ) do dec( SizeY );
    end;
  end;
```

The Draw Method

The Draw method was defined in the Button4 unit as a virtual method, but is redefined here because the ScrollBar object has different graphic drawing requirements:

```
procedure ScrollBar.Draw;
  var
    RectArr  : RectOutline;
    OldColor : word;
  begin
    OldColor := Graph.GetColor;
    Graph.SetColor( LineColor );
    SetViewPort( x, y, x+SizeX, y+SizeY, ClipOn );
```

The Draw method begins by saving the current color before setting a new drawing color and a new viewport to accommodate the scrollbar image. The next step is to draw the scrollbar outline as a solid bar:

```
SetOutline( RectArr, 1, 1, SizeX-1, SizeY-1 );

SetFillStyle( SolidFill, color );

SetLineStyle( SolidLn, 0, NormWidth );

FillPoly( sizeof(RectArr) div

        sizeof(PointType), RectArr );
```

This step could also be accomplished using the Bar procedure from the Graphics unit, but since the tools are already defined from the Button methods, the established format is repeated here.

Two arrow images are now drawn at each end of the solid bar using the thick line style:

```
Graph.SetColor( GetBkColor );

SetLineStyle( SolidLn, 0, ThickWidth );

case ScrollMove of

    Vertical:

        begin

            Line( 10, 4,  4, 12 );

            Line( 10, 4, 16, 12 );

            Line( 10, 4, 10, 16 );

            Line( 10, SizeY-4,  4, SizeY-12 );

            Line( 10, SizeY-4, 16, SizeY-12 );

            Line( 10, SizeY-4, 10, SizeY-16 );

        end;

    Horizontal:

        begin

            Line( 4, 10, 12,  4 );

            Line( 4, 10, 12, 16 );

            Line( 4, 10, 16, 10 );
```

```
            Line( SizeX-4, 10, SizeX-12,  4 );
            Line( SizeX-4, 10, SizeX-12, 16 );
            Line( SizeX-4, 10, SizeX-16, 10 );
        end;
end; {case}
SetLineStyle( SolidLn, 0, NormWidth );
```

At this point, the scrollbar image is a solid bar with an arrow at each end. The next step is to erase the center of the bar in order to leave two solid ends (the endpads) and also an outline along the length of the scrollbar:

```
Graph.SetColor( LineColor );
SetFillStyle( SolidFill, Graph.GetBkColor );
case ScrollMove of
    Vertical: SetOutline( RectArr, 1, 21,
                            SizeX-1, SizeY-21 );
  Horizontal: SetOutline( RectArr, 21, 1,
                            SizeX-21, SizeY-1 );
end; {case}
FillPoly( sizeof(RectArr) div
        sizeof(PointType), RectArr );
```

Finally, the Draw method restores the original color setting. It does so before calling the SetThumbPad method which creates the thumbpad image:

```
    Graph.SetColor( OldColor );
    SetThumbPad;
end;
```

The SetThumbPad Method

The SetThumbPad method draws a dot-patterned square within the scrollbar outline, beginning by saving the current color and then setting the viewport to the scrollbar outline:

```
procedure ScrollBar.SetThumbPad;

   var

      RectArr   : RectOutline;

      OldColor : word;

   begin

      OldColor := Graph.GetColor;

      Graph.SetColor( GetBkColor );

      SetViewPort( x, y, x+SizeX, y+SizeY, ClipOn );
```

The thumbpad image is created using the predefined CloseDotFill pattern and the current instance's Color, while the LineColor is used for the solid outline around the thumbpad:

```
Graph.SetColor( LineColor );

SetFillStyle( CloseDotFill, Color );

case ScrollMove of

    Vertical: SetOutline( RectArr, 2, SPos,

                                      18, SPos+19 );

    Horizontal: SetOutline( RectArr, SPos, 2,

                                      SPos+19, 18 );

end; {case}

FillPoly( sizeof(RectArr) div

        sizeof(PointType), RectArr );
```

Finally, the original color setting and viewport are restored:

```
   Graph.SetColor( OldColor );

   RestoreViewPort;

 end;
```

The EraseThumbPad Method

The EraseThumbPad method is essentially the same as the SetThumbPad method except that the background color and the SolidFill pattern are used, again ending by restoring the original color and viewport settings:

```
procedure ScrollBar.EraseThumbPad;

  var

     RectArr   : RectOutline;

     OldColor : word;

  begin

     OldColor := Graph.GetColor;

     Graph.SetColor( GetBkColor );

     SetViewPort( x, y, x+SizeX, y+SizeY, ClipOn );

     SetFillStyle( SolidFill, Graph.GetBkColor );

     case ScrollMove of

         Vertical: SetOutline( RectArr, 2, SPos,
                                         18, SPos+20 );

        Horizontal: SetOutline( RectArr, SPos, 2,
                                         SPos+19, 19 );

     end; {case}

     FillPoly( sizeof(RectArr) div

             sizeof(PointType), RectArr );

     Graph.SetColor( OldColor );

     RestoreViewPort;

   end;
```

The ScrollHit Method

The ScrollHit method is the heart of the scrollbar operations and it begins by setting a default value (NONE) for the local variable *Result*:

```
function ScrollBar.ScrollHit;

   var

      Result : HitType;

      BtnStatus, XPos, YPos : integer;

   begin

      Result := NONE;

      GMouse.GetPosition( BtnStatus, XPos, YPos );
```

Instead of calling the ScrollHit method with parameters for the mouse pointer location, ScrollHit calls the GMouse.GetPosition method directly to retrieve its own mouse button status and coordinate information. For simplicity, the button status information is not presently tested by the ScrollHit method, but could be used for confirmation of button down or button release status if desired.

Depending on whether the *ScrollMove* variable indicates the current instance is horizontal or vertical, the mouse coordinates are tested against the scrollbar position variables (with corrections from window coordinates to absolute screen coordinates) to decide if a scrollbar hit has occurred and if so, what type of hit has occurred:

```
case ScrollMove of

   Vertical:

      if( XPos >= x ) and ( XPos <= x+20 ) and

        ( YPos >= y ) then

         if YPos <= y+20

            then Result := UP    else

         if YPos <= y+SizeY-21

            then Result := VBAR else
```

```
        if YPos <= y+SizeY

            then Result := DOWN;

    Horizontal:

        if( YPos >= y ) and ( YPos <= y+20 ) and

            ( XPos >= x ) then

            if XPos <= x+20

                then Result := LEFT else

            if XPos <= x+SizeX-21

                then Result := HBAR else

            if XPos <= x+SizeX

                then Result := RIGHT;

end; {case}
```

Now, if you are a confirmed Pascal programmer, the preceding *if..then..else..* structure may look like something out of the dark ages — like it should be inscribed on vellum with floral elaborations — and your first thought is probably why not replace this mess with a *case* statement like this:

```
    Horizontal:

        if( YPos >= y ) and ( YPos <= y+20 ) then

        case XPos of

                        x..x+20 : Result := LEFT;

                x+21..x+SizeX-21 : Result := HBAR;

            x+SizeX-20..x+SizeX : Result := RIGHT;

        end; {case}

end; {case}
```

Obviously the same thought occurred to me, however, there is one problem: the compiler is not able to evaluate the expressions used in the case statement. A small matter perhaps, but in this case, the *if..then..else..* structure works and the case structure does not.

The current ScrollBar method tests for a hit anywhere along the scrollbar image. If the hit is not on either of the endpads or the thumbpad, the scroll position will jump abruptly to the selected location. In some applications, you may prefer to guard against such rapid movements by restricting hits to the endpads and to the thumbpad. In order to implement this provision, an alternate form appears in the listings at the end of this chapter.

At this point, ScrollHit has identified where the mouse hit occurred, but hasn't yet taken any action as a result. If *Result* is not NONE, then a response is appropriate:

```
if Result <> NONE then

begin

    GMouse.Show( FALSE );

    EraseThumbPad;
```

The response begins by turning off the mouse pointer and then erasing the current thumbpad.

Next, depending on where the mouse hit occurred, the thumbpad position (*SPos*) is adjusted either bythe *Step* increment if one of the endpads was hit or, if not, to move the thumbpad to the mouse pointer position:

```
case Result of

    LEFT,   UP: dec( SPos, Step );

          HBAR: SPos := XPos - ( x + 10 );

          VBAR: SPos := YPos - ( y + 10 );

    RIGHT, DOWN: inc( SPos, Step );

end; {case}
```

The resulting position is then checked, first against the scrollbar origin, then against the limit (size) of the scrollbar:

```
if( SPos < 21 ) then SPos := 21;
case Result of
   LEFT, HBAR, RIGHT:
      if( SPos > SizeX-41 ) then
         SPos := SizeX-41;
   UP, VBAR, DOWN:
      if( SPos > SizeY-41 ) then
         SPos := SizeY-41;
end; {case}
```

Last, the SetThumbPad method is called to restore the thumbpad image, the mouse pointer is turned on again and, *Result* is reported back to the calling application:

```
      SetThumbPad;
      GMouse.Show( TRUE );
   end;
   ScrollHit := Result;
end;
```

The ScrlTest Demo

The ScrlTest demo program creates the screen shown in Figure 6-1, allowing you to experiment directly with the scrollbar operations. The position of the included "Exit" button is controlled directly by the two scrollbars and will maneuver around the screen in response to the scroll operations selected.

Aside from these few comments, the ScrlTest program is essentially self-explanatory. Have fun.

Omissions

There are several methods, that have not been provided by the ScrollBar object definition — omissions intended to keep the present demonstration relatively simple — but which could be quite useful in actual applications.

First, while the ScrollHit method calls the GMouse.Position method directly to retrieve the mouse button status and position information, the mouse button status is not tested or used. However, the ScrollHit method could be rewritten so that, once a scrollbar hit was established, it would loop continuously, performing its own tests and moving the thumbpad until the mouse button was released or the mouse cursor moved away from the scrollbar. Now — and this is a loaded question — would this implementation be good or bad? If so, why or why not? I'll come back to this later.

Second, what about a provision, using the capabilities shown in Chapter 2, to change the mouse pointer from an arrow image to a glove pointer, either when the mouse pointer is over the scrollbar image or when the mouse button is pressed?

Third, how about a method provision to allow an application to directly control the thumbpad (slider pad) position along the scrollbar? This wouldn't be wanted for every application, but could be quite useful in many circumstances.

Fourth, should provisions be made to change the scrollbar colors without having to recreate the scrollbar from scratch?

Fifth, what about provisions to change the thickness of the scrollbar and the size of the endpads and thumbpads.

Sixth, what other provisions could be made to improve the efficiency and/or the performance of the scrollbar?

Here are a half-dozen questions to mull over and, after you have experimented with the ScrlTest program, you may have a half-dozen of your own. The first question concerned making the ScrollHit method essentially self-contained so that once called, it would conduct its own operations until the mouse button was released or the mouse pointer moved away from the scrollbar. What's wrong with this?

If you only want the scrollbars to control the scrollbar images, nothing. What about the external application which is calling the scrollbar to control its own operations? In the demo program, the scrollbars are used to move the Exit button image around the screen, but if the scrollbar instance does not exit until it can return a NONE result, how would the button image ever be updated?

If updating was done every time a ScrollHit method returned, regardless of the reported result, how would this look? Jerky? Large, sudden movements only? What about flicker when the mouse button was pressed somewhere other than over a scrollbar?

In some circumstances, a delayed response might be desired, but this would be relatively rare and could be implemented within the calling application without restricting the object methods to such a limited and unwieldy operation.

So, before making a method too efficient, consider how it affects the application using the object.

Summary

In this chapter, a new object type, the ScrollBar object, has been created using the extensibility feature of object-oriented programming. At the same time, several elements have been shown in the ScrollBar methods which could well be incorporated in the earlier Button and/or Point methods— including making them directly responsible for querying mouse position and button information and making each window-sensitive in terms of position.

For example, the Button object defined previously does not test the coordinate provided on either a Create or Move operation to see if these are valid for the screen size or for the window size — while the ScrollBar object does possess at least a rudimentary self-test capability to decide if it can be correctly displayed. Objects can be much more powerful than conventional procedures and functions, but to balance this power, they must also exercise some care to ensure proper operation.

If you are beginning to tire of the graphics objects used for demonstrations so far, Chapter 7 will begin with text-based objects to demonstrate a new aspect of object-oriented programming: **dynamic objects**.

```
unit Button4;   { BUTTON4.PAS / BUTTON4.TPU }

INTERFACE

uses Crt, Graph, Mouse;

type
   STR40 = string[40];
   RectOutline = array[1..5] of PointType;

   Point = object                          { no changes }

   ButtonType = ( Rounded, Square, ThreeD );
   Button = object( Point )
      Exist, State, Rotate : boolean;
      FontSize, TypeFace, SizeX, SizeY : integer;
      ThisButton : ButtonType;
      BtnTxt : STR40;
      constructor Init;
      procedure SetOutline(              { new method }
         var RectArr: RectOutline;
         x1, y1, x2, y2 : integer );
      procedure Draw; virtual;
                                        { no other changes }
   end;

var
   GMouse : GraphicMouse;                { new variable }

IMPLEMENTATION

{ SetOutline procedure moved to become Button method }
```

```
{=====================================}
{  no changes in Point implementation  }
{=====================================}

{=====================================}
{ implementation for object type Button }
{=====================================}
constructor Button.Init;
   begin
      Exist := FALSE;
      SetTypeSize( 10 );
      SetTypeFace( TriplexFont );
   end;


{==========================================================}
{ now method used by Button functions and descendants }
{==========================================================}
procedure Button.SetOutline;
   begin
      RectArr[1].x := x1;   RectArr[1].y := y1;
      RectArr[2].x := x1;   RectArr[2].y := y2;
      RectArr[3].x := x2;   RectArr[3].y := y2;
      RectArr[4].x := x2;   RectArr[4].y := y1;
      RectArr[5] := RectArr[1];
   end;

      { no further changes to Button methods }

      (* ======== end of methods ========== *)
end.
```

```
unit ScrlBar;   { SCRLBAR.PAS / SCRLBAR.TPU }

INTERFACE

uses Button4;

type
   HitType = ( NONE, RIGHT, UP, HBAR, VBAR, LEFT, DOWN );
   Direction = ( Vertical, Horizontal );
   ScrollBar = object( Button )
      ScrollMove : Direction;
      LineColor, SPos, Step : integer;
      VRef : ViewPortType;
     constructor Init( PtX, PtY, Size, C1, C2 : integer;
                           Orientation : Direction );
      procedure SetLoc( PtX, PtY : integer ); virtual;
      procedure RestoreViewPort;
      procedure Draw; virtual;
      procedure SetThumbPad;
      procedure EraseThumbPad;
      function  GetPosition: integer;
      function  GetDirection: Direction
      function  ScrollHit: HitType;
   end;

IMPLEMENTATION

uses Crt, Graph;
```

```
{============================================}
{ implementation for object type ScrollBar }
{============================================}
constructor ScrollBar.Init;
   begin
      GetViewSettings( VRef );
      if Size < 100 then Size := 100;
      ScrollMove := Orientation;
      SPos := 21;
      Step := Size div 100;
      case ScrollMove of
            Vertical : begin  SizeX := 20;
                              SizeY := Size;   end;
          Horizontal : begin  SizeX := Size;
                              SizeY := 20;     end;
      end; {case}
      SetLoc( PtX, PtY );
      Color   := C2;
      LineColor := C1;
      Exist   := TRUE;
      Draw;
   end;

procedure ScrollBar.SetLoc;
   begin
      X  := X1+PtX;
      Y  := Y1+PtY;
      while( X + SizeX > X2 ) do dec( SizeX );
```

```
        while( Y + SizeY > Y2 ) do dec( SizeY );
    end;

procedure ScrollBar.SetThumbPad;
    var
        RectArr  : RectOutline;
        OldColor : word;
    begin
        OldColor := Graph.GetColor;
        Graph.SetColor( GetBkColor );
        SetViewPort( x, y, x+SizeX, y+SizeY, ClipOn );
            {=== draw scrollbar thumbpad ===}
        Graph.SetColor( LineColor );
        SetFillStyle( CloseDotFill, Color );
        case ScrollMove of
            Vertical: SetOutline( RectArr, 2, SPos,
                                            18, SPos+19 );

          Horizontal: SetOutline( RectArr, SPos, 2,
                                            SPos+19, 18 );

        end; {case}
        FillPoly( sizeof(RectArr) div
                sizeof(PointType), RectArr );
          {=== restore default color settings ===}
        Graph.SetColor( OldColor );
        RestoreViewPort;
    end;

procedure ScrollBar.EraseThumbPad;
```

```
var
    RectArr  : RectOutline;
    OldColor : word;
begin
    OldColor := Graph.GetColor;
    Graph.SetColor( GetBkColor );
    SetViewPort( x, y, x+SizeX, y+SizeY, ClipOn );
            {=== erase thumbpad ===}
    SetFillStyle( SolidFill, Graph.GetBkColor );
    case ScrollMove of
        Vertical: SetOutline( RectArr, 2, SPos,
                                        18, SPos+20 );

      Horizontal: SetOutline( RectArr, SPos, 2,
                                        SPos+19, 19 );

    end; {case}
    FillPoly( sizeof(RectArr) div
            sizeof(PointType), RectArr );
     {=== restore default color settings ===}
    Graph.SetColor( OldColor );

    RestoreViewPort;

   end;

procedure ScrollBar.Draw;
   var
    RectArr  : RectOutline;
    OldColor : word;
   begin
    OldColor := Graph.GetColor;
```

```
Graph.SetColor( LineColor );
SetViewPort( x, y, x+SizeX, y+SizeY, ClipOn );
        {=== scrollbar outline ===}
SetOutline( RectArr, 1, 1, SizeX-1, SizeY-1 );
SetFillStyle( SolidFill, color );
SetLineStyle( SolidLn, 0, NormWidth );
FillPoly( sizeof(RectArr) div
         sizeof(PointType), RectArr );

        {=== scrollbar arrows ===}
Graph.SetColor( GetBkColor );
SetLineStyle( SolidLn, 0, ThickWidth );
case ScrollMove of
    Vertical:
        begin
            Line( 10, 4,  4, 12 );
            Line( 10, 4, 16, 12 );
            Line( 10, 4, 10, 16 );
            Line( 10, SizeY-4,  4, SizeY-12 );
            Line( 10, SizeY-4, 16, SizeY-12 );
            Line( 10, SizeY-4, 10, SizeY-16 );
        end;
    Horizontal:
        begin
            Line( 4, 10, 12,  4 );
            Line( 4, 10, 12, 16 );
            Line( 4, 10, 16, 10 );
            Line( SizeX-4, 10, SizeX-12,  4 );
```

```
                  Line( SizeX-4, 10, SizeX-12, 16 );
                  Line( SizeX-4, 10, SizeX-16, 10 );
            end;
      end; {case}
      SetLineStyle( SolidLn, 0, NormWidth );
          {=== clear scrollbar center ===}
      Graph.SetColor( LineColor );
      SetFillStyle( SolidFill, Graph.GetBkColor );
      case ScrollMove of
          Vertical: SetOutline( RectArr, 1, 21,
                                    SizeX-1, SizeY-21 );
        Horizontal: SetOutline( RectArr, 21, 1,
                                    SizeX-21, SizeY-1 );
      end; {case}
      FillPoly( sizeof(RectArr) div
              sizeof(PointType), RectArr );
       {=== restore default color settings ===}
      Graph.SetColor( OldColor );
      RestoreViewPort;
      SetThumbPad;
   end;

function ScrollBar.RestoreViewPort;
   begin
      with VRef do
         SetViewPort( X1, Y1, X2, Y2, Clip );
   end;
```

```
function ScrollBar.GetPosition;
   begin
      GetPosition := SPos;
   end;

function ScrollBar.GetDirection;
   begin
      GetDirection := ScrollMove;
   end;

function ScrollBar.ScrollHit;
   var
      Result : HitType;
      BtnStatus, XPos, YPos : integer;
   begin
      Result := NONE;
      GMouse.GetPosition( BtnStatus, XPos, YPos );
      case ScrollMove of
         Vertical:
            if( XPos >= x ) and ( XPos <= x+20 ) and
              ( YPos >= y ) then
               if YPos <= y+20
                  then Result := UP else
               if YPos <= y+SizeY-21
                  then Result := VBAR else
               if YPos <= y+SizeY
                  then Result := DOWN;
         Horizontal:
```

```
        if( YPos >= y ) and ( YPos <= y+20 ) and
           ( XPos >= x ) then
             if XPos <= x+20
               then Result := LEFT else
             if XPos <= x+SizeX-21
               then Result := HBAR else
             if XPos <= x+SizeX
               then Result := RIGHT;

    end; {case}

{=======================================================}
{ alternate form for thumbpad and endpad hits only  }
{=======================================================}
{ if( YPos >= y ) and ( YPos <= y+20 ) then         }
{ if( XPos >= x ) and ( XPos <= x+20 )              }
{    then Result := LEFT else                       }
{ if( XPos >= x+SPos ) and ( XPos <= x+SPos+20 )    }
{    then Result := HBAR else                       }
{ if( XPos >= x+SizeX-20 ) and ( XPos <= x+SizeX )  }
{    then Result := RIGHT;                          }
{=======================================================}

    if Result <> NONE then
    begin
       GMouse.Show( FALSE );
       EraseThumbPad;
    end;
    case Result of
        LEFT,   UP: dec( SPos, Step );
              HBAR: SPos := XPos - ( x + 10 );
              VBAR: SPos := YPos - ( y + 10 );
```

```
          RIGHT, DOWN: inc( SPos, Step );
      end; {case}
      if( SPos < 21 ) then SPos := 21;
      case Result of
         LEFT, HBAR, RIGHT:
            if( SPos > SizeX-41 ) then SPos := SizeX-41;
            UP, VBAR, DOWN:
            if( SPos > SizeY-41 ) then SPos := SizeY-41;
      end; {case}
      if Result <> NONE then
      begin
         SetThumbPad;
         GMouse.Show( TRUE );
      end;
      ScrollHit := Result;
   end;

(* =========== end of methods ============= *)

end.

program ScrollBar_Test; { SCRLTEST.PAS }

uses Crt, Graph, Mouse, Button4, ScrlBar;

var
   TMouse  : TextMouse;
   mButton : Position;
   Exit, Status : Boolean;
   GDriver, GMode, GError,
```

```pascal
      i, j, SButtons, BtnCount : integer;
var
   HScroll, VScroll : ScrollBar;
   ExitButton : Button;
begin
   GDriver := Detect;
   InitGraph( GDriver, GMode, '\TP\BGI' );
   GError := GraphResult;
   if GError <> grOk then
   begin
      writeln('Graphics error: ',GraphErrorMsg(GError));
      writeln('Program aborted...');
      halt(1);
   end;
   GMouse.Reset( Status, BtnCount );
   if Status then
   begin
      ClearDevice;
      Exit := FALSE;
      GMouse.Initialize;
      HScroll.Init( 0, GetMaxY, GetMaxX-60,
                    Green, LightGreen, Horizontal );
      VScroll.Init( GetMaxX, 0, GetMaxY,
                    Green, LightGreen, Vertical );
      with ExitButton do
      begin
```

```
      Init;
      SetButtonType( Rounded );
      Create( HScroll.Position-10, VScroll.Position,
              80, 20, White, 'Exit' );
  end;
  repeat
      GMouse.QueryBtnDn( ButtonL, mButton );
      if mButton.opCount > 0 then
      begin
          if ExitButton.ButtonHit( mButton.XPos,
                                        mButton.YPos )
          then Exit := TRUE else
          repeat
              case HScroll.ScrollHit of
                 LEFT, HBAR, RIGHT:
                 ExitButton.Move( HScroll.Position-10,
                                    VScroll.Position );
              end; {case}
              case VScroll.ScrollHit of
                 UP, VBAR, DOWN:
                 ExitButton.Move( HScroll.Position-10,
                                    VScroll.Position );
              end; {case}
              GMouse.QueryBtnUp( ButtonL, mButton );
          until mButton.opCount > 0;
      end;
```

```
        until Exit;
    end;
    CloseGraph;        { restore text mode and ...        }
    TMouse.Initialize; { reset mouse for text operation }
end.
```

CHAPTER 7

DYNAMIC OBJECT INSTANCES

All of the objects used so far in demo programs have been static instances; that is, instances of object types listed in the *var* declaration and statically allocated in the program's data segment and stack. References to *static* instances (or *static* objects) have no connection with the type of methods, static or virtual, that belong to the objects in question.

Static allocation is restrictive and cumbersome. With conventional record data structures, static allocation requires the determining of the maximum number of records that will be required at the time the program is written, and then the declaring of an array of records of the anticipated size. Of course, the traditional 64K data size limit has also been an unacceptable restriction for many applications.

More often, static record allocation is replaced by dynamic record allocation where memory pointers are used as reference links and where memory is dynamically allocated for data records as needed and deallocated when no longer wanted. This frees unnecessary memory for other uses.

Advantages of Dynamic Objects

Object instances, which are closely related to data records, can also be dynamically created, allocating memory as required, destroying the object and deallocating the memory when it is no longer needed. In this fashion, an application can create — within system memory limitations — as many objects as necessary and then release these from memory when they are no longer needed.

Obviously, for the Button or ScrollBar objects used in previous demonstrations, requirements for unanticipated numbers of objects are unlikely. Instead, in Chapter 8, a data record object type will be used to demonstrate dynamic object allocation in circumstances where prediction of the number of objects is not possible.

First, however, it will help to understand how objects are created using pointer references and dynamic memory allocation.

Pointers to Objects

Before dynamically creating an object instance, a handle or pointer to the object is necessary; otherwise, the object instance could not referenced or called by the application. An object instance can be allocated as a pointer referent using the New procedure:

```
var

   PHScroll : ^ScrollBar;


New( PHScroll );
```

Just as with a data record, the New procedure dynamically allocates sufficient memory space on the heap to contain an instance of the ScrollBar object — according to the size of the ScrollBar base type — and returns the address of the memory space allocated to the *PHScroll* pointer variable.

Since the ScrollBar object contains virtual methods, the Init method must be called for the constructor call as well to create the scrollbar image:

```
PHScroll^.Init( 0, GetMaxY, GetMaxX-60,

                Green, LightGreen, Horizontal );
```

After this, all method calls are made in the normal fashion except for using the pointer name and the caret (^) reference symbol in place of the instance name, which would have been used with a statically allocated object instance. Instead of:

```
case HScroll.ScrollHit of ...
```

the method is called as:

```
case PHScroll^.ScrollHit of ...
```

Grouped references can still be made to several methods as in the following example:

```
with PHScroll^ do

begin

   case ScrollHit of

   . . .

   end; {case}

   SetLoc( ... );

end;
```

The method calls internal to the object definition, of course, do not require the pointer referent and no changes to object definition units are required.

Allocation and Initialization

Beginning with Turbo Pascal 5.5, the syntax of the New procedure has been extended, allowing allocation and initialization of an object to be executed in a single operation:

```
New( PHScroll, Init( 0, GetMaxY, GetMaxX-60,

                  Green, LightGreen, Horizontal ) );
```

This extension of the New procedure (allowing New to be called with two parameters; the pointer variable as the first and the constructor invocation as the second) provides both convenience and a more compact program structure.

Obviously, for a pointer object, the constructor method (Init) cannot be called before the object is allocated by the New procedure because the instance being initialized does not exist yet. Instead, with New's extended syntax, the Init constructor performs the dynamic allocation via special entry code that is generated as part of a constructor's compilation, while the type of pointer passed as the first parameter tells the compiler which Init method to call.

A Second Extension for New

The New procedure has been extended in a second fashion too, allowing New to act as a function returning a pointer value. Used in this fashion, the calling parameter for New is the pointer type instead of the pointer variable:

```
type

   SPtr = ^ScrollBar;

var

   PHScroll : SPtr;

PHScroll := New( SPtr );
```

In this form, the New procedure can be used with the object's constructor as it was previously:

```
PHScroll := New( SPtr, Init( 0, GetMaxY, GetMaxX-60,

                  Green, LightGreen, Horizontal ) );
```

Note that this extension to the New procedure applies to all data types — not merely to object types — and the same format can be used; for example, with file data structure:

```
type

FPtr = ^FileRec;              { record type from Dos unit }

var

   PFile : FPtr;

PFile := New( FPtr );
```

Disposing of Dynamic Objects

Traditionally, data records are deallocated using the Dispose procedure when no longer required:

```
Dispose( DataItem );
```

For a dynamic object, there may be more required for disposal than simply releasing the heap space. This is because an object may contain its own pointers to other dynamic structures or to objects that also need to be released or that require special clean-up methods such as closing open files or restoring file records before exiting.

Instead of simply calling the Dispose method directly, complex objects should include a clean-up method, or multiple clean-up methods, to handle the special shutdown tasks. The *Turbo Pascal OOP Guide* suggests the standard identifier Done be used for such shutdown methods, just as Init is used as the standard constructor method name. This suggestion will be followed here.

The Destructor Method

Turbo Pascal 5.5 has provided a special method type — identified by the keyword *destructor* — which is used to clean up and deallocate dynamic objects. Unlike the constructor method call, the destructor call by itself does nothing directly to deallocate memory. Instead, the destructor method provides the means by which a program can combine a shutdown and clean-up method call with a Dispose instruction.

However, before going into the details of what the destructor call accomplishes and how, explanations will be simplified by looking first at how the destructor call is used.

Programming Destructor Methods

Using the ScrollBar object from Chapter 6 as an example, a destructor method could be declared as follows:

```
type

   ScrollBar = object( Button )

      ScrollMove : Direction;

      LineColor, SPos, Step : integer;

      VRef : ViewPortType;

      constructor Init( PtX, PtY, Size, C1, C2 : integer;

                        Orientation : Direction );

      destructor  Done; virtual;

      procedure   SetLoc( PtX, PtY : integer ); virtual;

      . . .

   end;
```

The destructor method, Done, might be implemented as follows:

```
destructor ScrollBar.Done;

   begin

      Erase;

      ResortViewPort;

   end;
```

In this case, the Done method calls the Erase method (which is inherited from the Button object type) to erase the scrollbar image.

Because the Button object resets the viewport (graphics window) to the entire screen, the Done method finishes its task by calling RestoreView-Port to restore the graphics window parameters that were originally found when the scrollbar was created.

Alternatively, the Done method — like the Init method — could be an empty procedure:

```
destructor ScrollBar.Done;

    begin

    end;
```

In other applications, a much more complex Done method may be desired — or more than one Done method — may be desired to execute different clean-up tasks. Unlike the constructor method type which normally needs only one version, it is practical for an object to have more than one destructor method, though only one destructor method can be called for any object instance.

Also, as with other methods, destructors can be inherited and may themselves be either static or virtual methods. Because each object type will generally require custom clean-up handling, it is recommended that destructors should always be virtual methods in order to ensure that the correct shutdown handling is called for each object type.

Using the Destructor Method

The destructor method is used in two different fashions, depending on whether the object instance is a static instance or was dynamically created. Because the destructor method is primarily concerned with dynamic object instances, these will be shown first. The simplest way to show how a destructor is used, is by example:

```
New( PHScroll, Init( 0, GetMaxY, GetMaxX-60,

                Green, LightGreen, Horizontal ) );

    . . .

Dispose( PHScroll, Done );
```

For dynamic instances, both the instance allocation (using New) and the deallocation (using Dispose) are handled by the application, not by the unit where the object type is defined (assuming, as is usually the case, that the object is defined separately from the calling application).

Destructor Calls and Static Instances

The destructor method identifier is not necessarily required for shutdown handling because the destructor method definition applies only to dynamically allocated objects to ensure that proper memory deallocation is executed. Destructor methods can also be used with statically allocated instances without incident or error:

```
var

   HScroll : ScrollBar;

HScroll.Init( 0, GetMaxY, GetMaxX-60,

              Green, LightGreen, Horizontal ) );

. . .

HScroll.Done;
```

In this case, the Done method is called for a static instance of ScrollBar and, as a result, the scrollbar image will be erased from the screen and the viewport settings will be restored, however, no memory deallocation is attempted. Here, the special properties of the destructor method call are not required and they do nothing.

Ergo, all object types can be supplied with destructor methods and, since you cannot predict that any object type will or will not eventually be used as a dynamic object, the best choice is to declare a destructor method for all object types.

The Destructor Mechanism

The destructor method is designed as a special method type for use principally with dynamic object instances and with polymorphic objects (see also Extended Type Compatibility), allowing dynamically allocated objects to be discarded or destroyed, releasing the memory used by the object for further use.

Before memory can be deallocated, however, the Dispose procedure needs to know not only where the memory should be released, but also how much memory should be released.

The Dispose Procedure

The Dispose procedure, like the New procedure, has been given an extended syntax in Turbo Pascal 5.5, allowing Dispose to accept a second parameter that specifies the amount of memory to be deallocated.

In conventional programming, the Dispose procedure is called as:

```
type
    Str : String;
var
    Ptr : ^Str;

    New( Ptr );
    Ptr^ := 'Now is the time for all good computers ...';
    Dispose( Ptr );
```

In this example, the Dispose procedure gets the size of the variable indicated by *Ptr* directly by looking at what *Ptr* indicates.

With objects, the sizes of object types vary tremendously. With polymorphic objects, the object identifier does not necessarily indicate the size of the allocated instance.

For this reason, the destructor offers the solution by accessing the object instance's Virtual Method Table. Each object type's VMT includes the size, in bytes, of the object type definition. The VMT for any object is available through the Self referent — an "invisible" referent which is passed to a method on any method call, providing a handle or address to the object type's Virtual Method Table.

When the destructor method is called, it returns the size indicated by the object type's VMT which is the size of the actual object instance. Even if the object instance is a polymorphic object where the object name no longer identifies the actual object instance, the instance's correct VMT is accessed and the appropriate instance size is still returned:

```
New( PHScroll, Init( 0, GetMaxY, GetMaxX-60,

                     Green, LightGreen, Horizontal ) );

. . .

Dispose( PHScroll, Done );
```

The Done destructor method, after calling the ScrollBar VMT, returns the size of the object instance to the Dispose procedure, ensuring that the appropriate memory deallocation is executed.

Note: the task of returning the instance size is not accomplished by the body of the destructor method, but by an epilog code generated by the compiler in response to the reserved word *destructor*.

Extended Type Compatibility

Turbo Pascal implements extended type compatibility rules that allow any object instance to be assigned to a variable of an ancestor object type. These are known as **polymorphic objects**.

Following the example object types used so far, an instance of object type ScrollBar can be assigned to a variable of type *Point*. In like fashion, a pointer to a variable of type *Point* can become a pointer to an instance of type ScrollBar.

Extended type compatibility will be used in later examples as pointers of an ancestor object type, List. The printers are assigned to a variety of descendant object types to create a mixed list of record object types.

Summary

In this chapter, two extensions to familiar Pascal procedures have been introduced — the extended New and Dispose procedures — and the theory of creating and handling dynamically allocated object instances has been discussed. A final graphics example, revising the ScrlTest.PAS program to use dynamic object instances is shown below.

In subsequent chapters, these techniques will be demonstrated further, together with handling practices for pointers and pointer-linked lists to

create a multipurpose address/telephone directory and to create special
methods allowing a linked list to conduct its own sorting operations, as
well as other custom activities.

```pascal
program ScrollBar_Test_2; { SCRLTST2.PAS }


{===============================================}
{ uses dynamically allocated ScrollBar objects }
{===============================================}

uses Crt, Graph, Mouse, Button4, ScrlBar;

var

   ...

   PHScroll, PVScroll : ^ScrollBar;

   ...

begin

   ...

     New( PHScroll, Init( 0, GetMaxY, GetMaxX-60,
                    Green, LightGreen, Horizontal ) );
     New( PVScroll, Init( GetMaxX, 0, GetMaxY,
                    Green, LightGreen, Vertical ) );

   ...

      Create( PHScroll^.GetPosition-10,
              PVScroll^.GetPosition,
              80, 20, LightRed, 'Exit' );

   ...

            case PHScroll^.ScrollHit of
               LEFT,

               HBAR,

               RIGHT: ExitButton.Move(
```

```
                           PHScroll^.GetPosition-10,
                           PVScroll^.GetPosition );
             end; {case}
             case PVScroll^.ScrollHit of
                  UP,
                VBAR,
                DOWN: ExitButton.Move(
                           PHScroll^.GetPosition-10,
                           PVScroll^.GetPosition );
             end; {case}
      . . .
      until Exit;
      Dispose( PHScroll,Done );
      Dispose( PVScroll,Done );
   end;
   . . .
end.
```

CHAPTER 8

DYNAMIC OBJECTS AND LINKED LISTS

While a simple example of dynamic object instances appeared in Chapter 7 and used the ScrollBar object type, there was nothing in this example that could not be accomplished as well using static instances. In this chapter, however, dynamic objects will be used in circumstances where static objects are impractical or inappropriate and, in order to show the uses of dynamic objects, two demo programs will be created: PHONE1.PAS and PHONE2.PAS.

Both of the demo programs read a data file titled PHONE.LST, sort and store the contents as pointer-linked dynamic objects and display the listings as shown in Figure 8-1. The PHONE.LST data file can be created using the MAKELIST program at the end of this chapter. Both the MAKELIST source code and a prepared PHONE.LST data file — as shown in Figure 8-1 — are provided on the program disk accompanying this book. Turbo's MemAvail function is used to show the available memory before the list is created, after the list is allocated and again after the dynamic objects are disposed.

Note that the index item appearing in Figure 8-1 is not a part of the data file, but shows the order in which the records were read from the file. Sorting, as you will see, is accomplished during the file read operation while the linked list is being created.

Figure 8-1: Text Display Generated By PHONE1 or PHONE2 demos

```
NAME OR COMPANY                    (INDEX)        PHONE NUMBER
Addison Wesley Publishing Co.      6              (617) 944-3700
Borland International              5              (408) 438 5300
Compuserve                        7              (800) 848-8990
Dr. Dobb's Journal                13             (415) 366-3600
Heart Interface Corporation       10             (800) 446-6180
... portions omitted ...
Sextant Magazine                  4              (202) 544 0900
Software Toolworks                1              (818) 986-4885
TurboGeometry                     16             (800) 636-7760
(*    Initial available memory: 116832 bytes    *)
(*         ... after list built: 115744 bytes    *)
(*           ... after disposal: 116832 bytes    *)
```

A Brief Explanation of Pointers

Before going into how a linked list of objects is created, a brief explanation of pointers and pointer operations is in order. When dynamic objects, or dynamic variables, are created, memory is dynamically allocated according to the size of the object or variable. At the same time, the allocation process returns the address of the memory that has been set aside for the object or variable (and also prevents the allocated memory from being used for any other purpose).

The address value returned is stored in a special type of variable known as a **pointer variable** or, more often, simply as a **pointer**. And these pointer variables provide the handles to access and also manipulate dynamic objects or dynamic variables. Without a pointer to an object, the object exists only in never-never-land — it's somewhere in the system's memory but it's also lost beyond recovery.

A pointer does not always have to point to a memory address — if a pointer has not yet been assigned to a dynamic object or variable the pointer is called a **nil** or **null pointer**, indicating that its value is undefined. Also, the value nil can be assigned to a pointer, indicating that the pointer is undefined.

Linked and Sorted Lists Using Pointers

Pointers and dynamic objects — or pointers and dynamic variables — are a natural combination for much more than simply finding or accessing the object. One of the primary applications of pointer variables is their use in sorting lists.

When a list of static objects (or variables or records) is sorted, the task is accomplished as a series of swap operations and, for each swap, two complete objects must be moved. This usually requires copying the first object to a temporary object variable, copying the second object variable to the first and finally, copying the temp object to the second for a total of three moves. Depending on the size of the object (or record), this can require quite a few CPU cycles to accomplish.

With dynamic objects or dynamic variables, however, the same swap operations are much simpler to accomplish because the objects or variable records are not moved at all. Instead, only the pointers to the object's memory locations are swapped and the CPU time required becomes constant, irrespective of the size of the list entries being sorted.

At the same time, objects or records can contain pointers. In this fashion, a linked list of objects can be created — as shown in Figure 8-2 — in which each object in the list contains a pair of pointers to the objects preceding and following. Note also that the first and last objects in the list each have a *nil* or undefined pointer.

There are, however, also two static pointers used, *FirstLink* and *LastLink,* which provide access to the ends of the list. In the sort routine and elsewhere, a third static pointer, *NPtr* (not shown) is used as a movable pointer to trace through the list. And, since the *FirstLink* and *LastLink* variables are static, they have the advantage of always being available (but must be assigned to the appropriate dynamic objects or they will be useless).

For more information on pointers and pointer applications, refer to Chapter 7 of *Programming The IBM User Interface*, available from Addison-Wesley Publishing Company.

Figure 8-2: A Linked-List Structure

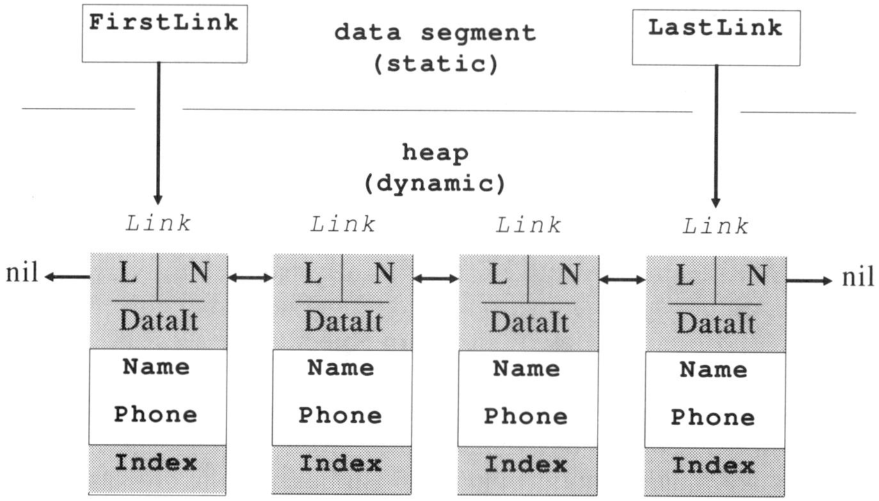

Sorting Lists

The data file used in both the PHONE1 and PHONE2 demonstrations has been deliberately disordered to show how the application can sort the list at the same time it is read from the disk file.

In the PHONE1 demo, both the disk read and sort operation are accomplished in a relatively conventional manner, but in the PHONE2 demo, both of these operations become object methods; thus the object is able not only to open and read its own data file, but at the same time sort itself.

The sort routine used here is called an Entry Sort. While this is not the fastest sort algorithm in existence, it is far from the slowest and offers adequate performance while using relatively simple coding. For applications that require sorting large quantities of data, you may prefer to use an Indexed Entry Sort or to rewrite the object method to use a Quick Sort algorithm.

Sorting algorithms, implementations and a comparison of performance speeds using different algorithms (both theoretical and practical), have already been covered at some length in Chapter 8 of *Programming The IBM User Interface*.

The Entry Sort Algorithm

Rather than leave you entirely in the dark, however, I will describe how the Entry Sort algorithm used in PHONE1 and PHONE2 works.

Since this is an Entry Sort, each item is sorted as it is read from the disk file source and, naturally, the first item read becomes a special case, and is used to initialize the sorting algorithm:

```
if FirstLink = nil then

begin
```

Each item read from the data file is written to a newly created dynamic object, NewEntry. For the first item read, the static variables *FirstLink* and *LastLink* are both assigned to (pointed at) the new entry and at each other, establishing an initial order even though the list contains only one item:

```
    FirstLink := NewEntry;
     LastLink := NewEntry;
    FirstLink^.Last := nil;
    FirstLink^.Next  := LastLink;
     LastLink^.Last := FirstLink;
     LastLink^.Next  := nil;
  end else
```

After this, since *FirstLink* now points to something, two initial tests are made, beginning by testing the Name field of the new entry against the Name field pointed to by *FirstLink*:

```
begin
    if Precede( NewItem.Name,

                 FirstLink^.Data.Name ) then
    begin
```

The Precede function returns TRUE if the first string argument precedes the second alphabetically. If so, then the current *FirstLink's* Last pointer is assigned to the new item:

```
FirstLink^.Last  := NewEntry;
```

the new entry's Next pointer is assigned to the first entry:

```
NewEntry^.Next   := FirstLink;
```

FirstLink itself is pointed at the new entry, making the new entry the new first entry:

```
FirstLink        := NewEntry;
```

and finally, the new *FirstLink's* Last pointer is assigned as nil:

```
    FirstLink^.Last := nil;

end else
```

If the new entry does not belong at the head of the list, it's tested to see if it belongs at the end of the list:

```
if Precede( LastLink^.Data.Name,

             NewItem.Name ) then
begin
```

If so, the new entry becomes the new *LastLink*:

```
     LastLink^.Next := NewEntry;

     NewEntry^.Last := LastLink;

     LastLink         := NewEntry;

     LastLink^.Next := nil;

  end else
```

When the new entry belongs neither first nor last, the pointer *ThisLink* is assigned to the top of the list and then stepped down through the list until an entry is found that should precede the current entry:

```
  begin

     ThisLink := FirstLink;

     while Precede( ThisLInk^.Data.Name,

                     NewItem.Name ) do

        ThisLink := ThisLink^.Next;

     ThisLink := ThisLink^.Last;
```

Once the location is found, the pointer *ThisLink* is actually one place beyond where the entry should go, so *ThisLink* is moved back one step. And NewEntry is added to the chain:

```
  NewEntry^.Last := ThisLink;
```

beginning by assigning the new entry's Last pointer to the current entry (*ThisLink*):

```
  NewEntry^.Next := ThisLink^.Next;
```

the Next pointer to the current entry's Next — thus preserving the existing forward link in the chain:

```
  ThisLink^.Next := NewEntry;
```

and the current entry's own Next.points to the new entry. The final step in this process is a bit of a trick because the entry following the current entry is not directly available, but still needs a pointer from the following item back to the new item. However, the following entry is indirectly available because the new entry's Next pointer does point forward to the next item:

```
NewEntry^.Next^.Last := NewEntry;
```

points forward to the next entry to assign the next link's *Last* pointer back to the new entry.

While the operations are a bit complex to explain, execution of the operation is quite simple and relatively fast, with the slowest part of the whole process writing the final list to the screen. See Table 8-1 for display times.

Table 8-1: Disk Read, Sort and Display Times (PHONE2.PAS)

File access time (16 items):	0.02060 seconds
Sort operations (16 items):	0.00955 seconds
Screen write (21 lines):	0.03680 seconds
Total:	0.06695 seconds

Operation times derived by averaging elapsed time for loop = 1..1000.

In PHONE2, the Sort method is implemented in a slightly different form than PHONE1 but works in essentially the same fashion as shown preceding.

Note that for longer lists, the Indexed Entry Sort routine, referred to earlier, can reduce search times tremendously while requiring only minimal additional overhead (less than a dozen lines of code plus index elements).

The Precede Utility

The Precede utility deserves a brief explanation and a recommendation. Too often, sort comparisons on lists containing alphabetical characters are made by the simple expedient of comparing the two entries directly; this results in *du Bois* following *Engles* and *MORSE* preceding *Miller*. For mixed alphanumerical entries such as *345-F-2469* and *345-a-2380*, ordering is not correct when the sort algorithm depends on the entry being made consistently using only upper- or lowercase characters.

Some programs attempt to avoid this problem by having all entries converted to uppercase as: *DU BOIS*, *ENGLES*, *MORSE* and *MILLER* — which is fine for a stock number, but inconvenient for a name and address file. The ideal for all sort routines is to make the ordering comparisons independent of the UPPERCASE/lowercase format of the entries (unless, of course, the entries are actually intended to be case sensitive). For this reason, the Precede function executes a comparison ignoring case.

The Precede function is called with two string arguments and begins by stepping through the string, by incrementing *j*, until the current characters in the two strings do not match:

```
function Precede( Str1, Str2 : string ): boolean;

   begin

      j := 0;

      i := ord( Str1[0] );

      while( upcase( Str1[j] ) = upcase( Str2[j] ) )

      and ( j <= i ) do

         inc( j );
```

The result reported is done, quite simply, by a comparison of the first two characters that do not match:

```
      Precede := upcase( Str1[j] ) < upcase( Str2[j] );

   end;
```

That's it — simple and fast.

The Phone1 Demo Program

The Phone1 demo begins by defining a record type, DataItem; an object type, DataObj; and a pointer to the object, DataPtr:

```
type
   DataItem = record  Name : string[40];
                     Phone : string[14];  end;
   DataPtr = ^DataObj;
   DataObj = object
              Last, Next : DataPtr;
                    Data : DataItem;
                   Index : integer;
              constructor Init( ThisIndex : integer;
                                ThisItem : DataItem );
              destructor  Done;
              procedure   Print;
          end;
```

In this first example, DataObj includes two pointers (*Last* and *Next*) which will be used as links to build a chain of DataObj, a record of DataItem (Data) and an integer field (Index) as well as three methods, Init, Done and Print.

The DataObj Methods

The first DataObj method, Init, is called — in this example — with two parameters: *ThisItem* which contains the information read from the disk file, and *ThisIndex* which is simply an integer value indicating the order in which the records were read and is used to show the sorting action:

```
constructor DataObj.Init;
   begin
      Last  := nil;
      Next  := nil;
      Index := ThisIndex;
```

```
    Data  := ThisItem;

end;
```

At the same time, simply as a precaution, the *Last* and *Next* pointers are set to *nil* — unassigned. The destructor method, Done, is declared, but has no tasks to perform:

```
destructor DataObj.Done;

  begin

  end;
```

And the final method, Print, lists the contents of the Data record and the index number:

```
procedure DataObj.Print;

  begin

    with Data do

      writeln( Name, Index:3, '        ', Phone );

  end;
```

At this time, the DataObj object is pretty simple and contains only the methods needed to demonstrate basic handling because the bulk of this demonstration is not accomplished by object methods, but by conventional programming procedures. In the Phone2 demo, however, this will not be the case.

The Phone1 Main Program

The main program begins by printing a header for the list, then checks the available memory and initializes the *FirstLink* pointer as *nil* to ensure that it does not contain some accidental value:

```
begin

  clrscr;

  gotoxy(  4,1 ); writeln('Name or Company');
```

```
gotoxy( 39,1 ); writeln('(index)      Phone Number');

Mem1 := MemAvail;

FirstLink := nil;

Read_File_Entries;
```

Next, the demo calls the Read_File_Entries procedure to open the diskfile and read and sort the contents using the algorithms previous shown.

The actual listing is accomplished by setting the static variable *This-Link* to the top of the list and then stepping down the list calling the indicated object's Print method to create the screen listing:

```
ThisLink := FirstLink;

while ThisLink <> nil do

begin

   ThisLink^.Print;

   ThisLink := ThisLink^.Next;

end;


Mem2 := MemAvail;
```

After the list is completed, it checks the available memory again.

Next, the pointer *ThisLink* is again set to the top of the list and stepped down, but this time, calling the Dispose procedure to deallocate the dynamically created objects:

```
ThisLink := FirstLink;

while ThisLink <> nil do

begin

   Dispose( ThisLink, Done );

      ThisLink := ThisLink^.Next;

   end;
```

Finally, the available memory found at each point is reported:

```
writeln;
writeln('(*  Available memory: initial: ',
        Mem1:6,      ' bytes    *)');
writeln('(*           ... after list built: ',
        Mem2:6,      ' bytes    *)');
writeln('(*           ... after disposal: ',
        MemAvail:6, ' bytes    *)');
readln;
end.
```

Now, the Phone1 demo is pretty simple to follow — which is the general idea — showing how pointers are used to create a linked list and to sort a list, but most of this example has been conventional programming and has not used the special capabilities of object-oriented programming.

The Phone2 Demo Program

The Phone2 demo accomplishes the same task as Phone1, but does so in a much more elegant manner. It creates a second object type, LinkObj, which takes over the task of both reading the data file and sorting the entries. Before introducing LinkObj, however, there are a couple of other changes from Phone1.

In this application, the linking pointers used to create the data list are not contained in the DataObj objects. Instead, the link elements themselves are a series of dynamically allocated records (*NodeRec*) that point to each other in order to create the list and, using a third pointer, also point to the DataObj objects (see Figure 8-3).

The record type, DataItem, appearing in Phone1, is still the same, but the associated object type, DataObj, has been revised. It loses the two pointer variables and the integer variable, *Index*:

```
DataObj  = object
              Data : DataItem;
              constructor Init( ThisItem : DataItem );
              destructor  Done;
              procedure   Print;
           end;
```

The constructor method, Init, now has only one calling parameter, the data record which is read from the disk file (or entered directly from the keyboard in an expanded application). The Done and Print methods remain unchanged.

Figure 8-3: Pointer-Linked Lists

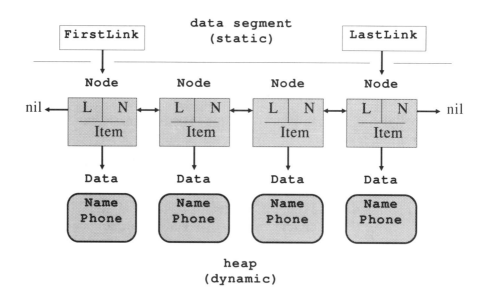

The NodeRec Definition

The two pointers that have been deleted from the DataObj object are still needed and now appear in a new record definition, NodeRec:

```
NodePtr = ^NodeRec;

NodeRec = record  Last, Next : NodePtr;
                          Item : DataPtr;  end;
```

This time, *Last* and *Next* are not *DataPtr* pointers, but are NodePtr pointers — pointers to other NodeRec records that will create a chain of NodeRec links instead of DataObj links. The NodeRec does contain a third pointer, *Item*, which is a pointer to a DataObj and, within the chain of NodeRec, will point to the associated DataObj entries.

The LinkObj Definition

More is involved here, however, than simply shifting the pointer links from being internal elements of the DataObj to external records. Instead, the NodePtr's do not stand alone, but are declared as elements within a new object type, LinkObj:

```
LinkPtr = ^LinkObj;

LinkObj = object
          Nodes : NodePtr;
          constructor Init;
          destructor Done;  virtual;
          procedure Add( ThisItem : DataPtr );
          procedure Sort( NewLink : NodePtr );
          procedure ReadFile( NameFile : string );
          procedure Print;
       end;
```

The LinkObj object consists of the single Node's data record and a series of methods that will replace most of the conventional programming used in the Phone1 demo program.

The LinkObj Methods

The LinkObj methods begin with the constructor method, Init, which establishes the link object type and sets both the Nodes and FirstLink pointer to *nil*, unassigned:

```
constructor LinkObj.Init;

   begin

      Nodes := nil;

      FirstLink := nil;

   end;
```

LinkObj's ReadFile method replaces the Read_File_Entry procedure used in Phone1, but in this example, is called with a parameter specifying the filename to be read. When called, the ReadFile method opens the specified filename, reading the contents and calling the Add method with each entry:

```
procedure LinkObj.ReadFile;

   var

      NewItem  : DataItem;

      DataFile : file of DataItem;

   begin

      assign( DataFile, NameFile );

      reset( DataFile );

      repeat

         read( DataFile, NewItem );

         Add( New( DataPtr, Init( NewItem ) ) );
```

```
      until EOF( DataFile );
      close( DataFile );
   end;
```

Each time a file record is read, the data is passed to a newly created DataObj — using the New procedure's extended nomenclature as described in Chapter 7, and passing the pointer value returned to the Add method.

In this example, the file type is predefined because only one type of record is intended to be read. In other applications, however, the file type might be set elsewhere or provided as a calling parameter.

LinkObj's Add method accepts a pointer to each DataObj as a calling parameter, again using the New procedure to dynamically allocate a new NodePtr and the NodePtr's Item pointer to the DataObj:

```
procedure LinkObj.Add;

   var

      NPtr : NodePtr;

   begin

      New( NPtr );

      NPtr^.Item := ThisItem;

      Sort( NPtr );

   end;
```

At this point, the new NodePtr is not connected to anything, except for pointing to the DataObj in its Item field. The Add method therefore calls the Sort method, using the *NPtr* variable as an argument, to link the new node into the list.

The Sort method in this example works almost exactly the same as demonstrated previously, the principal differences being in the nomenclature required to indicate the appropriate data fields for testing:

```
procedure LinkObj.Sort;

   var
```

```
      NPtr : NodePtr;

   function Precede( Str1, Str2 : string ): boolean;

      ... Precede subfunction — details omitted ...

   ... Sort method — details omitted ...
```

The main difference in the Phone2 version of the sort routine is in the parameters passed to the Precede function, with the denotation: *NewLink^.Item^.Data.Name* referring to the Name element in the Data record that is indicated by the Item pointer which, in turn, is indicated by the NewLink pointer (obviously, it's much easier to instruct the computer than it is to say it in English).

LinkObj's Print method is also new and replaces the list processing code in Phone1. While it accomplishes essentially the same task, it prints the entire list with a single call, using the local variable *NPtr* to step through the list's links:

```
procedure LinkObj.Print;

   var

      NPtr : NodePtr;

   begin

      NPtr := FirstLink;

      repeat

         with NPtr^.Item^ do Print;

         NPtr := NPtr^.Next;

      until NPtr = nil;

   end;
```

This Print method, however, does not actually print any information; instead, the LinkObj.Print method calls another object's Print method, in this case DataObj's Print method, to handle the actual display.

So, how does the LinkObj method know what Print method to call? After all, the LinkObj object and the DataObj object are totally unconnected and this is not a case of an ancestor object calling a descendant object or vice versa. Instead, the instruction *with NPtr^.Item^ do Print* tells the LinkObj.Print method which object's Print method is needed because the *NPtr^.Item^* specification points specifically to the DataObj method with no confusion and no errors.

Because the links will be dynamic, a destructor method, Done, is provided. In this case, however, the destructor method is considerably different from previous examples.

Previously, the destructor method has had little or nothing to do aside from providing the necessary epilog code when complied, a task which is accomplished by the keyword, *destructor*.

In this case, before a link node is deallocated, the object indicated by the Item field also needs to be deallocated; otherwise, only the ListObj objects would be released while the DataObj objects would still be in memory, taking up space, and lost in never-never-land.

What's wrong with this? Simple, the memory used by the still-allocated DataObj records is not available to the current program, nor to any other programs or applications even after the current program has terminated. If not deliberately and properly deallocated, the memory used will remain tied up until the computer is reset.

Therefore, the LinkObj.Done method begins by moving a local pointer (*NPtr*) to the head of the list and stepping down until the end of the list is reached. Beginning at the top, first the DataObj indicated by the Item pointer is released by a direct call to the Dispose procedure — again using the extended nomenclature discussed in Chapter 7:

```
destructor LinkObj.Done;
   var
      NPtr : NodePtr;
   begin
      NPtr := FirstLink;
      repeat
         Dispose( NPtr^.Item, Done );
```

Next, the static pointer, *FirstLink*, is pointed to the local pointer's Next field, moving *FirstLink* down one in the list:

```
FirstLink := NPtr^.Next;
```

The NodePtr record indicated by *NPtr* is released — remember, this was also a dynamically allocated record:

```
Dispose( NPtr );
```

Last, *NPtr* is again set to *FirstLink* before testing to see if the loop is finished:

```
    NPtr := FirstLink;

  until FirstLink = nil;

end;
```

Only after all of the objects and records held by the list are released, does the Done method itself return, allowing the list to be deallocated.

Warning, there's a catch here. Because the list itself does not need to be deallocated and cannot be deallocated (because the list itself is a static object), all that can be done has been done.

Still, if LinkList was a dynamic object, the same Done method would be necessary to release the elements of the list before the list was released and the only differences would be in the program code calling the Done method.

The Phone2 Main Program

The main program in Phone2 is considerably simpler than Phone1, primarily because most of the tasks accomplished in Phone1 are now handled by object methods in Phone2.

What's left, after writing the list header and reporting on memory usage, is very brief indeed:

```
with LinkList do

begin

   Init;

   ReadFile('PHONE.LST');
```

```
    Print;

    Done;

  end;
```

It should be self-explanatory at this point.

Memory Usage

Incidentally, the static object, LinkList, is moderately large and is reported by the SizeOf function as 3,816 bytes, most of which consists of the methods used by LinkList. In the example, the data — pointers, names and telephone numbers — only required 1,112 bytes, but this was a brief list. The LinkList overhead, of course, does not increase with an increase in the size of the data list created, only the memory allocated for the list elements themselves.

In many real-world applications, however, the savings in memory overhead by dynamically creating and releasing complex objects such as LinkList is almost as important as the conveniences of object-oriented programming itself. Dynamically created objects become a sort of super-convenient overlay.

Summary

In this chapter, two demonstrations have shown; first, how objects can be linked and sorted using pointers and; second, how a single object can manipulate a linked list and exercise methods controlling a series of other objects.

In Chapter 9, object lists will be taken a step further, creating a linked and sorted list of mixed dynamic object types, together with a stepped display and with the data presentation determined by the objects themselves.

```
        (*=============================*)
        (*  PHONE1.PAS Demo Program  *)
        (*=============================*)
program Phone_List_Demo_1;
```

```pascal
uses Crt;

type
   DataPtr  = ^DataObj;
   DataItem = record  Name : string[40];
                      Phone : string[14];  end;
   DataObj  = object
                  Last, Next : DataPtr;
                       Data : DataItem;
                      Index : integer;
                  constructor Init( ThisIndex : integer;
                                      ThisItem : DataItem );
                  destructor  Done;
                  procedure    Print;
               end;
var
   FirstLink, LastLink, ThisLink : DataPtr;
   Mem1, Mem2 : longint;

                   {=====================}
                   { Data implementation }
                   {=====================}

constructor DataObj.Init;
   begin
      Last := nil;
      Next := nil;
      Index := ThisIndex;
      Data  := ThisItem;
```

```pascal
      end;

destructor DataObj.Done;
   begin
   end;

procedure DataObj.Print;
   begin
      with Data do
         writeln( Name, Index:3, '      ', Phone );
   end;

                  {=====================}
                  { end of Data methods }
                  {=====================}
function Precede( Str1, Str2 : string ): boolean;
   var
      i, j : integer;
   begin
      j := 0;
      i := ord( Str1[0] );
      while( upcase( Str1[j] ) = upcase( Str2[j] ) )
      and ( j <= i ) do
         inc( j );
      Precede := upcase( Str1[j] ) < upcase( Str2[j] );
   end;

procedure Read_File_Entries;
   const
```

```
        NameFile = 'PHONE.LST';
var
    NewItem : DataItem;
   NewEntry : DataPtr;
   ReadFile : file of DataItem;
          j : integer;
begin
   j := 0;
   assign( ReadFile, NameFile );
   reset( ReadFile );
   repeat
      inc( j );
      read( ReadFile, NewItem );
      New( NewEntry, Init( j, NewItem ) );
      if FirstLink^.Data.Name = '' then
      begin
         FirstLink := NewEntry;
          LastLink := NewEntry;
         FirstLink^.Last := nil;
         FirstLink^.Next := LastLink;
          LastLink^.Last := FirstLink;
          LastLink^.Next := nil;
      end else
      begin                    { is this a new first?   }
         if Precede( NewItem.Name,
                   FirstLink^.Data.Name ) then
```

```
begin              { insert at top         }
   FirstLink^.Last := NewEntry;
   NewEntry^.Next  := FirstLink;
   FirstLink       := NewEntry;
   FirstLink^.Last := nil;
end else           { is this a new last?    }
if Precede( LastLink^.Data.Name,
         NewItem.Name ) then
begin              { insert at end          }
   LastLink^.Next := NewEntry;
   NewEntry^.Last := LastLink;
   LastLink       := NewEntry;
   LastLink^.Next := nil;
end else           { not first or last so,  }
begin              { start at top...        }
   ThisLink := FirstLink;
   while Precede( ThisLInk^.Data.Name,
               NewItem.Name ) do
      ThisLink := ThisLink^.Next;{ search }
   ThisLink := ThisLink^.Last;{ move back  }
   NewEntry^.Last := ThisLink;{ and insert }
   NewEntry^.Next := ThisLink^.Next;
   ThisLink^.Next := NewEntry;
   NewEntry^.Next^.Last := NewEntry;
end;
end;
```

```pascal
            until EOF(ReadFile);
            close(ReadFile);
        end;

begin
    clrscr;
    gotoxy(  4,1 ); writeln('Name or Company');
    gotoxy( 39,1 ); writeln('(index)     Phone Number');
    Mem1 := MemAvail;
    FirstLink^.Data.Name := '';
    Read_File_Entries;

    ThisLink := FirstLink;
    while ThisLink <> nil do
    begin
        ThisLink^.Print;
        ThisLink := ThisLink^.Next;
    end;

    Mem2 := MemAvail;

    ThisLink := FirstLink;
    while ThisLink <> nil do
    begin
        Dispose( ThisLink, Done );
        ThisLink := ThisLink^.Next;
    end;

    writeln;
    writeln('(*  Available memory: initial: ',
```

```
            Mem1:6,        ' bytes    *)');
   writeln('(*         ... after list built: ',
            Mem2:6,        ' bytes    *)');
   writeln('(*          ... after disposal: ',
            MemAvail:6, ' bytes    *)');
   readln;
end.


            (*============================*)
            (*  PHONE2.PAS Demo Program  *)
            (*============================*)
program Phone_List_Demo_2;
uses Crt;
type
   NodePtr = ^NodeRec;
   LinkPtr = ^LinkObj;
   DataPtr = ^DataObj;
   NodeRec = record  Last, Next : NodePtr;
                            Item : DataPtr;    end;
   LinkObj = object
                Nodes : NodePtr;
                constructor Init;
                destructor Done;  virtual;
                procedure Add( ThisItem : DataPtr );
                procedure Sort( NewLink : NodePtr );
               procedure ReadFile( NameFile : string );
                procedure Print;
             end;
```

```pascal
      DataItem = record   Name : string[40];
                          Phone : string[14];    end;
      DataObj = object
                  Data : DataItem;
                  constructor Init( ThisItem : DataItem );
                  destructor Done;   virtual;
                  procedure Print;
              end;
  var
    LinkList : LinkObj;
    FirstLink, LastLink : NodePtr;
    Mem1, Mem2 : longint;


                  {======================}
                  { Link implementation }
                  {======================}
constructor LinkObj.Init;
   begin
      Nodes := nil;
      FirstLink := nil;
   end;

destructor LinkObj.Done;
   var
      NPtr : NodePtr;
   begin
      NPtr := FirstLink;
      repeat
```

```pascal
        Dispose( NPtr^.Item, Done );
        FirstLink := NPtr^.Next;
        Dispose( NPtr );
        NPtr := FirstLink;
    until FirstLink = nil;
  end;

procedure LinkObj.Add;
  var
    NPtr : NodePtr;

  begin
    New( NPtr );
    NPtr^.Item := ThisItem;
    Sort( NPtr );
  end;

procedure LinkObj.Sort;
  var
    NPtr : NodePtr;

  function Precede( Str1, Str2 : string ): boolean;
    var
      i, j : integer;
    begin
      j := 0;
      i := ord( Str1[0] );
      while( upcase( Str1[j] ) = upcase( Str2[j] ) )
      and ( j <= i ) do
```

```
          inc( j );
      Precede :=
          upcase( Str1[j] ) < upcase( Str2[j] );
   end;

begin
   if FirstLink = nil then{ first entry from file  }
   begin
      FirstLink := NewLink;
       LastLink := NewLink;
      FirstLink^.Last := nil;
      FirstLink^.Next := LastLink;
       LastLink^.Last := FirstLink;
       LastLink^.Next := nil;
   end else
   begin                        { is this a new first?   }
      if Precede( NewLink^.Item^.Data.Name,
               FirstLink^.Item^.Data.Name ) then
      begin                     { insert at top           }
         FirstLink^.Last := NewLink;
         NewLink^.Next    := FirstLink;
         FirstLink        := NewLink;
         FirstLink^.Last := nil;
      end else                  { is this a new last?    }
      if Precede( LastLink^.Item^.Data.Name,
                  NewLink^.Item^.Data.Name ) then
      begin
```

```
            LastLink^.Next := NewLink; { insert at end }
            NewLink^.Last  := LastLink;
            LastLink       := NewLink;
            LastLink^.Next := nil;
         end else              { not first or last so,  }
         begin                 { start at top...        }
            NPtr := FirstLink;
            while Precede( NPtr^.Item^.Data.Name,
                       NewLink^.Item^.Data.Name ) do
               NPtr := NPtr^.Next; { search down...    }
            NPtr := NPtr^.Last;    { move back one... }
            NewLink^.Last := NPtr; { and insert entry }
            NewLink^.Next := NPtr^.Next;
            NPtr^.Next := NewLink;
            NewLink^.Next^.Last := NewLink;
         end;
      end;
   end;

procedure LinkObj.ReadFile;
   var
      NewItem  : DataItem;
      DataFile : file of DataItem;
   begin
      assign( DataFile, NameFile );
      reset( DataFile );
      repeat
```

```pascal
                read( DataFile, NewItem );
                Add( New( DataPtr, Init( NewItem ) ) );
           until EOF( DataFile );
           close( DataFile );
      end;

procedure LinkObj.Print;
   var
      NPtr : NodePtr;
   begin
      NPtr := FirstLink;
      repeat
         with NPtr^.Item^ do Print;
         NPtr := NPtr^.Next;
      until NPtr = nil;
   end;

                  {=====================}
                  { Data implementation }
                  {=====================}
constructor DataObj.Init;
   begin
      Data := ThisItem;
   end;

destructor DataObj.Done;
   begin
   end;
```

```pascal
procedure DataObj.Print;
   begin
      with Data do
         writeln( Name, Phone );
   end;

                  {=====================}
                  { end of Data methods }
                  {=====================}
begin
   clrscr;
   gotoxy(  4, 1 ); writeln('Name or Company');
   gotoxy( 42, 1 ); writeln('Phone Number');
   Mem1 := MemAvail;                { read available RAM }
   with LinkList do
   begin
      Init;                         { create a link list }
      ReadFile('PHONE.LST');        { read the data file }
   {  ReadFile('PHONE2.LST');  } {  ... optional...    }
   {  ReadFile('PHONE3.LST');  } {  ... optional...    }
      Print;                        { print out the list }
      Mem2 := MemAvail;             { read available RAM }
      Done;                         { dispose of list    }
   end;
   writeln;
   writeln('(*  Available memory, initial: ',
                   Mem1:6,      ' bytes  *)');
   writeln('(*         ... after list built: ',
```

```
                          Mem2:6,       ' bytes *)');
    writeln('(*            ... after disposal: ',
                          MemAvail:6, ' bytes *)');
    readln;
end.


              {====================}
              {    MAKELIST.PAS     }
              {====================}
program Create_Demo_Phone_List;
    uses Crt;
    const
        FileName = 'PHONE.LST';
        NullStr =                              { 40 spaces }
            '                                      ';

    type
        NameRecord = record
                        Name  : string[40];
                        Phone : string[14];
                     end;
    var
        ListFile : file of NameRecord;
        FileEntry : NameRecord;
          Finish : boolean;

function Read_Name : string;
    var
        TempStr: string;
    begin
```

```
         TempStr := '';

         write('Enter name: ');

         readln(TempStr);

         Read_Name := TempStr;

      end;

function Read_Number : string;

   var

      TempStr: string;

   begin

      TempStr := '';

      write('Enter phone number: ');

      readln(TempStr);

      Read_Number := TempStr;

   end;

begin

   ClrScr;

   Finish := false;

   writeln('Enter names and phone numbers ',
           'for demo program file');

   writeln('Enter blank line to exit: ');

   assign(ListFile, FileName);

   rewrite(ListFile);

   repeat

      FileEntry.Name := Read_Name+NullStr;

      FileEntry.Phone := Read_Number+NullStr;

      Finish := (FileEntry.Name = NullStr);
```

```
        if not Finish then write(ListFile,FileEntry);
    until Finish;
    close(ListFile);
end.
```

CHAPTER 9

LINKED LISTS AND MIXED OBJECTS

In the previous chapter, a simple linked-list was created with pointers to objects. Since all pointers are the same, consisting of segment and offset addresses, why not have the link Item pointers pointing to different object types and therefore, create a linked-list with mixed objects? In this manner, a single list could contain several different types of record while, at the same time, still treat each record in a different fashion. Sound useful?

One hopes so, because this is precisely what will be demonstrated in this chapter. It will be shown as a stepped display with the list object providing the display space and the data objects controlling the manner in which the information is presented within the list's frame. Figure 9-1 shows three examples though only one would be displayed at a time.

For the present application, a text display with keyboard controls will be used, but a graphics analog employing these same techniques may be used together with scrollbar controls (not with the text version), graphic control buttons and the mouse interface unit.

Figure 9-1: Three Data Records: Personal, Business and BBS

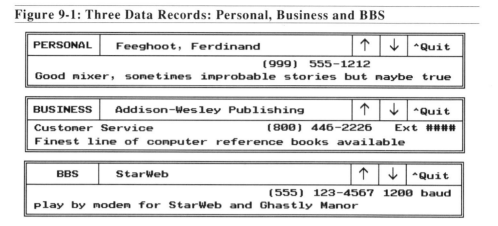

Mixing Objects Within a List

While all pointers are — in their internal structure — essentially the same, there do remain a few restrictions: pointers to object types are assignment compatible with pointers to ancestor object types. This means a pointer to an object may point to an instance of the object or to any descendant of the object type. But pointers to unrelated object types are not assignment compatible in Pascal.

As long as the NodeRec link elements have a pointer to the ancestor object type, these same pointers can be assigned to a variety of descendant object types to create a mixed list of object records. This allows a great deal of flexibility, particularly since each object type in the list can execute a different task in response to the method or methods called.

However this is also the reason that the entry sort task is executed by the list object and not the data objects — because the sorting job has to be executed in a consistent fashion and can't be done one way by one object and another way by another object; at least, not within a single list. (Anarchy among objects is all very well, but a degree of consistency is also necessary.)

Figure 9-2 shows a schematic structure for a linked list with varying object types — compare it with Figures 8-2 and 8-3 from the preceding chapter.

Figure 9-2: Linked-List With Mixed Object Types

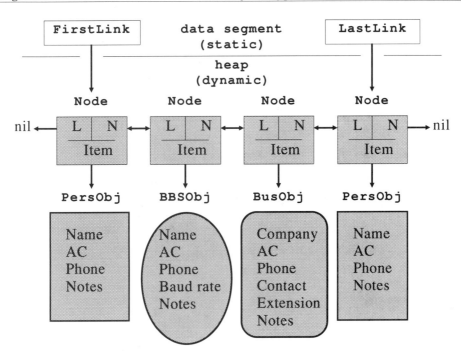

Multiple Sources vs. Single Source

Several approaches were possible in setting up this demo. One choice might have been to create a single source file using variant records for three different data types:

```
FileRec = record
    Name : string[30];        AC : string[3];
```

```
Phone : string[10];    Notes : string[60];
case ThisType : RecType of
   Personal: ( {empty} );
   Business: ( Contact: string[20];
                      Ext: string[5];  );
        BBS: (    Baud: string[4];  );         end;
```

As the data file is read, assign the file entries to different object types according to the record variant type (ThisType):

```
read( DataFile, NewItem );
case NewItem.ThisType of
   Personal: Add( New( PersPtr,
                      Init( NewItem ) ) );
   Business: Add( New( BusPtr,
                      Init( NewItem ) ) );
        BBS: Add( New( BBSPtr,
                      Init( NewItem ) ) );
end; {case}
```

The variant record approach has several advantages because only one data file is required; a single Init procedure declared by the original object type (PersObj) will serve for both descendant object types; and the program code is slightly simpler.

On the other hand, using three different data files has other advantages. First, three separate data files each devoted to a single data structure will be smaller overall than a single variant record file containing all three types of record data. More important than saving disk space (even though the program source code and the execute code are slightly larger to provide handling for multiple files of different types), the reduced memory usage for the dynamically allocated data records does result in an overall savings of active memory, particularly when larger data files are read in.

Also, if each data type is handled separately, then adding new record types becomes much simpler and does not require revising or re-entering the original data files. And, adding a new object descendant, object extensibility, is also enhanced. Ergo, the latter option — three separate data files — has been used here.

Three Data Files

The source listing for a utility program called MAKELSTS.PAS, appears at the end of this chapter. This program creates three separate data files for personal, business and BBS listings. These listings have record structures as follow:

```
PersRec = record
   Name: string[30];        AC: string[3];
   Phone: string[10];    Notes: string[60]; end;

BusRec = record
   ... PersRec data plus ...
   Contact: string[20];    Ext: string[5];   end;

BBSRec = record
   ... PersRec data plus ...
   Baud: string[4];                            end;
```

These same record structures are, obviously, also declared in the PHONE3.PAS program.

Three prepared data files, PHONEPRS.DAT, PHONEBUS.DAT and PHONEBBS.DAT, as well as the program source code for the MAKELSTS utility are also included on the program disk accompanying this volume. Note: the contents of the personal and BBS data files are, of course, fictitious.

Revising the LinkObj Object

While the linked list established in PHONE2 is easily adaptable for a mixed-object list, the LinkObj object does require some changes before it is able to read and accept the new data types — capabilities which will be provided by the ReadPers, ReadBus and ReadBBS methods replacing the earlier ReadFile method:

```
LinkObj = object
            Nodes : NodePtr;
            constructor Init;
            destructor Done;  virtual;
            procedure ReadPers( NameFile : string );
            procedure ReadBus( NameFile : string );
            procedure ReadBBS( NameFile : string );
            procedure Add( ThisItem : PersPtr );
            procedure Sort( NewLink : NodePtr );
```

At the same time, two additional methods, FWindow and Frame, are added to provide a text window and to draw the display frame:

```
    procedure FWindow( PosX,
                       PosY : integer );
    procedure Frame;
    procedure Print;
end;
```

Aside from replacing all DataPtr references with PersPtr — a pointer to the ancestor type of the three object types — the Init, Done, Add and Sort methods remain essentially as created. The remaining Print method has been revised to provide single entry handling and responds to the Up, Down, Home, End, Page Up and Page Down keys to step through the chain of data objects.

Accessing the Files

The three file access methods, ReadPers, ReadBus and ReadBBS, are essentially the same except for the DataFile types declared and the pointer type used calling the New procedure:

```
procedure LinkObj.ReadPers;

    var

        NewItem  : PersRec;

        DataFile : file of PersRec;

    begin

        assign( DataFile, NameFile );

        reset( DataFile );

        repeat

            read( DataFile, NewItem );

            Add( New( PersPtr, Init( NewItem ) ) );

        until EOF( DataFile );

        close( DataFile );

    end;

procedure LinkObj.ReadBus;

    var

        NewItem  : BusRec;

        DataFile : file of BusRec;

    begin

        ...

            Add( New( BusPtr,  Init( NewItem ) ) );

    end;

procedure LinkObj.ReadBBS;
```

```
var

   NewItem  : BBSRec;

   DataFile : file of BBSRec;

begin

   . . .

      Add( New( BBSPtr,  Init( NewItem ) ) );

end;
```

Each of the data read methods opens a file of data records, reading the contents until the end of the file is found and creating a new object instance for each data record — precisely the same as was done in the Phone2 program.

In the main program, access can be restricted to only one or two data types quite simply by limiting which data files are read or an active control could be created to select which data files were added to the listings.

The LinkObj FWindow and Frame Methods

The FWindow method is used to set up a text window at the X/Y coordinates specified, ensuring that the window coordinates are valid for the window size needed and ending by calling the Frame method to draw the outline for the display:

```
procedure LinkObj.FWindow;

   begin

      if PosX > 15 then PosX := 15;

      if PosY > 20 then PosY := 20;

      window( PosX, PosY, PosX+65, PosY+5 );

      Frame;

   end;
```

The destructor method, Done, has also been modified to reset the text window to the full screen after the linked list has been disposed:

```
destructor LinkObj.Done;

   ...

   begin

      ...

      Window(1,1,80,25);

   end;
```

The Frame method is provided to clear the text window and to draw the outline structure, ending by positioning the text cursor under the ^Quit prompt:

```
procedure LinkObj.Frame;

   var

      i : integer;

   begin

      clrscr;

      write(#$C9); for i :=  2 to 11 do write(#$CD);

      ...

      write(#$BC);

      gotoxy( 55, 2 );

   end;
```

The Frame method is essentially self-explanatory. The extended ASCII characters used for frame structure appear here and in the complete listing at the end of this chapter in hexadecimal format for two reasons: first, few editor programs support convenient entry of the extended ASCII characters and, second, even fewer typefaces support the extended ASCII character set at all.

The LinkObj Print Method

In this program, LinkObj's Print method not only displays the list, but becomes the primary control for the program. In this text version, the Up and Down keys step the listings one link along the chain and, at the top or bottom of the list, wrap the listings. The Page Up and Page Down keys step the listings by five entries (but do not wrap at top and bottom), while the Home and End keys move directly to the first or last links in the chain. Either the Return key or a Ctrl-Q entry exits:

```
procedure LinkObj.Print;
   var
      NPtr : NodePtr;
      Quit : boolean;
         i : integer;
      Key, Key2 : char;
   begin
      Quit := FALSE;
      NPtr := FirstLink;
      repeat
         TextAttr := LightRed;
         with NPtr^.Item^ do Print;
         TextAttr := Yellow;
         gotoxy( 59, 2 );
```

The LinkObj.Print method begins by setting the local pointer, *NPtr*, to the top of the linked list, initiating a repeat loop and then calling the Print method of the object indicated by the current link to display the data records held by that object instance. Next, the LinkObj.Print method waits on the keyboard, reading either a single key event or — when a function or keypad key is pressed — reading a second key event:

```
while not KeyPressed do;

Key := ReadKey;

if KeyPressed then Key2 := ReadKey;
```

If Key is a null character Ø, this indicates that a function or keypad entry was read and Key2 becomes the important item, identifying which key event occurred. Additional information on reading keyboard events can be found in Chapter 11, Trapping the Keyboard, and Appendix B, Keyboard Response Codes, of *Programming The IBM User Interface*, available from Addison-Wesley.

The first two key events — the Home or End keys — simply set the local pointer to the first or last links in the chain:

```
case Key of
   #$00: case Key2 of
 { Home }   #$47: NPtr := FirstLink;
 { End  }   #$4F: NPtr := LastLink;
```

The Up and Down keys each require a decision: if the local pointer is at the top or bottom of the chain respectively, then *NPtr* is jumped to the other end of the chain. Otherwise, the local point is move one link up or down the chain:

```
 { Up   }   #$48: if NPtr^.Last <> nil
                     then NPtr := NPtr^.Last
                     else NPtr := LastLink;
 { Down }   #$50: if NPtr^.Next <> nil
                     then NPtr := NPtr^.Next
                     else NPtr := FirstLink;
```

The Page Up and Page Down keys each move the local point five steps, but do not move beyond the top or bottom of the list:

```
{ PgUp }    #$49: for i := 1 to 5 do

                     if NPtr^.Last <> nil

                        then NPtr := NPtr^.Last;
{ PgDn }    #$51: for i := 1 to 5 do

                     if NPtr^.Next <> nil

                        then NPtr := NPtr^.Next;

            end; {case Key2}
```

Finally, if Key was set by either an Enter or a Ctrl-Q key event, Quit is set to TRUE in order to allow the ListObj.Print method to exit from the loop:

```
        #$0D,

        #$11: Quit := TRUE;

      end;

      Frame;

    until Quit;

end;
```

The last element in the loop is a call to the Frame method, erasing the current entry and redrawing the frame outline.

For a graphics version of this or any similar program, the same type of loop might be the primary control — except for waiting on button events instead of or as well as keyboard events and might look something like this:

```
repeat

    . . .

until QuitBtn.ButtonHit(...);
```

Three Data Object Types

In the Phone2 program, only two object types were used, but in Phone3, four object types are being employed: the list object, LinkObj, and three data objects, PersObj, BusObj and BBSObj. Of course, pointers to all of these have been declared:

```
PersPtr = ^PersObj;

BusPtr  = ^BusObj;

BBSPtr  = ^BBSObj;
```

The PersObj object is the ancestor object type for the remaining two and begins by declaring four data records and three methods:

```
PersObj = object

                Name : string[30];

                  AC : string[3];

               Phone : string[10];

               Notes : string[60];

               constructor Init( ThisItem : PersRec );

               destructor Done;   virtual;

               procedure Print;   virtual;          end;
```

The BusObj object is a descendant of PerObj and it inherits all of the ancestor's data records and methods, but begins by adding two new data records: Contact and Ext:

```
BusObj = object( PersObj )

               Contact: string[20];

                   Ext: string[5];

               constructor Init( ThisItem : BusRec );

               procedure Print;   virtual;          end;
```

The BusObj object also redefines the Init constructor to accept a different record type and creates its own version of the Print method. The BBSObj type is also a descendant of PersObj, not BusObj, adding one new record field, Baud, and redefining the same two methods as BusObj did:

```
BBSObj = object ( PersObj )

            Baud: string[4];

            constructor Init ( ThisItem : BBSRec );

            procedure Print;    virtual;          end;
```

Now, three object types have been declared for the three types of data record that will be read from files, but methods for these objects still require definition.

Three Constructor Methods

The three data object types have similar constructor methods, all titled Init and all defined in similar fashion. The first of these, PersObj.Init, assigns the four data record fields to the object's record fields:

```
constructor PersObj.Init;

    begin

        Name  := ThisItem.Name;

          AC := ThisItem.AC;

        Phone := ThisItem.Phone;

        Notes := ThisItem.Notes;

    end;
```

The BusObj version of Init duplicates PersObj.Init, but adds two other field assignments:

```
constructor BusObj.Init;

    begin
```

```
      . . .
      Contact := ThisItem.Contact;
          Ext := ThisItem.Ext;
   end;
```

BBSObj.Init also duplicates PersObj.Init with the addition of a single field assignment:

```
constructor BBSObj.Init;
   begin

      . . .

      Baud := ThisItem.Baud;
   end;
```

The Done Method

A single Done method is declared by the PersObj object and inherited by both descendants, but has no particular tasks aside from the epilog code supplied by the compiler in response to the *destructor* keyword:

```
destructor PersObj.Done;
   begin
   end;
```

Three Print Methods

The three data object types each have their own versions of the Print method. These versions position and display the appropriate data fields contained in each instance. The PersObj.Print method, see Figure 9-1, begins by writing a type caption in the upper left corner of the frame and then writes the four data fields to the frame:

```
procedure PersObj.Print;
   begin
```

```
      gotoxy(  3, 2 ); write('Personal');
      gotoxy( 15, 2 ); write( Name );
      gotoxy( 37, 4 );
      if( AC[1] <> ' ' ) then write( '(', AC, ')' );
      gotoxy( 44, 4 ); write( Phone );
      gotoxy(  3, 5 ); write( Notes );
   end;
```

Since local telephone numbers usually are not entered with the area code, the AC field is tested before writing anything to the screen.

The BusObj Print method begins by calling its ancestor's Print method, thus avoiding the need to duplicate a portion of code, and it overwrites the 'Personal' type caption with its own before adding the Contact field and testing to see if an extension is specified:

```
procedure BusObj.Print;
   begin
      PersObj.Print;
      gotoxy(  3, 2 ); write('Business');
      gotoxy(  3, 4 ); write( Contact );
      gotoxy( 54, 4 );
      if EXT[1] <> ' ' then write('Ext ', EXT );
   end;
```

The BusObj Print method also begins by calling PersObj.Print and then writes its own type caption and adds the Baud field:

```
procedure BBSObj.Print;
   begin
      PersObj.Print;
      gotoxy(  3, 2 ); write('   BBS ');
```

```
    gotoxy( 55, 4 ); write( BAUD, ' baud' );
end;
```

This completes the object methods for this version.

And One Question

Two of the three Print methods saved some code repetition by calling the PersObj.Print method to handle the printing of four of the data fields. At the same time, the three Read_XXX methods had completely separate field assignment statements.

And the question is: could the read methods have been simplified by having two of the methods call their ancestor method? Why or why not? (The answer in a moment.)

Summary

In this chapter, a new linked-list was created in which three different object types were organized and sorted — together, but with each object type holding different data records and treating the information in slightly different forms. At the same time, the list object (LinkObj) provided a framework and window for displaying the information and read keyboard events to step through the chain of objects.

But this was only a simple illustration of a much greater potential. For example, suppose that Dial methods were created for the three data objects. The Dial method might, for a personal or business call, send instructions to a smart-modem to initiate a telephone call, wait for an answer, dial an extension if necessary, and then finish by beeping the user and prompting them to pick up the hand-set. If the number selected was a BBS, then the program might still place the call, but then initiate a communications routine or call a communications package.

And you could also use a FaxObj object for fax connections. Or add PrintCard and PrintLabel methods to print out rolodex cards or adhesive labels.

The principles demonstrated are the only important elements in any of these demo programs — not the applications that were used to show how these principles worked — and the possibilities inherent in these object-oriented principles are limitless.

You've seen the basics of how to use object-oriented programming and how to use Turbo Pascal, both in graphics and text applications.

First, let's answer the question left hanging a few moments ago, about simplifying the Read_XXX methods.

Unfortunately, the answer is no, these cannot be simplified in the same fashion used for the Print methods because each Read_XXX method is called with a different type of record parameter derived from a different type of record file. The assignments in each method are specific about the record type being used.

```pascal
{=================================}
{        MAKELSTS.PAS   Utility        }
{   creates lists for PHONE3 demo   }
{=================================}

program Create_Mixed_Phone_List;

uses Crt;

var

    Select: char;       NullStr: string;

function Read_Str( Prompt: string; Length: integer ): string;
    var

        TempStr: string;
    begin
        while ord(Prompt[0]) < 12 do
            Prompt := ' '+Prompt;
        TempStr := '';
        write( Prompt, ': ');
        readln(TempStr);
        Read_Str := copy( TempStr+NullStr, 1, Length );
```

```pascal
      end;

procedure Write_Pers;
   type
      PersRec = record
          Name: string[30];
            AC: string[3];
         Phone: string[10];
         Notes: string[60];  end;
   var
      PersFile: file of PersRec;
      PersEntry: PersRec;
   begin
      writeln(' Personal Phone Entry ');
      with PersEntry do
      begin
         Name  := Read_Str( 'Name', 30 );
         AC    := Read_Str( 'AC', 3 );
         Phone := Read_Str( 'Phone', 10 );
         Notes := Read_Str( 'Notes', 60 );
      end;
      assign( PersFile, 'PHONEPRS.DAT' );
      {$I-} reset( PersFile ); {$I+}
      if( IOresult <> 0 ) then rewrite( PersFile );
      seek( PersFile, filesize( PersFile ) );
      write( PersFile, PersEntry );
      close( PersFile );
```

```pascal
        end;

    procedure Write_Bus;
        type
            BusRec = record
                  Name: string[30];
                    AC: string[3];
                 Phone: string[10];
                 Notes: string[60];
               Contact: string[20];
                   Ext: string[5];    end;
        var
            BusFile: file of BusRec;
            BusEntry: BusRec;
        begin
            writeln(' Business Phone Entry ');
            with BusEntry do
            begin
                Name    := Read_Str( 'Name', 30 );
                AC      := Read_Str( 'AC', 3 );
                Phone   := Read_Str( 'Phone', 10 );
                Contact := Read_Str( 'Contact', 20 );
                Ext     := Read_Str( 'Extension', 5 );
                Notes   := Read_Str( 'Notes', 60 );
            end;
            assign( BusFile, 'PHONEBUS.DAT' );
            {$I-} reset(BusFile); {$I+}
```

```
        if( IOresult <> 0 ) then rewrite( BusFile );
        seek( BusFile, filesize( BusFile ) );
        write( BusFile, BusEntry );
        close( BusFile );
    end;

procedure Write_BBS;
    type
        BBSRec = record
            Name: string[30];
              AC: string[3];
           Phone: string[10];
           Notes: string[60];
            Baud: string[4];    end;
    var
        BBSFile: file of BBSRec;
        BBSEntry: BBSRec;
    begin
        writeln(' Bulletin Board Entry ');
        with BBSEntry do
        begin
            Name  := Read_Str( 'Name', 30 );
            AC    := Read_Str( 'AC', 3 );
            Phone := Read_Str( 'Phone', 10 );
            Baud  := Read_Str( 'Baud Rate', 4 );
            Notes := Read_Str( 'Notes', 60 );
        end;
```

```pascal
        assign( BBSFile, 'PHONEBBS.DAT' );
        {$I-} reset( BBSFile ); {$I+}
        if( IOresult <> 0 ) then rewrite( BBSFile );
        seek( BBSFile, filesize( BBSFile ) );
        write( BBSFile, BBSEntry );
        close( BBSFile );
    end;

begin
    ClrScr;
    writeln('Create record files for Phone demo program');
    FillChar( NullStr, 80, ' ' );
    repeat
        writeln;
        write('Select type of entry: 1) Personal',
              ' 2) Business  3) BBS  4) Exit ');
        Select := ReadKey;
        writeln; writeln;
        case Select of
            '1': Write_Pers;
            '2': Write_Bus;
            '3': Write_BBS;
        end; {case}
    until Select = '4';
end.
```

```
             (*================*)
             (*    PHONE3.PAS   *)
             (*================*)
program Phone_List_Demo_3;

uses Crt;

type
    NodePtr = ^NodeRec;
    LinkPtr = ^LinkObj;
    PersPtr = ^PersObj;
    BusPtr  = ^BusObj;
    BBSPtr  = ^BBSObj;

    NodeRec = record  Last, Next : NodePtr;
                           Item : PersPtr;    end;

    LinkObj = object
                Nodes : NodePtr;
                constructor Init;
                destructor Done;  virtual;
                procedure Add( ThisItem : PersPtr );
                procedure Sort( NewLink : NodePtr );
                procedure FWindow( PosX,
                                     PosY : integer );
                procedure Frame;
               procedure ReadPers( NameFile : string );
                procedure ReadBus( NameFile : string );
                procedure ReadBBS( NameFile : string );
                procedure Print;
```

```pascal
                    end;

  PersRec = record
     Name: string[30];          AC: string[3];
     Phone: string[10];      Notes: string[60]; end;
  BusRec = record
     Name: string[30];          AC: string[3];
     Phone: string[10];      Notes: string[60];
     Contact: string[20];      Ext: string[5];  end;
  BBSRec = record
      Name: string[30];          AC: string[3];
     Phone: string[10];      Notes: string[60];
     Baud: string[4];                          end;
  PersObj = object
                 Name : string[30];
                   AC : string[3];
                Phone : string[10];
                Notes : string[60];
                constructor Init( ThisItem : PersRec );
                destructor Done;  virtual;
                procedure Print;  virtual;        end;

  BusObj = object( PersObj )
                Contact: string[20];
                    Ext: string[5];
                constructor Init( ThisItem : BusRec );
                procedure Print;   virtual;        end;
```

```
    BBSObj = object( PersObj )
                Baud: string[4];
                constructor Init( ThisItem : BBSRec );
                procedure Print;   virtual;           end;
var
   LinkList : LinkObj;
   FirstLink, LastLink : NodePtr;

                {=====================}
                { Link implementation }
                {=====================}
constructor LinkObj.Init;                    { no changes }

destructor LinkObj.Done;                      { REVISED }
   var
      NPtr : NodePtr;
   begin
      NPtr := FirstLink;
      repeat
         Dispose( NPtr^.Item, Done );
         FirstLink := NPtr^.Next;
         Dispose( NPtr );
         NPtr := FirstLink;
      until FirstLink = nil;
      Window(1,1,80,25);
   end;

procedure LinkObj.Add; { no changes in implementation }
                       { but declaration has changed  }
```

```pascal
procedure LinkObj.FWindow;                              { NEW }
   begin
      if PosX > 15 then PosX := 15;
      if PosY > 20 then PosY := 20;
      window( PosX, PosY, PosX+65, PosY+5 );
      Frame;
   end;

procedure LinkObj.Frame;                                { NEW }
   var
      i : integer;
   begin
   clrscr;
   write(#$C9); for i :=  2 to 11 do write(#$CD);
   write(#$D1); for i := 13 to 48 do write(#$CD);
   write(#$D1); for i := 50 to 52 do write(#$CD);
   write(#$D1); for i := 54 to 56 do write(#$CD);
   write(#$D1); for i := 58 to 64 do write(#$CD);
   writeln('');
   write(#$BA); for i :=  2 to 11 do write(' ');
   write(#$B3); for i := 13 to 48 do write(' ');
   writeln(#$B3, ' ', #$18, ' ',#$B3, ' ',
           #$19, ' ',#$B3, ' ^Quit ', #$BA );
   write(#$C7); for i :=  2 to 11 do write(#$C4);
   write(#$C1); for i := 13 to 48 do write(#$C4);
   write(#$C1); for i := 50 to 52 do write(#$C4);
   write(#$C1); for i := 54 to 56 do write(#$C4);
```

```
      write(#$C1); for i := 58 to 64 do write(#$C4);
      writeln(#$B6);
      write(#$BA); for i :=  2 to 64 do write(' ');
      writeln(#$BA);
      write(#$BA); for i :=  2 to 64 do write(' ');
      writeln(#$BA);
      write(#$C8); for i :=  2 to 64 do write(#$CD);
      write(#$BC);
      gotoxy( 55, 2 );
   end;

procedure LinkObj.Sort;                      { no changes }

procedure LinkObj.ReadPers;                        { NEW }
   var
      NewItem  : PersRec;
      DataFile : file of PersRec;
   begin
      assign( DataFile, NameFile );
      reset( DataFile );
      repeat
         read( DataFile, NewItem );
         Add( New( PersPtr, Init( NewItem ) ) );
      until EOF( DataFile );
      close( DataFile );
   end;

procedure LinkObj.ReadBus;                         { NEW }
```

```
    var
       NewItem   : BusRec;
       DataFile : file of BusRec;
    begin
       assign( DataFile, NameFile );
       reset( DataFile );
       repeat
          read( DataFile, NewItem );
          Add( New( BusPtr,  Init( NewItem ) ) );
       until EOF( DataFile );
       close( DataFile );
    end;

procedure LinkObj.ReadBBS;                          { NEW }
    var
       NewItem   : BBSRec;
       DataFile : file of BBSRec;
    begin
       assign( DataFile, NameFile );
       reset( DataFile );
       repeat
          read( DataFile, NewItem );
          Add( New( BBSPtr,  Init( NewItem ) ) );
       until EOF( DataFile );
       close( DataFile );
    end;

procedure LinkObj.Print;                         { REVISED }
```

```
var

    NPtr : NodePtr;

    Quit : boolean;

       i : integer;

    Key, Key2 : char;

begin

    Quit := FALSE;

    NPtr := FirstLink;

    repeat

        TextAttr := LightRed;

        with NPtr^.Item^ do Print;

        TextAttr := Yellow;

        gotoxy( 59, 2 );

        while not KeyPressed do;

        Key := ReadKey;

        if KeyPressed then Key2 := ReadKey;

        case Key of

           #$00: case Key2 of

         { Home }   #$47: NPtr := FirstLink;

         { End  }   #$4F: NPtr := LastLink;

         { Up   }   #$48: if NPtr^.Last <> nil

                             then NPtr := NPtr^.Last

                             else NPtr := LastLink;

         { PgUp }   #$49: for i := 1 to 5 do

                             if NPtr^.Last <> nil

                               then NPtr := NPtr^.Last;
```

```
        { Down }    #$50: if NPtr^.Next <> nil
                              then NPtr := NPtr^.Next
                              else NPtr := FirstLink;
        { PgDn }    #$51: for i := 1 to 5 do
                              if NPtr^.Next <> nil
                                then NPtr := NPtr^.Next;
              end; {case Key2}
        #$0D,                          { Return or        }
        #$11: Quit := TRUE;       { Ctrl-Q for Exit }
      end;

      Frame;

    until Quit;
  end;


                {=========================}
                { PersObj implementation }
                {=========================}
constructor PersObj.Init;                            { NEW }
   begin
      Name := ThisItem.Name;
        AC := ThisItem.AC;
    Phone := ThisItem.Phone;
    Notes := ThisItem.Notes;
   end;

destructor PersObj.Done;                             { NEW }
   begin
   end;
```

```
procedure PersObj.Print;                              { NEW }

   begin

      gotoxy(  3, 2 ); write('Personal');

      gotoxy( 15, 2 ); write( Name );

      gotoxy( 37, 4 );

      if( AC[1] <> ' ' ) then write( '(', AC, ')' );

      gotoxy( 44, 4 ); write( Phone );

      gotoxy(  3, 5 ); write( Notes );

   end;


                    {=======================}
                    { BusObj implementation }
                    {=======================}

constructor BusObj.Init;                              { NEW }

   begin

           Name := ThisItem.Name;

             AC := ThisItem.AC;

         Phone := ThisItem.Phone;

       Contact := ThisItem.Contact;

           Ext := ThisItem.Ext;

         Notes := ThisItem.Notes;

   end;


procedure BusObj.Print;                               { NEW }

   begin

      PersObj.Print;

      gotoxy(  3, 2 ); write('Business');

      gotoxy(  3, 4 ); write( Contact );
```

```
        gotoxy( 54, 4 );
        if EXT[1] <> ' ' then write('Ext ', EXT );
    end;

                {=======================}
                { BBSObj implementation }
                {=======================}

constructor BBSObj.Init;
    begin
        Name := ThisItem.Name;
          AC := ThisItem.AC;
       Phone := ThisItem.Phone;
       Notes := ThisItem.Notes;
        Baud := ThisItem.Baud;
    end;

procedure BBSObj.Print;                              { NEW }
    begin
        PersObj.Print;
        gotoxy(  3, 2 ); write('   BBS  ');
        gotoxy( 55, 4 ); write( BAUD, ' baud' );
    end;

                {====================}
                { end of Obj methods }
                {====================}

begin                                               { REVISED }
    clrscr;
    with LinkList do
```

```
    begin
        Init;                          { create a link list }
        ReadPers('PHONEPRS.DAT');      { read personal data }
        ReadBus( 'PHONEBUS.DAT');      { read business data }
        ReadBBS( 'PHONEBBS.DAT');      { read bulletin brds }
        FWindow( 10, 10 );             { window location    }
        Print;                         { print out the list }
        Done;                          { dispose of list    }
    end;
end.
```

CHAPTER 10

BINARY TREE OBJECTS

In previous examples, data was handled using pointer structures in linearly-linked lists. In this example, the linear list will be replaced by a binary-tree structure. Here, the organization of the data is — if confusing at first — faster both to sort and to access than in a linear structure.For additional information on the theory of tree structures in general, see *Algorithms and Data Structures* by Niklaus Wirth.

Binary-tree structures (called B-Trees or simply Tree structures) are generally recognized as the most efficient data structures possible for general applications. In some specialized cases, where the structure and arrangement of the data itself is highly predictable and ordered, other organizational structures may be more efficient, but these are exceptions.

Also, binary-sorts are actually more efficient when the source of the data is disordered than if the data source is already ordered or alphabetized; though, in either case, the binary sort is usually more efficient than a linear sort routine.

Binary Tree Structures

A binary tree structure is simply a data structure in which each element has two links to other elements and the elements are linked together in specific relationships. As an example, Figure 10-1 shows a binary tree created from the integer list: **6, 3, 4, 2, 8, 12, 11, 5, 1, 9, 7, 10**.

The rule ordering in this binary tree is very simple — smaller to the left, greater to the right — and the tree grows according to the order in which the data elements were added to the tree. Starting with **6** which forms the root of the tree, **3** is added to the left (smaller) and then **4** begins by taking the lesser (left) branch from **6** and then the greater (right) branch from **3**.

Each subsequent integer entry searches for its own appropriate position within the growing structure. Note that binary trees are usually illustrated upside down, beginning with the root at the top.

Figure 10-1: A Binary Tree of Integers

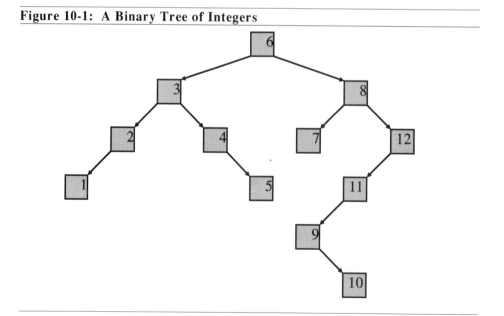

Notice that, when the tree is built, at no time is any established link changed to favor a newer entry. Therefore, **10** begins at the root, is greater than **6**, is greater than **8**, is less than **12**, is less than **11** and finally, finds its place as greater than **9**.

If the resulting tree appears confusing, consider how easy it is to locate any element in the tree. To locate the highest entry in the tree, for example, simply begin at the root, follow the greater (right) path and, after the third step, the entry **12** is located and identified as the greatest element in the tree. In a linear arrangement, this same result would require four times longer to accomplish.

Any element in the tree can be found in the same fashion.

Binary trees are not limited to numerical or alphabetical data lists. Instead, a binary tree can be created for any type of data for which a relationships can be described. For a second example, consider the formula — (**a** + **b** / **c**) - (**d** * **e** + **f**) — and the binary tree representing the values and operations involved (Figure 10-2).

In this structure, all variables (numerical values) are found at the ends of branches and all non-terminal nodes indicate operations. Notice also that the parentheses in the written formula do not appear in the binary tree. Instead, the groupings are implicit in the structure of the tree.

One simple application for a tree of this type might be a program to solve algebraic equations that were entered by the user in the text form similar to the preceding example.

Since the formula entered could take many different forms, any pre-defined structure would have to be unnecessarily complex to accept all of the possibilities. By using a binary tree structure similar to the one illustrated, any formula can be represented as a series of binary relationships.

A program using this structure would begin by finding the extremities of the tree; for example, beginning with the **d** and **e** elements, executing the * operation indicated by their mutual root, then replacing the operation with the resulting value and discarding the two terminal nodes.

By operating recursively on each branch until no subnodes remain, the root contains the final result of the formula. (Which is essentially how most programming languages handle formula processing in the first place.)

Figure 10-2: A Binary Tree for a Formula

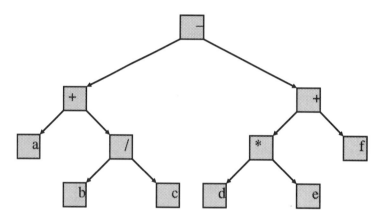

Naturally, if the formula is to be solved repeatedly for different values, instead of discarding nodes, the application would simply examine each node to see if it contained a value or only an operator, searching further if the node contained a solution.

Other, more familiar, examples of binary tree structures would include family genealogies, basketball or tennis tournaments, or race horse pedigrees.

A Binary Tree Application

In Figure 10-3, the same data list used in the previous examples is shown in a binary-tree using an alphabetical relationship. In this case, the tree is turned sideways (root element at left) and the numbers by each entry show the order in which the elements are read from the data file. This is essentially the binary tree structure that will be created by the PHONTREE program demonstrated in this chapter.

Figure 10-3: An Alphabetical Tree

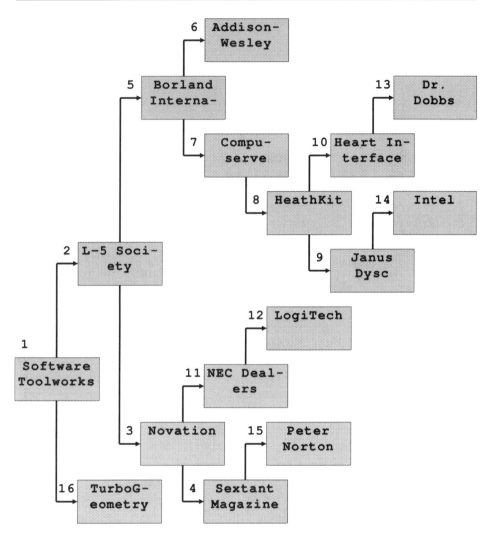

Before going into the intricacies of programming a binary tree, in Chapter 8 (Table 8-1) disk read, sort and display times were shown for a linearly-linked list. In Table 10-1, a time comparison is made between the linear sort used in Chapter 8 and the binary sort which will be demonstrated here.

Table 10-1: Comparing Disk Read, Sort and Display Times

	LINEAR SORT	BINARY TREE
File access time (16 items):	0.02060 seconds	0.02060 seconds
Sort operations (16 items):	0.00955 seconds	0.01071 seconds
Screen write (21 lines):	0.03680 seconds	0.01220 seconds
Total:	0.06695 seconds	0.04351 seconds

Operation times derived by averaging elapsed time for loop = 1..1000.

For the relatively short data list used in this example, the binary sort operations required a bit more time than the linear sort operations. For longer lists, when time becomes a real factor, the time requirements of the binary sort will be considerably shorter than for a linear sort with the discrepancy increasing as the number of handled entries grows.

This discrepancy is produced, in part, by the fact that both sort times include the time required to dispose of the data elements. For the linear sort, the dispose time itself is relatively short compared to the time required to build the list because, for disposal, the linear list simply begins at the top and works down without regard to the order of the list — in this example, requiring approximately $1/20$ of the time for disposal as was required to build the tree.

In order to accomplish disposal of the elements, the binary tree, has to execute essentially the same operations as were required to build the tree, retracing each branch and requiring equal time for both tasks.

However, the difference in execution speeds may be more obvious by looking at the *Screen write* times. Here, even though the linear sort is already ordered and has accomplished the screen write by stepping down an alphabetical list, the binary tree is still faster. It even uses a recursive process to search the tree for the proper order in which to write the data out to the screen.

In large part, of course, the times are a product of how each version of the program has compiled and, to some degree, it reflects the strengths of the Turbo Pascal compiler. The bottom line for application programming is not the theoretical speed of a system, but the actual real-time/real-world speed with which an application operates.

In the real world, data lists are not necessarily disordered; therefore, what happens when the data set is already in alphabetical order?

A third set of operation times appear in Table 10-2 using the same data list contents, but with the data entries pre-arranged in alphabetical order.

Table 10-2: A Binary Sort with Ordered and Disordered Sources

	DISORDERED	ORDERED
File access time (16 items):	0.02060 seconds	0.02060 seconds
Sort operations (16 items):	0.01071 seconds	0.01895 seconds
Screen write (21 lines):	0.01220 seconds	0.01219 seconds
Total:	0.04351 seconds	0.05174 seconds

Operation times derived by averaging elapsed time for loop = 1..1000.

Interestingly, the sort operations for the pre-ordered list have actually taken longer than for the randomly ordered list. This is not an unexpected outcome however, because in this case the binary tree result is the analog of a linear list and each subsequent element to be sorted has to step further down the tree to find its proper place than it did with a randomly ordered data set. The results are, even so, still faster than for the linear sort procedure.

You may also notice that the screen display time for the ordered list is faster — $1/10,000$ of a second — than for the disordered list, reflecting the difference in the number of recursive steps required to display the list in proper order. Most of the time required for the screen display is simply the time required to write the data to the video memory.

With either an ordered or disordered source, the handling time for the binary tree is significantly faster than for a linear listing.

Implementing a Binary-Tree Object

The PHONTREE program is similar to the PHONE1 demo in Chapter 8, using an instance of LinkObj to create a tree of DataObj. But there are also a few differences. PHONTREE will use recursive handling and the LinkObj definition changes to provide binary instead of linear linking.

```
type

   NodeRec = record  Root, Prev, Next : NodePtr;

                                 Item : DataPtr;  end;
```

In the PHONE1 and PHONE2 demos, the NodeRec definition had two pointers, *Prev* and *Next* which were used to create a chain. In this case, *Prev* and *Next* no longer point up and down the list, but point to elements that precede or follow the current element while the *Root* pointer points back to the root element of the current node or toward the root of the tree.

Also, where the original list could have been constructed with a single pointer linking the list only one way; for the binary tree, at least two links are essential and the third link, *Root*, will be necessary later before an item can be deleted from the tree without destroying the tree.

The definition of LinkObj is again similar — but the Add and Done methods now use the subprocedures, BuildTree and DisposeItem, for recursive handling and the implementation for these and the PrintList methods has been revised.

```
LinkObj = object

        Nodes : NodePtr;

        constructor Init;

        destructor Done;  virtual;

        procedure Add( ThisItem : DataPtr );

        procedure ReadFile( NameFile: string );
```

```
        procedure PrintList( ItemPtr: NodePtr);
        function  Find( RefLink : NodePtr;
                    SearchStr : string ): NodePtr;
        function  FindPartial( RefLink : NodePtr;
                    PartialStr : string ): NodePtr;
    end;
```

The DataObj definitions remain essentially the same as before.

Building the Tree

As previously, LinkObj's ReadFile method accesses the data file (or files), calling the Add with each entry. The Add method, however, has changed slightly.

```
procedure LinkObj.Add;
    var
        NPtr : NodePtr;
    begin
        New( NPtr );
        NPtr^.Root := nil;
        NPtr^.Next := nil;
        NPtr^.Prev := nil;
        NPtr^.Item := ThisItem;
```

In PHONE2, the Add method did nothing about assigning values to NPtr's pointers, simply assuming (correctly) that these would be handled by the Sort method. In this case, however, it is only provident to initialize all three of these pointers as *nil* because, if not, the unassigned pointers can quite easily clobber the stack the first time the program executes. When this happens, even though the program may execute correctly once, a system reset may be required afterwards before the program (or some other program) can operate again.

With this caution stated, the Add method proceeds by determining if the current entry is the first entry read.

```
if FirstLink = nil

    then FirstLink := NPtr

    else BuildTree( FirstLink, NPtr );

end;
```

If this is not the first entry, then the dynamic pointer to the current entry (*NPtr*) and the static pointer to the root entry (*FirstLink*) are passed to the BuildTree method for more handling.

The reason the Add method now uses a subprocedure instead of handling everything, is that PHONTREE's handling will be recursive and the BuildTree subprocedure can call itself recursively, which the Add method cannot.

```
procedure BuildTree( RefLink, NewLink: NodePtr );

    begin

        if Precede( NewLink^.Item^.Data.Name,

                    RefLink^.Item^.Data.Name ) then
```

As in previous examples, BuildTree begins by calling the Precede function to determine the order of the current and reference entries.

```
begin

    if RefLink^.Prev = nil then

    begin

        RefLink^.Prev := NewLink;

        NewLink^.Root := RefLink;

    end else BuildTree( RefLink^.Prev, NewLink );

end else
```

If the current entry precedes the reference entry, the next question is if the reference link's *.Prev* is already linked or if it is *nil* (empty).

If the latter case is true, then the new entry can be linked directly. If not, then *BuildTree* is called recursively using the reference link's *.Prev* pointer to step down the tree structure. If the current entry does not precede the reference entry, the same determination is made for the reference link's *.Next* pointer and the current item is either linked here or a recursive call is made to step down the tree until the appropriate location is found.

```
begin
    if RefLink^.Next = nil then
    begin
        RefLink^.Next := NewLink;
        NewLink^.Root := RefLink;
    end else BuildTree( RefLink^.Next, NewLink );
end;
end;
```

Disposing of the Tree

After building the tree, the next most important task is disposing of the tree. Remember, memory is being dynamically allocated for each item in the tree and, unless provisions are made to properly dispose of this memory, a lot of the available RAM can wind up allocated for defunct purposes and not available to other applications even after the current program has terminated.

```
destructor LinkObj.Done;
    procedure DisposeItem( ItemPtr : NodePtr );
        begin
            . . .
        end;
    begin
```

```
    DisposeItem( FirstLink );
end;
```

In the PHONE2 demo (Chapter 8), the destructor method, Done, included provisions to dispose of the linear list. For the binary tree, however, recursive handling is again required. Therefore, Done calls its own subprocedure, DisposeItem, with the static pointer, *FirstLink*.

The DisposeItem procedure is multiply recursive but begins with a test to determine if the current entry is *nil* and, if so, does nothing since nothing needs to be done (i.e., the end of a branch has been reached — that's all).

```
procedure DisposeItem( ItemPtr : NodePtr );

  begin

    if ItemPtr <> nil then

    begin
```

If ItemPtr is not empty, then the next step is to test the *.Prev* pointer. If this link points anywhere, then DisposeItem is called recursively to travel down this branch.

```
if ItemPtr^.Prev <> nil

  then DisposeItem( ItemPtr^.Prev );
```

The same test is then executed for the *.Next* pointer, again calling DisposeItem recursively if necessary.

```
if ItemPtr^.Next <> nil

  then DisposeItem( ItemPtr^.Next );
```

After disposing of the *Next* and *Prev* branches, the current entry's data elements, indicated by *.Item*, need to be handled.

```
if ItemPtr^.Item <> nil

  then Dispose( ItemPtr^.Item, Done );
```

Finally, the pointer itself, has to be disposed of:

```
    Dispose( ItemPtr );

  end;

end;
```

Printing the Tree

While building the tree and disposing of the contents after use are important, it also helps to be able to do something with the records in between. Even though the structure of the data is very different from the previous linear examples, the data will be displayed in essentially the same fashion — in alphabetical order.

This is quite easily accomplished here by making the PrintList method itself a recursive procedure.

In PHONE2, the Print method was called without arguments and handled the printing of the entire list by itself. The PrintList method, however, is initially called with the static pointer *FirstLink* and, thereafter, calls itself recursively until the entire list has been written to the screen.

```
procedure LinkObj.PrintList;

  begin

      if ItemPtr <> nil then

      begin
```

As with the DisposeItem method, PrintList begins by checking the current entry to see if it is empty. Assuming the entry is not empty, PrintList checks first to see if there are any items that preceded the current item. This is not done by calling the Precede function, but by checking the *.Prev* pointer and calling itself recursively to handle any prior entries.

```
if ItemPtr^.Prev <> nil then

    PrintList( ItemPtr^.Prev );
```

Only after checking the *.Prev* pointer is the current entry listed by calling DataObj's Print method.

```
with ItemPtr^.Item^ do Print;
```

After handling any prior items and the current item, the following items are handled, again by testing the *.Next* pointer and, again, calling PrintList recursively.

```
        if ItemPtr^.Next <> nil then

            PrintList( ItemPtr^.Next );

    end;

end;
```

Binary Searches, Insertions and Deletions

While the current program does not do searches or insert and delete items from the tree, methods are provided for two of these purposes: searching and deleting.

For inserting new items in the tree however, unlike linear-lists, no special provisions are required because the same method used to build the tree is used to add new items and new entries are always made at an existing free node instead of attempting to insert the new element within the existing structure.

Searching a Binary Tree

Searching a binary tree is different than searching a linear list and, for this purpose, two methods — Find and FindPartial — are provided.

The Find method is called with two arguments; the static pointer, *FirstLink*, and a string argument to be located. It returns a pointer to the located entry or a *nil* pointer if the entry is not found. The Find method, however, requires an exact match beginning at the first of each Name field though the search string can be only part of the name field.

The FindPartial method is called in the same fashion as the Find method, but will attempt to find a match for the search string anywhere within the Name field, not merely beginning from the first of the field.

Of course, the FindPartial method searches the entire binary tree until a match is found while the Find method searches the tree according to where a matching entry should occur. And the trade-off here is that the Find method is faster, but the FindPartial method is more accurate (and more forgiving of human foibles).

Note: the program listing at the end of this chapter shows one way that these two methods might be used in combination, using the Find method first for speed and then FindPartial second for accuracy.

The Find Method

The Find method searches recursively, looking for an exact match for the search string beginning at the first of the Name field.

```
function LinkObj.Find;

   var

      Result : NodePtr;

   function Match( Str1, Str2 : string ): boolean;

      begin

         . . .

      end;
```

The Match function used by the Find method simply compares two strings, disregarding case, to determine if the strings match. It returns a boolean result.

```
begin

   Result := nil;

   if RefLink <> nil then

      if Match( SearchStr,
```

```
          RefLink^.Item^.Data.Name ) then

     Result := RefLink else
```

The Find method begins by testing the current item for a match. If a match is found, then the *RefLink* pointer is returned to the calling function.

If no match is found, Find compares the search string with the current name field to decide if the search string would precede or follow the current entry within the tree structure, then calls itself recursively.

```
     if Precede( RefLink^.Item^.Data.Name,

                  SearchStr )

        then Result := Find( RefLink^.Next,

                              SearchStr )

        else Result := Find( RefLink^.Prev,

                              SearchStr );

  Find := Result;

end;
```

The FindPartial Method

The FindPartial method searches the entire binary tree and identifies a match for the search string anywhere within the Name field, returning a pointer to the first matching entry found.

```
function LinkObj.FindPartial;

   var

      Result : NodePtr;

   function Match( Str1, Str2 : string ): boolean;

      begin

         . . .

      end;
```

The Match function used by the FindPartial method converts both strings to uppercase before executing a comparison, then uses the Pos function to determine if the search string occurs anywhere within the Name field, again returning a boolean result.

```
begin
    Result := nil;
    if RefLink <> nil then
    begin
        if RefLink^.Prev <> nil then
            Result := FindPartial( RefLink^.Prev,
                                        PartialStr );
```

FindPartial executes recursively in order to begin at the alphabetical top of the binary tree and searches down until a match has been found.

If a match has been found and, therefore, the *Result* pointer is no longer *nil*, there's no point checking the current Name field. Otherwise, the local Match function is used and, if a match occurs, *Result* returns the *RefLink* pointer.

```
        if Result = nil then
            if Match( PartialStr,
                        RefLink^.Item^.Data.Name ) then
                Result := RefLink;
```

If Result is still *nil*, FindPartial continues recursively down the tree.

```
        if Result = nil then
            if RefLink^.Next <> nil then
                Result := FindPartial( RefLink^.Next,
                                            PartialStr );
    end;
```

```
    FindPartial := Result;
  end;
```

If no match has been found, then a *nil* result is returned to the calling procedure.

Removing an Item from the Tree

The DeleteItem method is used to remove a specific entry from the binary tree, but obviously, before an item can be deleted from the tree, provisions to locate a specific entry were needed and have been supplied by the Find and FindPartial methods.

Of course, the real trick is not deleting an entry from the binary tree structure, but doing so *without losing other elements* that were linked to the deleted item — kind of like cutting out the center of a tree branch without cutting off the limb.

One method that could be used would be to delete the data element while leaving the node element in place. This will work, but it is hardly an elegant solution and could leave a lot of useless, empty nodes within the tree. A better method is to remove both the data and node elements, relinking the affected portions of the tree. Figure 10-4 shows an entry being deleted from the tree. The affected links are shown as heavy lines.

Now, as you can see, after deleting the Novation entry, the L-5 entry has one free pointer but both the Sextant and NEC entries are left dangling with no connections to the rest of the tree. Obviously, only one of these can be linked back to the L-5 node, so the question becomes which branch takes the immediate link and where does the other branch reconnect.

The choices are not completely arbitrary because there are restrictions that need to be observed to preserve the ordering of the tree.

In the illustrated example, since the L-5 node's free link is a *Next* pointer, the obvious choice is to reconnect the Novation node's *Next* link, maintaining the correct ordering.

Now, the NEC node was previously connected to a *Prev* link so a new *Prev* link is needed to reconnect and this is done simply by stepping down this branch of the tree until a free *Prev* pointer is found. The results for

Figure 10-4: Deleting an Element

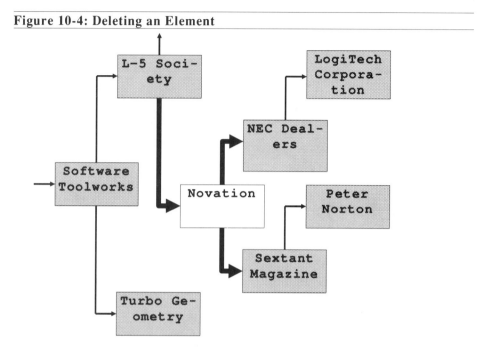

this branch of the binary tree are shown in Figure 10-5, again with the new links appearing as heavy lines.

If the broken link to the main body of the tree had been a *Prev* pointer, then the descendant *Prev* link, if any, would have been reconnected first and the remaining branch stepped down until an empty *Next* pointer was found.

The fact that this will always result in a correct ordering is not entirely obvious, but it should become clear if you will consider for a moment how entries are added to the tree.

Any entry that followed the L-5 entry, but would have preceded the Novation entry, would have originally connected to the tree either at the NEC entry or further along this branch and could not have been found on the Sextant branch. Therefore, everything on the NEC branch must precede all entries that are descended from Sextant and all entries that

Figure 10-5: Relinking After Deletion

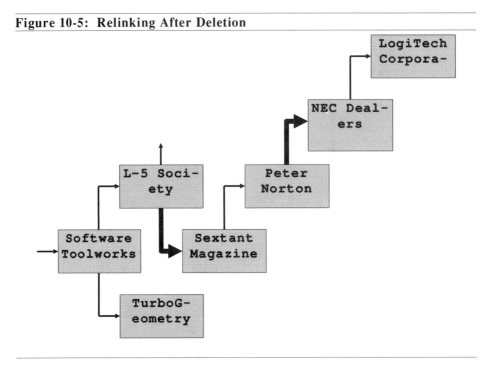

are descended from the Sextant node must be lower than entries on the NEC branch.

Now, if you are not completely confused (try drawing a few examples for yourself — unless you make an error, you will find this ordering correct), there still remain special cases where the preceding handling is not sufficient.

First, if the deleted item is linked to only one subbranch — which can be either a *Prev* or *Next* link — this single link is reconnected to the deleted item's root node.

Second, if the deleted item is the end of a branch and has no dependent links then the deleted item's root must be set to *nil*.

Last, if the deleted item is the root of the binary tree, the static pointer *FirstLink* must be updated to point to the new root element.

The DeleteItem Method

The requirements and conditions described preceding make the DeleteItem method a relatively complex *if..then..else* decision tree; at least, complex compared to the other methods used here.

```
procedure LinkObj.DeleteItem;

   var

      APtr, BPtr : NodePtr;

   begin

      APtr := ItemPtr;

      if APtr = FirstLink then

         if FirstLink^.Prev  nil

            then FirstLink := FirstLink^.Prev

            else FirstLink := FirstLink^.Next;
```

The DeleteItem method uses two static pointers, imaginatively named *APtr* and *BPtr*, to track positions through the binary tree. *APtr* begins by taking the pointer links of the item that will be deleted and then handles the first special case: is the current pointer the root of the entire tree?

If so, then *FirstLink* is moved to either the *Prev* link or, if there is no *Prev* link, to the *Next* link.

Of course, if the tree is empty except for this root item, then there is neither a *Prev* nor a *Next* link ... so, what happens then? Is this another special case? And is more special handling required?

While the case is special, additional handling shouldn't be necessary because — if the deleted item is the only remaining item in the tree — FirstLink will now be pointing to a *nil* pointer and nothing else needs to be done. In this instance, the special case has taken care of itself.

The next decision is to determine if the item to be deleted, indicated by *APtr*, was connected to a *Prev* or *Next* link and this is accomplished by calling the Precede function with the Name fields of the current item and its root. If there is no root item (i.e., if the current item is the root), then the Precede function returns a fail-safe FALSE result and, once more, no special handling is necessary.

```
if Precede( APtr^.Item^.Data.Name,

            APtr^.Root^.Item^.Data.Name ) then

begin
```

Beyond this point, the code becomes two symmetrical branches, each reflecting the other.

Following this decision branch, the current entry was determined to be descended from its root entry by a *Prev* link so this branch begins by deciding if the current entry has a *Next* link that will require handling.

If there is no descendant *Next* link, the situation is simplified and the next question is whether there is a descendant *Prev* link or is this the end of the branch.

```
if APtr^.Next = nil then

begin

   if APtr^.Prev = nil then

     APtr^.Root^.Prev := nil else

     begin

        APtr^.Root^.Prev := APtr^.Prev;

        APtr^.Prev^.Root := APtr^.Root;

     end;

end else
```

If the current entry is the end of the branch then the Root node is set to *nil* and that's all that needs to be done, the current entry has been cut free. The current entry's Prev entry is connected back to the Root and the Root to the Prev entry. If the current entry did have a *Next* link then the situation is slightly more complex and begins by assigning *BPtr* to the Next entry, ensuring that a handle is available when needed.

The next step is to decide — since it's already known that there is a *Next* link — if a *Prev* link exists.

```
begin
    BPtr := APtr^.Next;
    if APtr^.Prev = nil then
    begin
        APtr^.Root^.Prev := APtr^.Next;
        APtr^.Next^.Root := APtr^.Root;
    end else
```

If there is no *Prev* link, then the Next link is connected back to the Root and that's it — all's well and the *BPtr* was unnecessary. If there is *Prev* link, however, then it takes precedence and is connected back to the *Root*, leaving the old *Next* link, saved as *BPtr*, to find its new location.

```
    begin
        APtr^.Root^.Prev := APtr^.Prev;
        APtr^.Prev^.Root := APtr^.Root;
        APtr := APtr^.Prev;
        while APtr^.Next <> nil do
            APtr := APtr^.Next;
        BPtr^.Root := APtr;
        APtr^.Next := BPtr;
    end;
  end;
end else
```

Following the rules previously described, *APtr* is stepped down the branch, always taking the *Next* link, until an empty *Next* link is found where *BPtr* can be connected. This connection can be made anywhere along the branch or, if nothing is found sooner, will occur at the end of the branch.

At this point, new links have been established for any and all descendant elements in the tree and all that remains is to dispose of the memory allocated to the current item and its node pointers — which is easily accomplished:

```
Dispose( ItemPtr^.Item, Done );

Dispose( ItemPtr );
end;
```

The static local pointers, *APtr* and *BPtr*, were used so that these could be manipulated freely without losing track of the essential pointer, *ItemPtr*, which is needed, in the final step, to call the Dispose utility.

One feature worth comment: deletions within the binary tree tend to produce linear branches while new additions tend to sprout subbranches. As the tree evolves, assuming a balance between additions and deletions, the structure of the tree will tend to simplify, approaching a linear structure (as demanded by the laws of entropy).

Even in a linear format, however, the binary tree tends to be faster to transmit than the equivalent, purely linear structure and this will remain true regardless of size. (Actually, binary tree efficiency increases with size compared with the equivalent linear structures.)

Other Methods

A variety of other methods could be created for use with the binary structure. For example, the Find and FindPartial methods could both be improved to meet probable application requirements.

Taking the FindPartial method as a sample, an enhancement might be to include provisions, when a partial match is found, to inquire if this is the desired element or if a further search — continuing from the present, recursive location rather than beginning again at the root — should be executed.

The same could be applied — though in a more limited fashion — to the Find method to provide for the circumstances where several entries might begin identically: as would be the case with *Jones, Bill, Jones, Sarah* and *Jones, John J.*

Search methods do not need to be limited specifically to the Name field of an entry and, with complex data fields, might well be designed to execute partial searches on several fields within an entry. They might also execute different searches on different fields within a single trip though the tree.

For complex data, multiple binary trees can be constructed, each linking through a different field or through different rules (or both). Figure 10-6 shows the same tree organization as illustrated in Figure 10-3 and adds a second binary tree — using the same data — but linked through the Phone field instead of the Name field. For simplicity, the data entries have been replaced by integers showing the order in which each record was added to the tree and these are, of course, consistent for both trees.

As you can see, both trees have the same root entry since the root entry is simply the first record read from the file and, purely by coincidence, the second and fifth entries have the same relationship in both trees. Beyond this, however, the two trees are distinctly different.

Even if the data source is ordered for one data field, it will most certainly be disordered for the second and third fields. Disorder, with binary trees, is an advantage rather than a liability.

When working with multiple tree indexes, however, it may help to work out and test the rules for each tree organization separately. Once two or more trees are combined in an application, complex searches can be made very quickly by comparing the pointer addresses returned by separate search methods.

Figure 10-6: Two Binary Trees

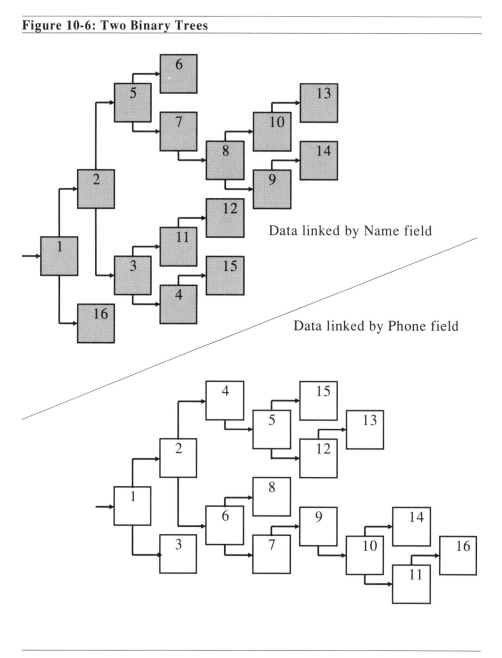

Data linked by Name field

Data linked by Phone field

Remember, even though the organization used by different tree structures will be different, the addresses of the data elements indicated by the separate link nodes will be the same; that is, assuming that both trees' nodes are pointing to the same data element.

All is not well, however, because multiple trees will also require additional handling in the DeleteItem method to ensure that all trees are correctly updated before an item is actually deleted. Since the data items do not have pointers to their nodes — only the nodes have pointers to the data — each tree's nodes would need to be searched independently and some care taken to ensure that each tree's node was indeed pointing to the same data element.

Of course, with multiple trees, a pointer for each tree could be added to the data element, pointing back to the data element's node for each separate tree. This could simplify several processes.

There are no simple answers for multiple trees but the results can be very powerful and very fast, especially when large data bases and complex data fields are used — keep these possibilities in mind.

Summary

Binary tree structures are powerful and fast as well as compatible with object methods.

Notice particularly that the PhonTree demo has not only created a binary tree organization, but provides methods by which the tree object manipulates itself, adding, arranging, searching and deleting data elements, even deleting the tree itself, all without requiring intervention by the application.

This is the heart and soul of object-oriented programming. Once an object has been created and supplied with the appropriate methods, it is capable of acting by itself, exercising considerable powers of decision and, in general, carrying out complex tasks without requiring supplemental programing.

Some of the objects demonstrated have been static objects, declared by the program and remaining in memory until the program exits. Others have been dynamic object capable of requesting their own memory allocation when created and, when no longer wanted, erasing themselves and releasing the memory used for other tasks. Some have appeared both as static and as dynamic objects in different instances.

You've seen objects as graphic control elements, not only controlling their own presentation, but even querying the mouse object to find out if a mouse hit has occurred and reacting accordingly. These are only a few of the ways in which objects can be created and only a few of the tasks that objects can undertake. An object can be virtually anything from a simple scrollbar in a graphics program to a complex binary tree organizing data to an entire editor utility called on by an application as needed and released when no longer required.

The choices are yours — use simple objects for simple tasks or create complex objects for complex tasks. Virtually anything which you can program can be programmed as an object or using objects. The only real limits — because this is always true — are those of your imagination.

So, unshackle your familiar fetters and habits and let yourself go and have fun!

PHONTREE.PAS

```pascal
program Phone_Tree_Demo;

uses Crt, Dos;

type
    NodePtr = ^NodeRec;

    LinkPtr = ^LinkObj;

    DataPtr = ^DataObj;

    NodeRec = record  Root, Prev, Next : NodePtr;

                                    Item : DataPtr;  end;

    LinkObj = object
      Nodes : NodePtr;

      constructor Init;

      destructor Done;  virtual;

      procedure Add( ThisItem : DataPtr );
```

```
    procedure DeleteItem( ItemPtr : NodePtr );

    procedure PrintList( ItemPtr : NodePtr );

    procedure ReadFile( NameFile : string );

    function Find( RefLink : NodePtr;

                SearchStr : string ): NodePtr;

    function FindPartial( RefLink : NodePtr;

                    PartialStr : string ): NodePtr;

    function Precede( Str1,

                    Str2 : string ): boolean;

  end;
DataItem = record   Name : string[40];

                    Phone : string[14];    end;
DataObj = object

        Data : DataItem;

        constructor Init( ThisItem : DataItem );

        destructor Done;  virtual;

        procedure Print;

      end;
var

  LinkList   : LinkObj;

  FirstLink  : NodePtr;

  Mem1, Mem2 : longint;

  Hr, Min, Sec, Hun : word;

  i : integer;
```

```pascal
                    {=====================}
                    { Link implementation }
                    {=====================}
constructor LinkObj.Init;
    begin

    end;

destructor LinkObj.Done;

    procedure DisposeItem( ItemPtr : NodePtr );
        begin
            if ItemPtr <> nil then
            begin
                if ItemPtr^.Prev <> nil then
                    DisposeItem( ItemPtr^.Prev );
                if ItemPtr^.Next <> nil then
                    DisposeItem( ItemPtr^.Next );
                if ItemPtr^.Item <> nil then
                    Dispose( ItemPtr^.Item, Done );
                Dispose( ItemPtr );
            end;
        end;

    begin
        DisposeItem( FirstLink );
    end;

procedure LinkObj.Add;
    var
```

```
   NPtr : NodePtr;

procedure BuildTree( RefLink, NewLink : NodePtr );
   begin
      if Precede( NewLink^.Item^.Data.Name,
                  RefLink^.Item^.Data.Name ) then
      begin
         if RefLink^.Prev = nil then
         begin
            RefLink^.Prev := NewLink;
            NewLink^.Root := RefLink;
         end else
         BuildTree( RefLink^.Prev, NewLink );
      end else
      begin
         if RefLink^.Next = nil then
         begin
            RefLink^.Next := NewLink;
            NewLink^.Root := RefLink;
         end else
         BuildTree( RefLink^.Next, NewLink );
      end;
   end;

begin
   New( NPtr );
   NPtr^.Root := nil;
```

```
      NPtr^.Next := nil;

      NPtr^.Prev := nil;

      NPtr^.Item := ThisItem;

      if FirstLink = nil

         then FirstLink := NPtr

         else BuildTree( FirstLink, NPtr );

   end;

procedure LinkObj.ReadFile;

   var

      NewItem  : DataItem;

      DataFile : file of DataItem;

   begin

      assign( DataFile, NameFile );

      reset( DataFile );

      repeat

         read( DataFile, NewItem );

         Add( New( DataPtr, Init( NewItem ) ) );

      until EOF( DataFile );

      close( DataFile );

   end;

procedure LinkObj.PrintList;

   begin

      if ItemPtr <> nil then

      begin

         if ItemPtr^.Prev <> nil then
```

```
            PrintList( ItemPtr^.Prev );
        with ItemPtr^.Item^ do Print;
        if ItemPtr^.Next <> nil then
            PrintList( ItemPtr^.Next );
        end;
    end;

procedure LinkObj.DeleteItem;
    var
        APtr, BPtr : NodePtr;
    begin
        APtr := ItemPtr;
        if APtr = FirstLink then
            if FirstLink^.Prev  nil
                then FirstLink := FirstLink^.Prev
                else FirstLink := FirstLink^.Next;
        if Precede( APtr^.Item^.Data.Name,
                    APtr^.Root^.Item^.Data.Name ) then
        begin
            if APtr^.Next = nil then
            begin
                if APtr^.Prev = nil then
                    APtr^.Root^.Prev := nil else
                    begin
                        APtr^.Root^.Prev := APtr^.Prev;
                        APtr^.Prev^.Root := APtr^.Root;
```

```
            end;
        end else
        begin
            BPtr := APtr^.Next;
            if APtr^.Prev = nil then
            begin
                APtr^.Root^.Prev := APtr^.Next;
                APtr^.Next^.Root := APtr^.Root;
            end else
            begin
                APtr^.Root^.Prev := APtr^.Prev;
                APtr^.Prev^.Root := APtr^.Root;
                APtr := APtr^.Prev;
                while APtr^.Next <> nil do
                    APtr := APtr^.Next;
                BPtr^.Root := APtr;
                APtr^.Next := BPtr;
            end;
        end;
    end else
    begin
        if APtr^.Prev = nil then
        begin
            if APtr^.Next = nil then
                APtr^.Root^.Next := nil else
                begin
```

```
                APtr^.Root^.Next := APtr^.Next;
                APtr^.Next^.Root := APtr^.Root;
            end;
      end else
      begin
         BPtr := APtr^.Prev;
         if APtr^.Next = nil then
         begin
            APtr^.Root^.Next := APtr^.Prev;
            APtr^.Prev^.Root := APtr^.Root;
         end else
         begin
            APtr^.Root^.Next := APtr^.Next;
            APtr^.Next^.Root := APtr^.Root;
            APtr := APtr^.Next;
            while APtr^.Prev <> nil do
               APtr := APtr^.Prev;
            BPtr^.Root := APtr;
            APtr^.Prev := BPtr;
         end;
      end;
   end;
   Dispose( ItemPtr^.Item, Done );
   Dispose( ItemPtr );
end;
```

```
function LinkObj.Find;
   var
      Result : NodePtr;

   function Match( Str1, Str2 : string ): boolean;
      var
            i, j : integer;
         Result : boolean;
      begin
         Result := TRUE;
         i := ord( Str1[0] );
         j := ord( Str2[0] );
         if j < i then i := j;
         for j := 1 to i do
            if Result then
               Result :=
                  upcase(Str1[j]) = upcase(Str2[j]);
         Match := Result;
      end;

   begin
      Result := nil;
      if RefLink <> nil then
         if Match( SearchStr,
                   RefLink^.Item^.Data.Name ) then
            Result := RefLink else
            if Precede( RefLink^.Item^.Data.Name,
```

```
                        SearchStr )
              then Result := Find( RefLink^.Next,
                                    SearchStr )
              else Result := Find( RefLink^.Prev,
                                    SearchStr );

      Find := Result;
    end;

function LinkObj.FindPartial;
    var
        Result : NodePtr;

    function Match( Str1, Str2 : string ): boolean;
        var
            i, j : integer;
        begin
            for i := 1 to ord( Str1[0] ) do
                Str1[i] := upcase( Str1[i] );
            for i := 1 to ord( Str2[0] ) do
                Str2[i] := upcase( Str2[i] );
            j := pos( Str1, Str2 );
            Match := j <> 0;
        end;

    begin
        Result := nil;
        if RefLink <> nil then
        begin
```

```pascal
        if RefLink^.Prev <> nil then
          Result := FindPartial( RefLink^.Prev,
                                       PartialStr );
        if Result = nil then
          if Match( PartialStr,
                    RefLink^.Item^.Data.Name ) then
            Result := RefLink;
        if Result = nil then
          if RefLink^.Next <> nil then
            Result := FindPartial( RefLink^.Next,
                                        PartialStr );
      end;
    FindPartial := Result;
  end;

function LinkObj.Precede;
  var
    i, j : integer;
  begin
    i := ord( Str1[0] );
    j := 1;
    while( upcase(Str1[j]) = upcase(Str2[j]) )
       and ( j <= i ) do
         inc( j );
    Precede := upcase(Str1[j]) < upcase(Str2[j]);
  end;
```

```
                { Data implementation }
constructor DataObj.Init;
   begin
      Data := ThisItem;
   end;

destructor DataObj.Done;
   begin
   end;

procedure DataObj.Print;
   begin
      with Data do
         writeln( Name, Phone );
   end;

                { end of Data methods }
var
   LocPtr : NodePtr;
   LocStr : string;
begin
   clrscr;
   gotoxy(  4, 1 ); writeln('Name or Company');
   gotoxy( 42, 1 ); writeln('Phone Number');
   Mem1 := MemAvail;              { read available RAM }
   FirstLink := nil;
   GetTime( Hr, Min, Sec, Hun );
```

```pascal
with LinkList do
begin
   Init;                          { create a link list }
   ReadFile('PHONE.LST');         { read the data file }
   PrintList( FirstLink );        { print out the list }

{=====================================================}
{      demo for Find... and DeleteItem methods        }
{=====================================================}
   writeln;
   LocStr := 'Borland';
   LocPtr := Find( FirstLink, LocStr );
   if LocPtr <> nil then
      begin
         write('Found: ');
         LocPtr^.Item^.Print;
      end else writeln( LocStr, ' not found');
   if LocPtr = nil then
   begin
      LocPtr := FindPartial( FirstLink, LocStr );
      if LocPtr <> nil then
         begin
            write('Found: ');
            LocPtr^.Item^.Print;
         end else writeln( LocStr, ' not found');
   end;
   if LocPtr <> nil then
```

```
    begin
       DeleteItem( LocPtr );
       writeln( '***', LocStr, ' deleted***' );
       writeln;
       PrintList( FirstLink );
    end;
{=================================================}

    Mem2 := MemAvail;              { read available RAM }
    Done;                          { dispose of list    }
  end;

writeln;
writeln('Available memory, initial: ', Mem1:6,
       ' bytes' );
writeln('      ... after list built: ', Mem2:6,
       ' bytes' );
writeln('        ... after disposal: ', MemAvail:6,
       ' bytes' );
readln;
end.
```

CHAPTER 11

DEBUGGING OBJECT-ORIENTED PASCAL

Together with the new extensions creating object-oriented Pascal, Borland has also extended the integrated debugger to support object-oriented debugging within the **Integrated Development Environment** (IDE).

For stand-alone testing, version 1.5 (or later) of the Turbo Debugger also supports object-oriented debugging, including several special features that allow access and examination of object-oriented elements. An example of the Turbo Debugger main window appears in Figure 11-1.

Debugging in the IDE

Debugging object-oriented programming within Turbo's IDE does not require any special preparations or special code considerations. The integrated debugger fully supports objects and object elements, treating them in the same fashion as procedures, functions and records. Just as the integrated debugger allows you to examine, trace or alter variables and values in procedures, the same handling is extended to methods and other object elements.

Figure 11-1: Turbo Debugger's Main Window (#1)

```
  File    View    Run    Breakpoints    Data    Window    Options
┌CPU 80286══════════════════════════════════════════════════════════1┐
│BUTTON_TEST_3.62:                              ax 0000   │c=0│
│  cs:0295 9A0000DA82       call    82DA:0000   bx 0000   │z=0│
│  cs:029A 9A00007882       call    8278:0000   cx 0000   │s=0│
│  cs:029F 9A2216F27E       call    7EF2:1622   dx 0000   │o=0│
│  cs:02A4 55               push    bp          si 0000   │p=0│
│  cs:02A5 89E5             mov     bp,sp       di 0000   │a=0│
│  cs:02A7 81EC0001         sub     sp,0100     bp 0000   │i=1│
│BUTTON_TEST_3.63                               sp 3FFE   │d=0│
│  cs:02AB 31C0             xor     di,0884     ds 7D62   │   │
│  cs:02AD A38408           mov     [0884],ax   es 7D62   │   │
│BUTTON_TEST_3.64                               ss 84C6   │   │
│  cs:02B0 BF8408           mov     di,0884     cs 7D72   │   │
│  cs:02B3 1E               push    ds          ip 0295   │   │
│                                                         │   │
├─────────────────────────────────────────────┬─────────────┤
│  ds:0000   CD 20 00 A0 00 9A F0 FE =..á.Ü≡.  ss:4004 047E │
│  ds:0008   1D F0 53 03 23 57 20 03 ↔≡S♥#W.♥  ss:4002 C402 │
│  ds:0010   23 57 2D 02 AC 5D 12 40 #W-.¼].@  ss:4000 0EEC │
│  ds:0018   O1 01 01 00 02 FF FF FF ........  ss:3FFE 0000 │
└───────────────────────────────────────────────────────────┘
```

Tracing Method Calls

Method calls are handled by the debugger in exactly the same fashion as a procedure or function. Thus, the F8 hot key (**Step**) handles a method the same as a procedure, executing it without displaying the processes within the method. The F7 hot key (**Trace**) loads the method's code if it is available, tracing through the individual steps. Obviously, if a method's code is derived as a descendant of an external unit, the source code will not be available for **Trace** and will be treated as if the **Step** option had been chosen.

Static vs. Virtual Methods

Both static and virtual method calls are traced in the same fashion. Since virtual methods — at run time when the debugging is carried out — have already been resolved, no ambiguities remain. The debugger, therefore, is not faced with any unresolved references and has no problems determining which object's method should be executed next.

The Call Stack Window

The Call Stack window displays the method names with the object type's prefix. Note: the method prefix is the object type defining the object, not the variable name of the object instance. For example, the Call Stack window would display *ScrollBar.Init* rather than *Init* or *HScroll.Init*.

The Evaluate Window

Normally, when only an object name is specified for the Evaluate window, only the data fields are displayed. In the Evaluate window, the object's data fields are displayed in essentially the same format as a date record. The same record format specifiers apply and all expressions that are valid for records are accepted for objects.

When a specific method name is evaluated — either for virtual or static methods — a pointer value is displayed indicating the address of that method's code. Since the debugger handles virtual method evaluations in the same manner as the object code itself, by looking in the instance's VMT, the address reported for a virtual method is the correct address for the virtual method code for the instance.

Within the IDE, the debugger can also evaluate or watch the *Self* parameter and *Self* can be traced with format and field specifications or method qualifiers.

The Watch Window

Any object can be assigned to the Watch window just as a record might. All qualifiers that are valid for records are valid for objects.

The Find Procedure Command

Under Turbo 5.5, the Find Procedure command from the Debug menu permits entry of expressions that evaluate to an address within the code segment. This applies to procedural variables and parameters as well as object methods.

The Turbo (Stand-Alone) Debugger

The Turbo Debugger version 1.5 (or later) also supports stand-alone debugging for object-oriented programs. Several new features are provided by Turbo Debugger version 1.5, including Object Hierarchy, Object Type Inspector and Object Instance Inspector windows that will be examined later in this chapter.

As with conventional programming, the **D**ebug/Stand-alone Debugging option must be turned on when the program is compiled and, of course, the Compile/**D**estination option must be set to disk.

For units, the Debug Information flag (**{$D+}** or, from the menu, Options/Compiler/**D**ebug Information) must be enabled.

Also for units, the **D**ebug/Stand-alone Debugging and the Options/**L**inker/**M**ap File switch can be used with the **{$D+}** switch to record debug information in the compiled unit's object code. This information increases the size of the .TPU file and requires additional space when compiling programs using the unit, but does not affect the size or speed of the resulting .EXE program. No other special options or switches are required to debug object-oriented programs.

Just as with the integrated debugger, the Turbo Debugger treats method calls in the same fashion as conventional functions or procedures with the **S**tep command (F8) treating a method call as a single statement and stepping over it and the **T**race command (F7) calling the method's source code, if available, and following it step by step.

Symbols and Scope

The scope of a symbol establishes where the debugger looks for the symbol and the Turbo Debugger uses the cursor position to determine the current scope. If no module window is open, the Turbo Debugger derives the scope from the CS:IP values in the CPU window. (See Chapter 9 in the Turbo Debugger manual — Implied Scope — for expression evaluation.)

If a symbol is not in the current scope, the symbol can be qualified with a path:

```
[unit] [object-type.method] {proc} [variable]
```

Items in square brackets are optional, but should appear only once. Items shown in french brackets are also optional, but may be repeated.

The Evaluate Window

Object instances in the Evaluate window are treated just as they are by the integrated debugger under the IDE. By default, only the object's data fields are displayed but, if a method is specified, the pointer address for that method is displayed. Also, as within the IDE, the debugger can evaluate the *Self* parameter and *Self* can be traced with format and field specifications or method qualifiers.

Method Evaluation

Methods can also be called from the Evaluate window by typing the object instance name — not the object type name — followed by a period (dot) and the method name, and then followed by the calling parameters in parentheses or empty parentheses if there are no calling parameters.

For example, using the Button object type (from Chapter 3) with the type declarations:

```
type

   Button = object( Point )

      . . .

      procedure Draw;

      procedure Create( PtX, PtY,

                       Width, Height, C : integer;

                       Text : STR40 );

      procedure Erase;

      procedure Invert;

      procedure Move( PtX, PtY : integer );

      procedure SetColor( C : integer );

      . . . .
```

```
    end;

var

    GButton : array[1..10] of Button;
```

the expressions listed in Table 11-1 could be entered in the Turbo Debugger's Evaluate window.

Note: constructor or destructor methods cannot be executed in the Evaluate window.

Table 11-1: Examples Using the Evaluate Window

EXPRESSION	RESULT

GButton[1]
   (shows all values which)
   (belong to GButton[1])
	(10, 10, 9, FALSE, FALSE
	   FALSE, 10, 1, 100, 40,
	   ThreeD, 'TEST 1')

GButton[2].X	120 ($78) : integer
GButton[3].Move	Procedure @7E26:076C
GButton[4].Move(100, 100)	calls method Move
GButton[5].Invert()	calls method Show
The following expressions produce errors:	
GButton.X	Left side not a record, structure or union
GButton.Move	
GButton[4].Move( )	Syntax error

The Watch Window

Objects can be entered in the Watch window just as records are. The expressions above, used in the Evaluate window, can also be used in the Watch window.

The Object Hierarchy Window

The Object Hierarchy window is a new feature of Turbo Debugger 1.5 that allows the examination of complete object hierarchies. Select Hierarchy under the View menu item.

The Object Hierarchy window — see Figure 11-2 — is a two frame display providing information about object types, not object instances. The left frame lists, in alphabetical order, all object types used by module being debugged. The right frame shows the object types arranged in hierarchy order with lines showing ancestor/descendant relationships. Descendant object types appearing below and to the right of their ancestor types.

Figure 11-2: The Object Hierarchy Window (#4)

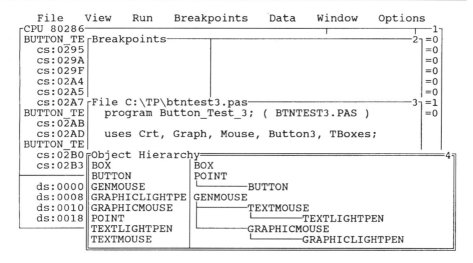

```
     File    View    Run    Breakpoints   Data   Window    Options
 ┌CPU 80286────────────────────────────────────────────────────┬1┐
 │BUTTON_TE┌Breakpoints──────────────────────────────────────2┐ │=0
 │  cs:0295│                              │                    │ │=0
 │  cs:029A│                              │                    │ │=0
 │  cs:029F│                              │                    │ │=0
 │  cs:02A4│                              │                    │ │=0
 │  cs:02A5│                              │                    │ │=0
 │  cs:02A7┌File C:\TP\btntest3.pas───────────────────────────3┐=1
 │BUTTON_TE│   program Button_Test_3; ( BTNTEST3.PAS )          │=0
 │  cs:02AB│                                                    │
 │  cs:02AD│   uses Crt, Graph, Mouse, Button3, TBoxes;         │
 │BUTTON_TE│                                                    │
 │  cs:02B0┌Object Hierarchy═══════════════════════════════════4┐
 │  cs:02B3│BOX                  │BOX                            │
 │         │BUTTON               │POINT                          │
 │  ds:0000│GENMOUSE             │       └────BUTTON             │
 │  ds:0008│GRAPHICLIGHTPE│GENMOUSE                              │
 │  ds:0010│GRAPHICMOUSE  │      ├────────TEXTMOUSE              │
 │  ds:0018│POINT                │        └────────TEXTLIGHTPEN  │
 │         │TEXTLIGHTPEN         │        └────GRAPHICMOUSE      │
 └─────────│TEXTMOUSE            │                └────────GRAPHICLIGHTPEN│
```

F1-Help F2-Bkpt F3-Close F4-Here F5-Zoom F6-Next F7-Trace F8-Step

In addition to using the cursor keys to search through lists of object types, an incremental match feature provides a speed search for long lists. With the highlight bar in the left frame, begin typing the name of the object type desired and — key by key — the highlight bar will select the first object type matching the string entry.

The Enter key opens an Object Type Inspector window for the selected object type. Two local menu options are also supported by hot keys:

- Inspect (Ctrl-I) Calls the **Object Type Inspector** window for the selected object type (see Figure 10-3).

- Tree (Ctrl-T) Shifts to the object hierarchy tree, placing the highlight bar on the object type selected in the alphabetical list. The Tab key can also be used to move between frames.

Hot key (Ctrl-key) selections must be enabled through the TDINST utility before hot key selection will function (default is enabled).

The Object Type Inspector Window

The Object Type Inspector window displays type information, data fields and methods, about a selected object type (not an object instance). The window is divided horizontally into two frames: the upper frame showing the data fields belonging to the object type (including inherited data fields); the lower frame showing the method's names, indicating the method is a procedure or a function with the function return type, but does not show calling parameters for either procedures or functions — see Figure 11-3.

Local menu items for the top frame include:

- Inspect (Ctrl-I) Opens a new Object Type Inspector window if the highlighted field is an object type or a pointer to an object type. Pressing Enter also selects highlighted field.

- Hierarchy (Ctrl-H) Opens an Object Hierarchy window for the object type selected.

- Show Inherited (Ctrl-S) <YES/NO> Toggles with YES as default value, showing all data fields and methods regardless of whether they are defined within the inspected object type or inherited from an ancestor object type. When NO is selected, only those fields and methods defined within the inspected object type are shown.

Local menu items for the bottom frame include:

- Inspect (Ctrl-I) Opens a new Object Type Inspector window if the highlighted field is an object type or a pointer to an object type. Pressing Enter also selects highlighted field.

- Hierarchy (Ctrl-H) Opens an Object Hierarchy window for the object type selected.

- **S**how Inherited (Ctrl-S) <YES/No> Toggles with YES as default value, showing all methods regardless of whether they are defined within the inspected object type or inherited from an ancestor object type. When NO is selected, only methods defined within the inspected object type are shown.

Figure 11-3: The Object Type Inspector Window (#5)

```
     File    View    Run    Breakpoints    Data    Window    Options
┌CPU 80286────────────────────────┬──────────────┬────1┐
│BUTTON_TE┌Breakpoints────────────┤              2┐ =0
│  cs:0295│                        │               │=0
│  cs:029A│                        │               │=0
│  cs:029F│                        │               │=0
│  cs:02A4│                        │               │=0
│  cs:02A5│                        │               │=0
│  cs:02A7┌File C:\TP\btntest3.pas─────────────────3┐=1
│BUTTON_TE│    program Button_Test_3; ( BTNTEST3.PAS )│=0
│  cs:02AB│                                           │
│  cs:02AD│    uses Crt, Graph, Mouse, Button3, TBoxes;│
│BUTTON_TE│                                           │
│  cs:02B0┌Object Hierarchy────────────────────────4┐
│  cs:02B3│BOX           │BOX                        │
│         ┌Object Type GENMOUSE══════5┐              │
│  ds:0000│X : INTEGER                 │             │
│  ds:0008│Y : INTEGER                 │             │
│  ds:0010│VISIBLE : BOOLEAND          │E            │
│  ds:0018│                            │TEXTLIGHTPEN  │
│         │                            │OUSE          │
│         │FUNCTION TESTMOUSE : BOOLEAN│GRAPHICLIGHTPEN│
│         │PROCEDURE SETACCEL          │              │
│         │PROCEDURE SHOW              │              │
└─────────└────────────────────────────┘──────────────┘
 F1-Help F2-Bkpt F3-Close F4-Here F5-Zoom F6-Next F7-Trace F8-Step F
```

The Module Window

The Module Window remains unchanged from Turbo Debugger version 1.0, but deserves mention here because it will be used to select object instances for display in the Object Instance Inspector window. The Module window is selected from the **V**iew / **M**odule commands or using the Alt-F3 hot key.

Note: do not confuse the Module window — see Figure 11-4 — with the File window (window #3 in Figures 11-2 and 11-3). Object instances cannot be selected from the File window, only from the Module window.

Before attempting to select a module, go to the **O**ptions menu, select **P**ath for Source and enter the drive/path specification where the program source files are located. If you will be working regularly with programs from a specific directory, use the **S**ave Options command to save the current drive/path. After selecting the desired module, use the cursor to select an object instance in the Module window and enter Ctrl-I.

Figure 11-4: The Module Window (#4)

```
      File    View    Run    Breakpoints    Data    Window    Options
 ┌CPU 80286──────────────────────────────┬──────────────────┬─1┐
 │BUTTON_TE┌Breakpoints─────────────┬──────────────────2┐=0│
 │  cs:0295│                        │                    │=0│
 │  cs:029A│                        │                    │=0│
 │  cs:029F│                        │                    │=0│
 │  cs:02A4│                        │                    │=0│
 │  cs:02A5┌Module: BUTTON_TEST_3 File: C:\TP\BTNTEST.3.PAS=4┐=0│
 │  cs:02A7│            Init;                               │=1│
 │BUTTON_TE│            SetButtonType( ThreeD );            │=0│
 │  cs:02AB│            Create( (i-1)*110+10, (i-1)*50+10,  │
 │  cs:02AD│                    100, 40, i+8, 'Test'+TempSt │
 │BUTTON_TE│          end;                                  │
 │  cs:02B0│          GButton[6].Init;                      │
 │  cs:02B3│          GButton[6].SetButtonType( ThreeD );   │
 │         │          GButton[6].Create( 10, 260, 100, 40, W│─│
 │ ds:0000│      end;                                      │
 │ ds:0008│                                                │
 │ ds:0010│      procedure Init_TBox;                      │
 │ ds:0018└────────────────────────────────────────────────┘
 └──────────────────────────────────────────────────────────┘
```

F1-Help F2-Bkpt F3-Close F4-Here F5-Zoom F6-Next F7-Trace F8-Step

---

The Object Instance Inspector Window

The Object Instance Inspector window displays information about a specific object instance, using an extended form of the record inspector window.

In the past, the Data Record Inspector window has used two frames: the top frame summarizing the record's field names and their current values and the bottom frame displaying the field type highlighted in the top frame. The Object Instance Inspector window — Figure 11-5 —it adds a third (middle) frame which summarizes the object instance's methods and shows the code address of each. (The code address shown uses the VMT and is correct for polymorphic objects.)

The top frame summarizes the object's data fields, supporting the following local menu commands. Local menus for the active frame are shown by pressing Alt-F10.

- **R**ange (Ctrl-R) Allows the range of array items to be displayed — selected item must be an array or a pointer.

- **C**hange (Ctrl-C) Permits loading a new value into the highlighted data field.

- **M**ethods (Ctrl-M) <YES/NO> Toggles with YES as default and methods summarized in middle frame. When set to NO, middle frame does not appear. The Methods setting is retained by the next Inspector window opened. (New with Turbo Debugger 1.5.)

- **S**how Inherited (Ctrl-S) <YES/NO> Toggles with YES as default, showing all data fields and methods regardless of whether they are defined within the inspected object type or inherited from an ancestor object type. When NO is selected, only those fields and methods defined within the inspected object type are shown.

- **I**nspect (Ctrl-I) Opens a new Data Type Inspector window for the highlighted field. Pressing Enter also selects highlighted field.

- **D**escend (Ctrl-D) Highlighted items replace the item currently in the Inspector window — no new window is opened. Does not permit return to the previously inspected field as can be done using the **I**nspect option. Descend is used to trace through complex data structures without opening separate Inspector windows for each element.

- **N**ew Expression (Ctrl-N) Prompts for a new data item or expression to inspect. New item replaces contents of current window.

- **H**ierarchy (Ctrl-H) Opens Object Hierarchy window.

The middle pane summarizes the methods belonging to an object, supporting the same local menu items as the top frame with the exception of the Change command since methods cannot be changed during execution.

The bottom frame displays the item type highlighted in the upper two frames and has no local menu.

In Figure 11-5, the Draw method has been selected in the middle frame and, in the bottom frame, is shown as a Virtual Procedure.

Figure 11-5: Object Instance Inspector Window (#6)

```
    File    View    Run    Breakpoints    Data    Window    Options              READY
┌Inspecting GButton[6]══════════════════════════════════════════════════════════6┐
│@60CE:0404
│X                           10 ($A)
│Y                           260 ($104)
│COLOR                       15 ($0F)
│EXIST                       True
│STATE                       False
│ROTATE                      False
│FONTSIZE                    4 ($4)
│TYPEFACE                    0 ($0)
├──────────────────────────────────────────────────────────────────────────────
│INIT                        @5B02:0095
│CREATE                      @5B02:0626
│MOVE                        @0072:5B02
│DRAW                        @071B:5B02
│SETCOLOR                    @0000:0000
│SETLOC                      @076C:5B02
│DESTROY                     @1FFF:5B02
│GETCOLOR                    @0000:0000
│GETX                        @0000:0000
├──────────────────────────────────────────────────────────────────────────────
│VIRTUAL PROCEDURE
└──────────────────────────────────────────────────────────────────────────────┘
F1-Help F2-Bkpt F3-Close F4-Here F5-Zoom F6-Next F7-Trace F8-Step F9-Run
```

New Error Messages

Two new error messages are generated by the Turbo Debugger:

Constructors and destructors cannot be called   Attempts to evaluate constructor or destructor methods are not allowed.

Not an object Pascal program   An attempt to open an Object Hierarchy window is only possible if objects are included in the program being examined.

APPENDIX A

OOP TERMINOLOGY

Abstract Data Types   A set of data structures (data types) defined strictly in terms of the features of the structures and the operations executed on these structures. In OOP, **object types** (that is, classes) are abstract data types.

Ancestor Type   Any type from which another object type inherits. *See also* **immediate ancestor.**

Binding   The process by which the address of a procedure is given to the caller. This may be **early binding** occurring at compile/link time or **late binding** occurring at run time when the procedure is called. Traditional compilers such as C and Pascal support early binding only, while C++ and OS/2 (.DLL libraries) compilers support both early and late binding. *See also* **early binding** and **late binding**.

C++   An object-oriented superset extension to the C compiler language developed by Bjarne Stroustrup.

Classes   Term used by Smalltalk and others — synonymous with **object types**.

Client Relationship   Not implemented in object-oriented Turbo Pascal. In other OOP systems, objects may be clients of other objects in addition to the inheritance relationship. A client relationship means that the implementation of the client object (class) relies on the implementation of the supplier object (class).

Concurrency   Not implemented by DOS languages at present, concurrency is a potential implementation of object-oriented programming for systems employing concurrent or parallel processors or multitasking systems such as OS/2. The capability of object-oriented programs to communicate by messages removes some of the difficulty of synchronization between concurrent or parallel processes. For examples, see OS/2, but note that while OS/2 uses object-oriented programming methods, it is not recommended as a good example of how object-oriented programming should be implemented.

Constructor   A special type of **method** — defined by the reserved word constructor — which initializes an object containing **virtual methods**. An **instance**'s constructor must be called before calling its virtual methods; otherwise, a run-time error will occur.

Descendant Type   Any type that inherits from an **object** type. *See also* **inheritance**.

Destructor   A special type of **method.** This is defined by the reserved word destructor — which determines the size of an **object**, at run-time, immediately before deallocating the object from the heap. Destructors allow **polymorphic** objects to be correctly deallocated, even though their exact type and; therefore, exact size, is not known at compile time.

Dynamic Binding   Late or delayed binding. *See* **late binding**.

Dynamic Instance   Any object instance that is created by dynamic memory allocation. *See also* **static instance**.

Early Binding The traditional method of compiling in which the addresses of procedures or functions are determined at compile/link time. Object-oriented language compilers, however, may use **late binding** in which the procedures' address code is not known at compile/link time, but is only determined at run time when the procedure is actually called. *See also* **virtual methods**.

Encapsulation The wedding of code to data within an **object** unit. This is modularity applied to data — combining records with procedures and functions that manipulate data to form a new data type which is called an object. Encapsulation renders an object's data ''invisible'' to the user of the object while the methods for manipulating the data remain ''visible.''

Extensibility A feature allowing the user of object-oriented code to extend the code without having the source code. Descendant object types can be made to inherit the ancestor object type's properties even though the ancestor object type belongs to an externally compiled module. Extensibility allows sharing or selling object libraries without revealing trade secrets or algorithms. Also, extensibility allows existing objects to be customized for new applications by extending these as new object types.

Hybrid Paradigms Some systems such as Smalltalk (and OS/2) are pure object-oriented programming systems, operating solely by message passing. Others such as Object Pascal, Objective C or C++ are hybrids which provide both OOP and non-OOP programming features. Hybrids are popular largely for ease of development, the presence of familiar capabilities and speed in execution and creation.

Immediate Ancestor An object type may have several ancestors, but the ancestor named in the object's type definition is the type's immediate ancestor. *See also* **ancestor type**.

Information Hiding Information hiding is a feature of modular programming in which the information within a module is private to the module except as made public through an interface definition (method). *See* **encapsulation**.

Inheritance   The property of all object types that allows a type to be defined which "inherits" all data and method definitions that were contained in a previously defined type. It does so without restating these definitions. Any type inheriting from another type is called a **descendant type**. Inheritance is a property of objects, allowing creation of a hierarchy of objects with descendants of objects implicitly inheriting access to their ancestors' code and data structures.

Instance   A variable of type object or an instance of a specific object type. Also, in conventional usage, the term **object** refers to an instance of an object type.

Late Binding   A method of calling procedures in which the address of the procedure — the address to which control is passed when the procedure is called — is not known at compile/link time and is only determined at run time when the procedure is actually called. Late binding is characteristic of object-oriented language compilers and, in conjunction with **inheritance**, late binding makes **polymorphism** possible. *See also* **early binding** and **virtual methods**.

Messages   Action parameters or orders passed to object calls, instructing the object to execute specific capabilities or features.

Method   A procedure or function which is defined as belonging to an **object type**. Methods may be **static** or **virtual**.

Modularity   Program construction in modules, blocks or units that are combined to build complete programs. Ideally, the redesign or reimplementation of a unit or module can be accomplished without affecting the operation of the rest of the program or system. The DOS, CRT and GRAPH units in Turbo Pascal and Turbo C are good examples of modularity, while other unit examples are shown and developed in this book. Modularity is one of the primary objects of object-oriented programming.

Multiple Inheritance Not implemented in Object Pascal. A few OOP systems (such as Eiffel) possess multiple inheritance, allowing an object to inherit features and data from two or more ancestor objects. With single inheritance, the inheritance structure is a tree. With multiple inheritance, the inheritance structure is a web or maze with multiple ancestors contributing separate data and methods (complementary). They may contribute identical or entirely different versions of the same method, the latter case generally leading to confusion.

Object Reserved word indicating object type definition or any variable of an object type — may also be called an **instance** of an object type.

Object Hierarchy A group of object types related through **inheritance**. The Turbo Debugger, executing an object-oriented module, can be used to display a graphic representation of an object hierarchy by selecting Views, Hierarchy from the menu.

Object Type A special structure that may contain procedure and function definitions — called **methods**. The **object type** structure is similar to the Pascal **record** structure. Object types may be defined as including all data and method definitions which were defined within some previously object type. *See* **ancestor type**, **descendant type** and **inheritance**.

Object-oriented Term for programming practices or compilers that collect individual programming elements into hierarchies of classes, allowing program objects to share access to data and procedures without redefinition.

Polymorphic Object An instance of an object with a descendant object is a polymorphic object because the descendant object inherits the ''shape'' of any of the ancestor type, but can ''polymorph'' into a new ''shape.''

Polymorphism Polymorphism is the property of sharing a single action (and action name) throughout an object hierarchy, but with each object in the hierarchy implementing the action in a manner appropriate to its specific requirements.

Range Checking ($R)   In Turbo Pascal 5.5, the **$R+** compiler option (active) tests the initialization status of all object instances making virtual methods calls that prevent uninitialized calls from producing a system hang up. After a program is debugged, the **$R−** (inactive) setting can be used to speed program execution.

Redefinition   The mechanism which allows the client programmer to employ the same name to refer to different things depending on the class to which each is applied. For example, both Point and Circle possess the property of location, but this property may be redefined from one object to the next. For Point, location would be a single pixel on the screen, but for Circle, location may be either the center of the circle or the corner of the screen rectangle in which the circle was created. *See also* **selective inheritance**.

Repeated Inheritance   Not implemented in Object Pascal. Repeated inheritance is a special case of multiple inheritance in which an object D is the descendant of A by more than one path.

Reusability   A principal feature and objective of object-oriented programming, to allow software to be reused instead of reinvented. Libraries and include files are early examples of reusability, while the Turbo Pascal Units (TPUs) are a later development.

Selective Inheritance   Not implemented by Object Pascal (or by anyone else), selective inheritance would allow objects to discard data or features belonging to their ancestor objects. Currently, redefinition is the only method of changing inheritance features, but selective inheritance may appear at a later time.

Self   An invisible identifier which is automatically declared within an object — may be used to resolve identifier conflicts by qualifying data fields belonging to an method's object.

Simula-67   The original object-oriented language, Simula-67 was designed for writing test simulations of physical objects such as mechanical devices.

Smalltalk   An early object-oriented language, Smalltalk is an interpreter language (like BASIC), not a compiler.

Static Instance Any instance of an object which is named in a **var** declaration and, therefore, is statically allocated in the stack and data segment. *See also* **dynamic instance**.

Static Method A **method** implemented using **early binding**. The method's address is determined at compile/link time, just as the address of any conventional procedure or function is known at compile time. Static method calls require less overhead and should be used as optimization when the flexibility of virtual methods is not required.

Static Object Similar to static data definitions, static object definitions are allowed in C++, but not in Object Pascal. *See also* **static instance**.

Types Templates or definitions for creating **objects**.

Virtual Method Any **method** implemented with **late binding** by using the reserved word **virtual**. In actual operation, a virtual method is usually a group of methods with identical procedure or function headers within an object hierarchy. When a virtual method is executed, a special mechanism determines which implementation of the virtual method is appropriate to the object type of the calling instance. The selection mechanism is installed by calling the object's **constructor**.

Virtual Method Table (VMT) A table appearing in each virtual object type's data segment. The VMT contains the size of the object type (record size) and pointers to the procedures and functions implementing the object type's methods. Each object instance's **constructor** creates a link between the calling instance and the VMT, with the VMT used to call the method implementations.

APPENDIX B

THE OBJECT MOUSE UTILITY

The Object Mouse unit (MOUSE.TPU) is an object-oriented mouse unit for use with Turbo Pascal application programs. It supplies four mouse types for general use: a graphics mouse, text mouse, and both graphics and text lightpen mouse object types that provide the following procedures and functions:

General Mouse Object Procedures

GetPosition   Reports mouse position and button status (all).

QueryBtnDn   Reports requested button down event and position.

QueryBtnUp   Reports requested button up event and position.

ReadMove   Reports mouse movement.

Reset   Resets mouse to default status.

SetAccel   Sets acceleration point for enhanced mouse movement.

SetLimits   Restricts mouse movement to selected screen area.

SetPosition   Sets position of mouse cursor on screen.

SetRatio   Sets ratio of physical mouse movement to screen movement.

TestMouse   Reports mouse and driver present on system.

Show   Shows or hides mouse cursor.

Text Mouse Object Procedures

Initialize   Sets initial conditions for text mouse.

SetCursor   Sets hardware or software text cursor.

Graphic Mouse Object Procedures

ConditionalHide   Selects screen area where graphic cursor is hidden.

Initialize   Sets initial conditions for graphic mouse.

SetCursor   Selects graphics mouse cursor.

LightPen Mouse Object Procedures

LightPen   Enables or disables lightpen emulation for both text and graphics lightpen mouse objects.

The type definitions for each mouse are available to any application program including the statement *uses Mouse* in the header, but each application must declare a local variable using one of the following appropriate types:

```
var

    TMouse  = TextMouse;              { standard text mouse }
    GMouse  = GraphicMouse;    { standard graphics mouse }
    LTMouse = TextLightPen;          { text with lightpen }
    LGMouse = GraphicLightPen; { graphic with lightpen }
```

General Mouse Procedures and Functions

Many of the procedure and functions supplied by the mouse unit are common to all of the object mouse types. Two record structures and seven constants are also defined globally in the mouse unit and are available to the application using the mouse unit.

The first structure, defined as *type Position*, is used by all mouse object types to report mouse button events:

```
type

   Position = record

      BtnStatus,

      opCount,

      xPos, yPos : integer;

   end;
```

The second structure, defined as type *GCursor*, is used by the Graphic-Mouse object type to set the graphics mouse cursor:

```
type

   GCursor = record

      ScreenMask,

      CursorMask : array[0..15] of word;

      hotX, hotY : integer;

   end;
```

The seven constants shown in Table B-1 are globally defined by the mouse.

Table B-1: Constants

CONSTANT	VALUE	APPLICATION
ButtonL	0	left button
ButtonR	1	right button

Table B-1: Constants

CONSTANT	VALUE	APPLICATION
ButtonM	2	middle button
Software	0	used to set software text cursor
Hardware	1	used to set hardware text cursor

TestMouse

The TestMouse function returns a boolean result indicating the presence or absence of a mouse driver in the system. This is generally used by an application to determine if a mouse is already in use. For most applications, the Reset procedure is preferred.

Reset

The Reset procedure is used to reset the mouse driver to its default state. Two arguments are required, returning a Boolean status and the number of buttons supported by the physical mouse. The procedure is called as:

```
var

    Status : Boolean;

    BtnCount : integer;

    GMouse.Reset( Status, BtnCount );
```

Status will return TRUE if the mouse and mouse driver are present and installed; FALSE if the mouse cannot be used. *BtnCount* will return with a value of 2 or 3 indicating the number of buttons supported by the physical mouse.

In graphics applications, the default mouse cursor is enabled by the Reset function, but see also the Initialize procedure supplied by the GraphicMouse.

Show

The Show procedure is used to turn the mouse cursor on or off and is called with a single booleanargument specifying the desired state. The Show procedure is called as:

```
GMouse.Show( TRUE )                    { shows mouse cursor }

GMouse.Show( FALSE )                   { hides mouse cursor )
```

Initially, the mouse cursor is always hidden and must be explicitly rendered visible. The visible or invisible state of the mouse, however, does not affect tracking the mouse position or reporting on mouse button events.

Note: conventional mouse Show and Hide functions decrement or increment a cursor counter such that two or more calls to hide the mouse cursor will require two or more calls to make the mouse cursor visible again and vice versa. The object mouse avoids this potential problem and multiple calls to Show(ON) do not require multiple calls to Show(OFF).

GetPosition

The GetPosition procedure is called with three integer arguments: *BtnStatus*, *XPos* and *YPos*. These are returned with the current status of the mouse buttons and the x- and y-axis mouse pointer coordinates and are called as:

```
var

    BtnStatus, XPos, YPos : integer;

    GMouse.GetPosition( BtnStatus, XPos, YPos )
```

The *BtnStatus* variable returns with the three least-significant-bits — beginning with bit 0 — indicating the status of the left, right and middle buttons respectively. If the button is down, the bit is set. If the button is up, the bit is cleared. The *XPos* and *YPos* variables return the current screen coordinates of the mouse cursor.

In text modes, the coordinates are always returned in incremental steps determined by the character cell width and height, but are still in pixel coordinates. For example, if the system is in text mode and the mouse cursor is in the third column, second row, the coordinates returned would be 24, 16 (assuming an 8x8 character cell).

In graphics modes, the coordinates returned are the pixel coordinates of the graphics cursor's hotspot.

See also QueryBtnDn, QueryBtnUp and SetLimits.

SetPosition

The SetPosition procedure allows the application program to position the mouse cursor independent of the movement of the physical mouse. The SetPosition function is called with two integer arguments establishing the x- and y-axis position for the mouse cursor:

```
GMouse.SetPosition( 315, 200 );
```

In text modes, the x- and y-axis coordinates are rounded to the nearest character boundaries in pixel coordinates. Assuming an 8x8 character cell, the arguments shown would position the cursor at column 39, row 25. In graphics modes, the mouse cursor would be positioned with the cursor hotspot at the specified coordinates.

All subsequent movements generated by the physical mouse will begin at the location established by the SetPosition function.

QueryBtnDn and QueryBtnUp

The QueryBtnDn and QueryBtnUp procedures require two arguments: a integer argument selecting the mouse button to be reported and a variable of *type Position* (globally defined by the mouse unit) which returns the button status, event count and coordinates of the button event requested.

QueryBtnDn reports button pressed events; QueryBtnUp reports button released events.

```
var

   BtnEvent : Position;

   QueryBtnDn( ButtonL, BtnEvent );
   QueryBtnUp( ButtonM, BtnEvent );
```

The returned *BtnEvent* structure reports the number of times (if any) the queried button has been pressed (or released), the current status (up or down) of the queried button, and the screen coordinates of the mouse cursor when the most recent button event occurred.

The button event counter — for the specific button and type of event — is reset by this call.

ReadMove

The ReadMove procedure requires two integer arguments to return the horizontal and vertical step counts. The values returned are always in the range -32768..32767 with positive counts indicating motion from left to right or from top to bottom:

```
var

    XMove, YMove : integer;

    ReadMove( XMove, YMove );
```

The horizontal and vertical step counters are reset to zero by this call. See also SetAccel.

SetAccel

The SetAccel procedure is used to set a physical speed threshold (in mickeys/second) over which the mouse driver adds an acceleration component. With an acceleration threshold set, fast mouse movements move the cursor further than slow movements over the same physical distance, allowing fine positioning by slow movements and broad changes with fast movements:

```
SetAccel( 300 );
```

Mouse acceleration can be disabled by setting an arbitrarily high threshold value (such as 7FFFh). See also SetRatio.

SetLimits

The SetLimits procedure sets minimum and maximum screen limits, restricting cursor movement to the selected area. If the cursor is outside the area set, the cursor is immediately moved just inside the new borders:

```
SetLimits( 0, 0, GetMaxX, GetMaxY );
```

The shown call sets the mouse boundaries to cover the entire graphics screen. If either minimum value is greater than the corresponding maximum, the two values are swapped.

SetRatio

The SetRatio procedure uses two integer arguments to set the ratio of physical mouse motion to horizontal and vertical screen mouse motion:

```
SetRatio( 16, 16 );
```

Default movement ratios are 8 mickeys (units of physical movement) to 8 pixels horizontal and 16 mickeys to 8 pixels vertical. Ratio values may be in the range 1..32767 mickeys. See also SetAccel.

The Text Mouse Object

The Text Mouse object includes all of the general mouse procedures with one addition:

SetCursor

The SetCursor procedure is used to select either a *Software* or *Hardware* text cursor and to set the cursor style. The *Software* and *Hardware* constants are predefined by the mouse unit.

If the *Hardware* cursor is selected, the second and third parameters specify the start and stop scan lines for the cursor:

```
SetCursor( Hardware, 8, 7 );
```

If the *Software* cursor is selected, the second and third parameters set the screen and cursor masks (see Chapter 2 for details):

```
SetCursor( Software, $0000, $8F18 );
```

The Graphic Mouse Object

For the graphics mouse, the SetCursor procedure is also implemented, but in a different form from the text mouse. Two additional graphics procedures — ConditionalHide and Initialize — are provided as well.

ConditionalHide

The ConditionalHide procedure is called with four integer parameters: left, top, right and bottom, in this order — establishing an area of the screen where the mouse cursor is automatically concealed:

```
var

    left, top, right, bottom : integer;


    ConditionalHide( left, top, right, bottom );
```

The ConditionalHide procedure can be used to guard an area of the screen which is about to be repainted. If the mouse is in the area selected, the cursor visible counter is decremented just as if Show(OFF) was called.

Any subsequent call to Show(ON) reenables the cursor within the entire region established by the SetLimits procedure.

Initialize:

The Initialize procedure is called without parameters and provides a convenient method of setting initial conditions for a graphics mouse:

```
    Initialize;
```

The Initialize procedure enables mouse movement over the entire graphics screen, selects the arrow cursor, renders the cursor visible and positions the mouse at the center of the screen.

SetCursor

With the graphics mouse, the SetCursor procedure is slightly different than with the text mouse and is called with a single parameter that must be *type GCursor* as defined in the mouse unit:

```
SetCursor( arrow );
```

Five graphic cursors are predefined in the mouse unit, including arrow, check, cross, glove and ibeam, the latter four appear in Figure B-1.

Additional graphics cursors can be created using the MOUSEPTR utility from Chapter 2 and may be included directly in the application program or added to the mouse unit.

Figure B-1: Four Graphic Mouse Cursors

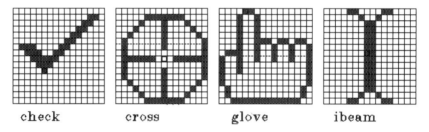

check   cross   glove   ibeam

The LightPen Mouse Object

Two versions of the LightPen Mouse are provided by the mouse unit: TextLightPen and GraphicLightPen. These are descendants, respectively, of the text and graphics mouse objects, but add lightpen handing to each.

LightPen

The LightPen procedure is the same for both text and graphics versions and is called with a single Boolean parameter to either enable or disable lightpen emulation by the mouse:

```
LightPen( TRUE );                    { lightpen enabled  }

LightPen( FALSE );                   { lightpen disabled }
```

A

Abstract data types, 353
Allocation
    static, 217
Ancestor, 9
    ancestor type, 353
    immediate, 355
ASCII characters, 273

B

Binary sort, 305
Binary trees, 299
Binding
    defined, 353
    early versus late, 155
Borland, 107
Button objects
    for graphics and text, 97
    foreground and background,
        103
    and the virtual method table,
        164
Buttons
    styles, 106-107
    test program, 120
    for text, 97-98

C

C++, 353
Caret symbol, 219
Classes, 353
Clients, 354
Communications package, 281
Compiler operations
    for static methods, 152
Compuserve, 154
Concurrency, 354
Constructor method, 171
    defined, 170, 354
    executing, 318
Create method, 20
Cursors
    for software and hardware, 53
    and the Turbo Debugger, 344

D

Data abstraction, 139
Data fields
    accessing, 16
    inheritance, 159
Data records, 266, 277
Declarations
    forward, 153

object versus record, 3
of virtual methods, 169
Deleting, 317-318
Descendant, 10
    of altered objects, 144
    and its constructor method,
      172
Destroy method, 20, 23
Destructor method, 223-224
    defined, 354
    executing calls, 318
    programming, 222
Dispose, 225
Dot referencing, 149
    purposes of, 151
Dynamic instances, 217
    defined, 354
Dynamic objects, 218
    allocation and initialization
      of, 219
    disposing of, 221
Dynamic variables. *See* Dynamic
    objects

E
Early binding, 155
    defined, 355
Encapsulation, 16
    defined, 1, 355
Errors
    duplicate method names, 116
    and encapsulation, 26
    involving Destroy method, 25
    and redundant constructor dec-
      larations, 173
    and uninitiated objects, 116

Exist flag, 106
Extended type compatibility, 235
Extending objects, 145
Extensibility, 168, 181
    defined, 355
    procedure and function avail-
      ability, 183
    programming for, 182

F
Files
    accessing, 271-272
Fonts
    from Borland, 107

G
Global variables, 151
Graphic buttons
    states and colors, 99

H
Handle. *See* Pointers
Hierarchy
    sample hierarchy, 3-5
    See also Inheritance
Hot keys, 342
Hybrids, 355

I
Inheritance
    within data fields, 152
    defined, 1-2, 356
    of objects, 9
    selective, 358
Initialize function, 51
Instances, 217

defined, 356
   statically allocated, 224
Integrated Development Environment (IDE), 341

K
Keywords
   destructor, 247, 279
   virtual, 169

L
Late binding, 155
   defined, 356
Linked lists, 232, 267
   pointer-linked lists, 242
Lightpens, 54
Logitech mouse, 49, 116

M
Memory usage, 249, 268-269, 309
Menu options
   and hot keys, 348
Methods, 10
   constructor, 171
   cursor editor, 55
   defining for objects, 17
   destructor, 223-224
   done, 224, 273, 279
   duplicate method names, 116
   evaluation, 345
   initialization of, 172
   static versus virtual, 342-343
   tracing calls, 342
Mickeys
   defined, 48
Microsoft mouse, 116

Mixed objects and lists, 280
Modularity, 356
Mouse
   button mouse selection, 104
   coordinates, 110
   defining buttons for, 37
   object procedures, 361-362
   and step counts, 47

N
New, 226, 227
Nil pointer, 231
Nodes, 252
Null character, 275

O
Objects
   assigning values, 9
   binary-tree, 306
   declaration of, 3
   dynamic, 218
   and extensibility, 181
   hierarchy, 5
   instances, 218
   pointers to, 218
   polymorphic, 226
   and statically-linked calls, 154
   type declaration, 17
   uninitiated objects, 116
Object libraries, 17
Object methods. *See* Methods
Object-oriented programming
   and binary trees, 325
   debugging, 341
   and extensibility, 168, 181
   and source code, 182

Organization
    of data, 299
    in programs, 17-18

P
Pascal, 16-17
    editor facilities, 25
    extending objects, 151
Point object
    and the virtual method table,
      164
Pointers, 230-231
    null pointers 231
    to objects, 266
Polymorphism, 19
    defined, 1, 357
    and late binding, 356
    and objects, 224, 357
Precede utility, 247
Print method, 279-281
    for a binary tree, 311
Program
    organization, 17
    structure, 220

R
Range checking, 172-173, 358
Record declaration, 3
Record structure
    fields, 12
Redefinition, 358
Reset function, 42

S
Screen updates
    display times, 236, 304-305

and mouse, 44
Scrollbar
    constructor,196
    Draw, 199
    EraseThumbPad, 202
    RestoreViewPort, 198
ScrollHit, 203
SetLoc, 198
SetThumbPad, 201
Scrollbar object, 191
    creation of, 193
Searches, 312-313
Self, 234
SetColor methods, 23
SetGraphMode, 36
SetLoc function, 11-12
Show function, 44
Simula-67, 358
Smalltalk, 16, 358
Sorting lists, 232-233
Static allocation, 217
Static instances, 217, 359
Static methods
    compiler operations, 152
    defined, 359
    and early binding, 155
    inheritance, 149
    overriding, 152
    redefinition as virtual, 168-
      169
    versus virtual methods, 342-
      342
Static pointers, 231

T
TBoxes, 100-101, 106

Text button
  states and colors, 98
  using the Create method, 107
Trees
  binary trees, 299
Turbo Debugger, 341, 344
Turbo Pascal
  and the compiler directive,
    172
  and the Dispose procedure,
    225
  and the linker, 144
Turbo Pascal OOP Guide, 36, 217
Type Declaration, 17
Typefaces
  support, 273

V

Variables
  in binary trees, 311

global, 17-18, 151-152
  renaming, 144
Viewport, 114
Virtual methods, 149, 359
  creation of, 169
  and late binding, 155
  range checking, 172
  versus static methods, 342-
    343
Virtual method table, 163
  and constructor methods, 171
  defined, 359
  examples of, 166-167
VMT, 163

W

Windows
  module window, 349
  call stack and evaluate, 343